10 FLASHPOINTS
20 YEARS

It is rare for a senior political leader to write on national security. But Manish Tewari does this admirably, with his political acumen especially on display while discussing civil-military tensions. His book is essential reading for those of us trying to understand Indian political thinking on national security issues.

—**Rahul Roy-Chaudhury**,
Senior Fellow for South Asia,
International Institute for Strategic Studies (IISS) London

In this important volume, Manish Tewari invites us to reflect on some of the crucial national security challenges that continue to limit the realization of India's full potential at home and abroad. Tewari's rich insights are based on a discussion of 10 major recent developments—from the 1998 nuclear weapon tests to the 2019 reorganization of Jammu and Kashmir—and provide a strong basis for a vigorous discussion of India's unfinished agenda of national security reform.

—**C. Raja Mohan**,
Director, Institute of South Asian Studies,
National University of Singapore

Manish Tewari's thoughtful reflections on two decades of national security challenges offer hope that India will master the tests that confront it in its neighbourhood and beyond—provided it sustains a peaceful society at home and engages with confidence abroad. As India's external environment grows more challenging, his candid analysis illumines why growing material—including military—capabilities, institutional effectiveness and adroit statecraft will all be required for the success of India's political experiment in a tumultuous world.

—**Ashley J. Tellis**,
Tata Chair for Strategic Affairs,
Carnegie Endowment for International Peace (CEIP), Washington D.C.

With clarity of analysis and strength of argument, Manish Tewari's *10 Flashpoints; 20 Years* delves into the policies and actions at the heart of the most politically charged events of our time, from the rise of China to the abrogation of Article 370. An insightful examination of the challenges that have characterized Indian foreign policy in recent years by one of our more thoughtful political figures.

—**Dr Shashi Tharoor**,
Member of Parliament, Lok Sabha

10 FLASHPOINTS 20 YEARS

National Security Situations that Impacted India

MANISH TEWARI

RUPA

Published by
Rupa Publications India Pvt. Ltd 2021
7/16, Ansari Road, Daryaganj
New Delhi 110002

Sales centres:
Allahabad Bengaluru Chennai
Hyderabad Jaipur Kathmandu
Kolkata Mumbai

ISBN: 978-93-5520-091-4

First impression 2021

10 9 8 7 6 5 4 3 2 1

The moral right of the author has been asserted.

Printed at Parksons Graphics Pvt. Ltd, Mumbai

CONTENTS

PROLOGUE
by Happymon Jacob

Nations that refuse to engage in ruthless truth-telling and honest introspection hardly learn from their past mistakes and are therefore more likely to repeat them. One of the wonderful things about India, despite the occasional shortcoming, is its vibrant political and intellectual environment that allows for critical discussions and self-reflection. This constitutionally guaranteed, argumentative political culture has routinely prompted self-correction and thrown up out-of-the-box ideas for the country's future trajectory.

10 Flashpoints; 20 Years: National Security Situations that Impacted India by Manish Tewari is an intellectually curious, historically accurate, often charitable towards non-Congress dispensations and deeply honest attempt at stock-taking India's national security performance. A well-read and equally well-travelled politician, Tewari rose through the ranks of the Congress party and went on to become the union minister of Information and Broadcasting in the United Progressive Alliance (UPA-II) government of Prime Minister Manmohan Singh. At 55, a Member of Parliament (MP) from Punjab's Anandpur Sahib, Tewari has a long political career ahead of him. And yet, such a promising political career ahead hasn't stopped him from being critical of how various governments have made national security choices in the country: that is what makes this book impressive and promising.

I have known the author for several years, most recently through our joint work on conflict resolution in the region, in particular, between India and Pakistan. Representing a parliamentary constituency adjacent to Pakistan, his desire for peace with Pakistan is a product of hard-nosed realism as well as the deep conviction that the people of Pakistan and India could talk, trade and live in peace with each other. Neither is his realism inflexible nor is his conviction about a peaceful subcontinent bereft of the considerations of realpolitik. Tewari believes in a brand of politics, to use the words of Otto von Bismarck, which is the art of the possible.

Tewari tells us a compelling story about the 20-year journey India undertook. In doing so, he picks up 10 national security flashpoints during this period and offers us his reflections on each of them with a view to guiding the government towards better policy formulation, and encouraging the general public to critically discuss them. We have read the author's engaging and provocative weekly columns in the Indian media: this book is a more scholarly, reflective and statesmanlike treatment of the themes he has often covered in those columns.

Tewari has caveated the book by stating that it uses only publicly available information, meaning that he has steered clear of any confidential information to which he would have been privy as a minister and the spokesperson of the party in office from 2004-14. But that caveat should be no reason to view the author's reflections as removed from how they might have actually taken place when they did. Put differently, this book provides deep insights into 20 years of India's national security journey through the mind of someone who has been in the government and knows how the system works. The author's policy experience and his political existence within New Delhi's policy ecosystem make the book immensely valuable to those of us who have not been part of the policy or political ecosystem in India. It has advice for those in the government, and insights for those outside of it.

One of the persistent complaints amongst researchers or journalists working on Indian foreign policy or national security is that documents relating to national security and foreign policy are not declassified even after half a century. Therefore, memoirs, or books—such as this one—in my opinion, remain closest to how events may have unfolded or choices may have been made within the government. This book therefore must be read as such: not as an official account but as reflections of someone who continues to inhabit the policy and political space in India.

KEY TAKEAWAYS

Among the several well-researched arguments that Tewari makes in this book, I wish to highlight five of them here. One of the clearly articulated themes that runs through the book is regarding the importance of pacifying India's neighbourhood. Be it Pakistan or the neighbourhood consisting of smaller South Asian states, the author believes that India's rise is largely dependent on a peaceful and harmonious neighbourhood. Conflict resolution with Pakistan, therefore, is crucial to this goal. Building bridges to countries such as Nepal, Bangladesh and Sri Lanka are equally important—failure to do so would lead India to 'strategic claustrophobia' (not his words). The increasing dominance of China in the region, displacing traditional Indian primacy, would only serve to exacerbate tensions between India and its neighbours. The solution then is a straightforward one: we must build peace with our neighbours.

Second, contrasting the policies of UPA and the National Democratic Alliance (NDA) towards China, Tewari argues that India must have a long-term strategy to deal with China. This is all the more important given the fundamental shifts that have taken place in Sino-Indian relations in the summer of 2020. India and China may have reached a point of no return in the foreseeable future and therefore India must develop a smart strategy to deal with it, both by preparing itself to deal with any unforeseen eventualities and by engaging in carefully calibrated external balancing.

Third, having painstakingly revisited the Kargil conflict, Operation Parakram, 26/11 Mumbai attacks and the problems in civil–military relations in India, he argues that there has been, and continues to be, a slow progress in reforming the country's national security architecture. More significantly, perhaps, the country doesn't have a national security doctrine. India may not even have readied itself to withstand the technology solutions that the enemy might employ against it in the days ahead. Clarity and a sense of purpose, the author emphasizes, are essential in national security management.

Another noteworthy argument that Tewari makes is regarding the increasing domestic politicization of India's foreign policy. When domestic political calculations interfere with foreign policy pursuits, the outcomes could become suboptimal, compromised or controversial. Both the Citizenship (Amendment) Act (CAA), 2019 and the NDA government's Kashmir policy are excellent examples in this regard.

Finally, Tewari underlines a basic fact about the nature of politics in complex societies: it takes political flexibility and statesmanship to deal with domestic political contestations such as the Kashmir conflict. In a complex country with a multitude of internal challenges, the political class must also be guided by moralpolitik, not just realpolitik.

I am delighted to present to you this important book with crucial insights and lessons on India's national security and foreign policy.

Happymon Jacob teaches Diplomacy and Disarmament Studies at the School of International Studies, Jawaharlal Nehru University, and is the founder of the Council for Strategic and Defense Research, New Delhi.

PREFACE

This book attempts to capture time. It endeavours to contextualize the national security challenges that India has faced over the past two decades and its responses to them. It asks a very simple and central question: have India's reactions and subsequent actions if any, to these multifarious situations made the nation any safer today than it was when that particular predicament had manifested itself?

Answering that question would have meant writing this book with a predetermined mindset. That was neither the intent nor the objective of the current exertion. The narration of facts and events are so designed to enable the reader to arrive at their own conclusions. This is an invitation to reflect on some of the events that have fundamentally transformed India's national security and not a guidebook to prefabricated answers.

This book is neither a practitioner's account nor an insider's tale but an observer's reflection. These are ruminations of someone who has followed, with some degree of interest, developments and decisions with regard to India's strategic trajectory over the past 20-odd years. It is based entirely and purposefully on the public record and analysis available in the public space.

If one was to take a wide-angle view of history, it is fairly evident that the contours of India as a modern nation state started emerging only after the unsuccessful First War of Independence in 1857 and the subsequent transfer of suzerainty from the East India Company to the British Crown in 1858. This is notwithstanding the civilizational continuity that is repetitively delineated, commencing with the Mauryan dynasty encompassing the Kushan, Gupta and Sultanate periods before finally culminating with the Mughals to establish that the Idea of Hindustan as a homogenous entity preceded the arrival of the British Crown by a couple of millennia.

Hypothetically, even if one were to assume that the idea of Hindustan was indeed a homogenous entity, at least in the geographical sense of the term, the fact nevertheless remains that nobody was able to guarantee its security. The safety of the Indian subcontinent had been in constant peril going as far back as 1500 BCE. It has perhaps been the most invaded entity in human history. Between the tenth and eighteenth century CE, at least 70 invaders came down the Khyber Pass to continuously loot, pillage and impoverish the Indian subcontinent. The question, therefore, is not why India was such an attractive destination for foreign invaders, but why the subcontinent, through the millennia, was unable to protect itself. Why, even today, is there an absence of a strategic culture in its principal successor state—India—despite all this accumulated experience of travesty?

When India looks ahead at the remaining decades of the twenty-first century what does the future behold? A certain degree of multipolarity in the past decade or so has replaced two decades of US hegemony. This paradigm of unipolarity was preceded by a bipolar world. This multipolarity is a necessary and a welcome change. It therefore requires a new pair of lenses and a novel set of policy prescriptions to navigate through and across these shifting sands.

The recent victory of the Taliban in Afghanistan or the virtual surrender by the United States (US) in Doha, disregarding the enormous amounts of blood and treasure invested over 20 long years, would have significant implications on Pax Americana going forward. It may see a realignment of the global balance of power—l'équilibre des pouvoirs. This evolving yet fluid reality would challenge both the intellectual and even physical capacities of the Indian state to navigate this uncharted territory.

However, what is India's most immediate requirement? Space and time for internal consolidation. For that, it requires peace on its periphery and a tranquil South Asia for at least three decades, if not more. This is an imperative to effectively surmount both its human and social development challenges. Thirty years is not even a blip in the long march of India as a civilization in continuum as opposed to a Westphalian nation state, which as pointed out above, is of rather recent vintage.

Additionally, as India aspires to become a player on the global stage, the inescapable fact is that it still continues to be locked in its neighbourhood. It has been unable to break out. Over the past seven decades, the baggage of the Partition with regard to Pakistan coupled with unsettled borders vis-à-vis China continue to be its principal bugbear inhibiting both its great power aspirations on one hand, and holding South Asia's potential hostage on the other. It therefore needs to get out of this gridlock. In order to do so, India requires a new National Security Doctrine.

As pointed out earlier, India lacks a tradition of coherent and consistent strategic analysis dovetailed into viable plans of action. This becomes all the more intimidating given the immediate need of ensuring peace on India's periphery over the next three decades. India confronts a landscape where both the nature and means of conflict are undergoing a complete metamorphosis. The variegated challenges that India has faced in the past two decades—including conventional war, repeated terror outrages and even a plane hijack executed by state-sponsored actors—were of a completely different order to the dares that it will face in the decades ahead.

The digital revolution over the past three decades has transformed the trajectory of future military engagements. This revolution has transformed every area of human enterprise into a veritable battlefield. India needs to be cognizant of the fact that the cyber domain has become weaponized. A question that national security practitioners should apply themselves to is: at what point does a cyber-attack become an act of war that necessitates a conventional response by utilizing formal military means? Similarly, if India or one of its critical facilities were to be attacked by autonomous weapons, how would it then tailor a rejoinder, more so if the identity of the architect of such an assault remains shrouded in anonymity?

This digital makeover has also ensured that the fighting model has now evolved from fighting the fight that fits the arsenal to customizing the arsenal to fit the fight. Notwithstanding the instrument of aggression utilized, conflict among nations is invariably war by other means. An alteration, therefore, in the means used must not deflect attention from viewing such an action through the prism of both traditional and enduring principles of war.

Notwithstanding the futuristic scenario delineated above, it still remains germane to look back at the preceding two decades to discern the conceptual construct through which India has viewed and responded to the various inflection points that have defined its security milieu. Have the comebacks been episodic or was there ever an attempt made to look at situations in a holistic manner, discern patterns and craft preemptive responses that could have neutered both intrinsic hostility and the consequent acts of violence?

Another question that India needs to answer is why it has not utilized the doctrine of offensive defence to a greater degree to neutralize challenges, especially from semi-state actors. This assumes importance, given that the biggest challenge it has faced for close to over four decades is cross-border state-sponsored terror. Why have non-conventional means not been actively explored and actioned as a means of thwarting the terrorist threat? Does it have something to do with the moral dilemma of being a democracy and not adopting means and methods outside the pale of both constitutionalism and law? Can this be a sustainable format for the future also?

A connected question is with regard to nuclear deterrence given that the India-Pakistan-China nuclear triangle is a convoluted, if not complicated, state of play. China is a first age nuclear power while both India and Pakistan are second age nuclear powers. Is the theology of the first nuclear age, predicated essentially on Mutually

Assured Destruction (MAD),[1] the abiding template for the second nuclear age also? Instead, can a process of dialling back be crafted with all the three countries moving to a clearly articulated No First Use Policy? Pakistan's nuclear force posture does not currently abide by this code. If it were to happen, would it not make the security environment more stable and relaxed?

Based on the experiences of the past two decades, the motivation for this endeavour is to incite a collective think about India's new national security doctrine for the remaining decades of the twenty-first century.

My experience after serving on the Parliamentary Standing Committees of Defence and External Affairs during 2009-12 and on the Parliamentary Consultative Committee of Defence during the same period as well as again on the Defense Consultative Committee from 2019 onwards convinced me that there is virtually no serious debate or informed introspection of our national security calculus even within the rarefied echelons of the legislature.

There is hardly any parliamentary oversight, unlike the kind of rigorous scrutiny that other legislatures around the world undertake of their national security and defence establishments, particularly those who live in extremely hostile and challenging environments. My work on the Private Members' Bill that I had moved in Parliament in 2011 and again in 2019 to provide a proper legislative architecture to our intelligence agencies and the Central Bureau of Investigation (CBI), as well as the various policy platforms that I have been associated with for close to over two decades now, gave me an opportunity to interact with and observe some of India's finest national security professionals. It further convinced me that a wider national consciousness of our national security imperatives is a must, both inside and outside our legislative organs.

This book, therefore, is not only meant for those fine men and women who serve the cause of our national security. They perhaps

---

[1]'MAD doctrine,' *The Hindu*, 12 July 2017, https://www.thehindu.com/opinion/op-ed/mad-doctrine/article19259265.ece. Accessed on 15 March 2021.

know and understand far more than I have possibly attempted to comprehend. Rather, this attempt is aimed at a wider audience of those people who are intellectually curious about issues pervading our defence and national security ecosystem. Those who are interested in a sober reflection and a civilized debate on these issues, those who are worried about the absence of a strategic culture in India and those who are trying to craft the intellectual underpinnings of a new security doctrine for India.

This book is finally also aimed at my colleagues in Parliament and the state legislatures whose preoccupation with the cut and thrust of retail politics and the daily grunt work of delivering to the aspirations of their constituents hardly leaves them with any time to look at the bigger picture of where India should be headed and how to get there, which is their primary responsibility as law makers and policy formulators.

ONE

1998: TESTING TIMES

It all really began in the 1960s as the development of nuclear technology in India gathered steam. However, the initial impetus was given much earlier; in fact, right after Independence, with the foundation of the Atomic Energy Commission (AEC) in 1948, spearheaded by Homi Bhabha. This was followed by the establishment, in 1954, of the Atomic Energy Establishment, Trombay (AEET), later renamed the Bhabha Atomic Research Centre (BARC), to shepherd India's nuclear energy development programme. The passage of the Atomic Energy Act of 1962 provided for the '...development and control of atomic energy...' Prime Minister Jawaharlal Nehru was opposed to nuclear weaponization, but he was clear that if the need arose, India would make use of nuclear energy as seen fit, which would not necessarily preclude weapon systems.[1]

After the 1962 border war with China, a systematic nuclear weapons development program was set in motion. In fact, the genesis of India's nuclear program can be traced back to Operation 59-6, the code name for China's first nuclear foray on 16 October 1964. It would nonetheless take India nearly a decade to test the first nuclear prototype (as a forerunner to the 1998 tests).

In his captivating account, 'India's Nuclear Bomb', George Perkovich chronicles the origins and the theological debates that

---

[1]'Indian Nuclear Program', *Atomic Heritage Foundation*, 23 August 2018, https://www.atomicheritage.org/history/indian-nuclear-program. Accessed on 10 November 2020.

marked this quest.[2] The principal actors were former prime minister Lal Bahadur Shastri, the brilliant but mercurial nuclear physicist Homi Bhabha and the Indian National Congress (INC). Since Independence, Bhabha had worked relentlessly to further India's nuclear aspirations, but was hamstrung by Mahatma Gandhi's legacy of non-violence. It virtually proscribed any public discussion on 'going nuclear'. Even after the Chinese test, Bhabha found it difficult to persuade Shastri to embark on a weapons program, given the latter's qualms about nuclear weapons. However, Bhabha was eventually able to convince Shastri to fast-track India's nuclear power program, and to sanction a project for 'peaceful nuclear explosions (PNEs)'—a major milestone in India's nuclear journey.

Within a decade, India carried out its first PNE, code-named 'Smiling Buddha', on 18 May 1974 at Pokhran, a remote location in the deserts of Rajasthan.

The credit for this undoubtedly goes to Prime Minister Indira Gandhi, who never shied away from taking bold and even contentious decisions. Three and a half years earlier, in December 1971, she had redefined the political map of South Asia and shepherded Bangladesh into existence. Her decision to cleave Pakistan into two halves in the face of tremendous international pressure, especially from the United States (US) and its western allies, probably made her clear-eyed about India's need for a nuclear shield.

The alleged role of an intelligence agency that she referred to as the ubiquitous 'foreign hand' in India, between 1972–5, may well have been the tipping point, if not the trigger, for the decision to go ahead with the 1974 test. This particular aspect has never been the subject of any sustained and serious research by academics,

---

[2]George Perkovich, *India's Nuclear Bomb: The Impact on Global Proliferation,* University of California Press, 2001.

strategic experts, biographers or even historians.[3][4][5]

The Pokhran test came at a price that PM Gandhi must have surely contemplated. Sanctions were imposed by the P-5—the US, Russia, the United Kingdom (UK), France and China—five countries recognized by the Nuclear Non-Proliferation Treaty (NPT) as nuclear weapon states. The Nuclear Suppliers Group (NSG), or the London Club, set up in 1975, was essentially a reaction to India's nuclear tests. It had a straightforward objective: to prevent other nations from going nuclear by denying them access to nuclear material.

The members of the London Club at that moment were the US, the Union of Soviet Socialist Republics (USSR), the UK, France, Canada, Federal Republic of Germany, Japan, Belgium, Czechoslovakia, German Democratic Republic, Italy, Netherlands, Poland and Sweden. They decided to adopt a set of guidelines, a gentlemen's agreement not amounting to a treaty. These guidelines aspired to control the export of certain sensitive nuclear materials, equipment and technology.

In the wake of the 1974 sanctions, there were agonizing moments of both vacillation and tentativeness in India's nuclear journey, underscored by the untested weaponization of the 1980s, and Prime Minister P.V. Narasimha Rao's aborted mission to carry out India's second nuclear test (December 1995) due to alleged international sensitivities. Rao's attempt at conducting a nuclear test during his tenure as prime minister (1991–6) had been allegedly preempted by the US. When Rao handed over the reins to Atal Bihari Vajpayee in May 1996, he reportedly told Vajpayee, '*Saamagri tayyar hai* (the

[3]Rudra Chaudhuri, 'India Has a Lesson for Trump: National Emergencies Are a Disaster for Democracy,' *Foreign Policy*, https://foreignpolicy.com/2019/02/21/india-has-a-lesson-for-trump-national-emergencies-are-a-disaster-for-democracy/. Accessed on 15 March 2021.

[4]Rajiv Dogra, *India's World: How Prime Ministers Shaped Foreign* Policy, Rupa Publications, 2020.

[5]Prashant Reddy, 'Foreign Funding of NGOs,' *Open Magazine*, 22 February 2013, https://openthemagazine.com/features/business/foreign-funding-of-ngos/. Accessed on 15 March 2021.

ingredients are ready [for the nuclear test]). You can go ahead.'[6] He subsequently handed Vajpayee a chit prompting the latter to finish the task he had initiated.[7]

Finally, on 11 and 13 May 1998, India carried out a series of five nuclear tests at the Pokhran test range, which coincided with the second innings of Atal Bihari Vajpayee as prime minister. His first term had lasted barely a fortnight in May 1996. His second term had begun barely two months earlier on 19 March 1998. The National Democratic Alliance (NDA)—a 24-party Bharatiya Janata Party (BJP)-led coalition, which he was heading—was far from stable, given the unwieldy and disparate nature of the arrangement, temperamental alliance partners and simmering disagreements right from the outset.

For the BJP, this attempt at governance was critical. This was the first right-wing-led coalition government formed since India's first post-Independence general elections held in 1951–2. Although there had been six non-Congress governments earlier, these had been led either by former Congressmen or people with a broadly permissive ideological orientation, namely Morarji Desai (1977–9), Charan Singh (1979–80), V.P. Singh (1989–90), Chandra Shekhar (1990–1), H.D. Deve Gowda (1996–7) and Inder Kumar Gujral (1997–8).

It was also important for the Vajpayee government to establish a distinction from those that had governed India between 1947 and 1998. The sphere where they thought this point of departure lay was in their approach to national security via muscular nationalism.

---

[6]Vinay Sitapati, 'Narasimha Rao, Not Vajpayee, Was the PM Who Set India on a Nuclear Explosion Path,' Scroll.in, 1 July 2016, https://scroll.in/article/810874/narasimha-rao-not-vajpayee-was-the-pm-who-set-india-on-a-nuclear-explosion-path. Accessed on 15 March 2021.
[7]Ashok Tandon, 'Narasimha Rao Passed on a Chit to Vajpayee During His Swearing-In. Here's Why,' News18, 17 August 2018, https://www.news18.com/news/opinion/opinion-narasimha-rao-passed-on-a-chit-to-vajpayee-during-his-swearing-in-heres-why-1847817.html. Accessed on 15 March 2021.

SAVIOUR OF THE SAFFRON GOVERNMENT

On the vital nuclear issue, the BJP's stand had always been distinctive from other conventional political parties. Its political predecessor, the erstwhile Bharatiya Jana Sangh, had always been a fervent supporter of India going nuclear.[8] As far back as 1964, the Jana Sangh, in one of its initial resolutions on the nuclear issue, proclaimed,

> The Bharatiya Jan Sangh has always been of the view that the nation's determination to build up military strength adequate enough to frustrate the gravest challenge to its independence and integrity should not be limited by pseudo pacifist inhibitions. Since the last two years, India has been at undeclared war with China. No price can be considered too high where the country's defence is involved.[9]

Their words turned out to be swiftly prophetic, considering China's first nuclear test took place in October 1964.

After the first PNE in May 1974, the Jana Sangh passed another resolution on 2 June that year declaring 18 May 1974 as a 'red letter day in Indian history'. L.K. Advani, then president of the Jana Sangh, who also headed the BJP in later years, wrote that India should build a nuclear arsenal 'to protect our independence'. He further added that the demand was no longer confined to a niche bomb lobby. It was the nation's collective demand.[10]

The only dilution in the pro-nuclear weapons posture of the Jana

[8]Manoj Joshi, 'Political and Diplomatic Overview of the Run Up to the 1965 India-Pakistan War', *Observer Research Foundation*, 3 September 2015, https://www.orfonline.org/research/political-and-diplomatic-overview-of-the-run-up-to-the-1965-india-pakistan-war/. Accessed on 16 November 2020.

[9]'Resolutions on Defence and External Affairs, Vol. 3', July 1973, http://library.bjp.org/jspui/handle/123456789/197. Accessed on 15 March 2021.

[10]Sitakanta Mishra, 'Role of Political Parties in Formulating India's Nuclear Weapons Policy', Jawaharlal Nehru University, 2011. http://hdl.handle.net/10603/133031. Accessed on 15 March 2021.

Sangh occurred when it melded into the Janata Party government and deferred to the Morarji Desai line of nuclear dovishness.[11] However, this was but a brief abatement considering that Morarji's prime ministerial tenure lasted a little over two years, from March 1977 to July 1979.

After the fall of the Morarji government in 1979 and the formation of the BJP a year later, the party reverted to its original position. Speaking on the demand for grants of the Ministry of Defence (MoD) (on 18 July 1980 in the Lok Sabha), Vajpayee said the government must keep all its options open and build a second-strike capability in view of Pakistan's repeated efforts to acquire resources for nuclear capability.

Thereafter, the BJP's stand had been consistent, vociferously supporting India's need to go nuclear. In its 1989 election manifesto, the BJP stated, 'we must go for the nuclear option'. It went further in its 1991 election manifesto, stating that if the party came to office, it would give 'our defence forces nuclear teeth'. In the election manifesto of 1996, the party expanded on its earlier position, promising to 're-evaluate the country's nuclear policy and exercise the option to induct nuclear weapons'.[12]

During the general elections of 1998 that propelled the BJP to power, the party was perhaps most emphatic when its manifesto underscored that 'the BJP rejects the notion of nuclear apartheid and will actively oppose attempts to impose a hegemonistic nuclear regime. We will not be dictated to by anybody in matters of security requirements and in the exercise of nuclear option'.[13] Over the years, the BJP's nuclear proclamations have been sharp, undeviating, with nothing left to conjecture.

---

[11]'Foreign Relations of the United States, 1977–1980, Volume 19,' *Office of the Historian*, https://history.state.gov/historicaldocuments/frus1977-80v19/d74. Accessed on 15 March 2021.

[12]BJP Election Manifesto Collection, *BJP Central Library*, http://library.bjp.org/jspui/handle/123456789/260, Accessed on 15 March 2021.

[13]'BJP Election Manifesto, 1998,' *BJP Central Library*, http://library.bjp.org/jspui/handle/123456789/241. Accessed on 15 March 2021.

The 1998 Manifesto assertion was also perhaps grounded in the rather polarizing proceedings that played themselves out in the Conference on Disarmament in Geneva in 1996, qua the Comprehensive Nuclear-Test Ban Treaty (CTBT). Despite India vetoing the treaty, the US took it to the United Nations (UN) General Assembly. The CTBT was adopted by the General Assembly as a resolution (A/RES/50/245) on 10 September 1996. The Treaty opened for signature on 24 September 1996. Ironically, the US Senate is yet to ratify the treaty after refusing to provide either advice or consent on 13 October 1999.[14]

In the initial days of the Vajpayee government, it seemed the contradictions of coalition politics would prohibit the BJP from taking that radical nuclear step. The National Agenda for Governance, the bedrock of the BJP's tryst with executive power, declared that a National Security Council (NSC) would be formed to carry out the first-ever strategic defence review. The document stated that in the course of the review, the government would 're-evaluate the nuclear policy' and 'exercise the option to induct nuclear weapons.'[15]

Even George Fernandes, India's defence minister, in an expansive conversation, stated, 'Our National Agenda has said that at the end of doing a strategic review, which will be the first of its kind, if we come to the conclusion that things have reached a stage with China and Pakistan—one an acknowledged nuclear power and the other claiming to be a nuclear power—and that India now needs to take the plunge, then so be it.'[16]

---

[14]'The Status of the Comprehensive Test Ban Treaty: Signatories and Ratifiers', *Arms Control Association*, https://www.armscontrol.org/factsheets/ctbtsig. Accessed on 15 March 2021.

[15]'National Agenda for Governance', https://www.scribd.com/presentation/289571714/National-Agenda-for-Governance. Accessed on 15 March 2021.

[16]Manoj Joshi, 'Confronted with Pakistani Sabre-rattling, India Gears up to Meet the Challenge', *India Today*, 4 May 1998, https://www.indiatoday.in/magazine/nation/story/19980504-confronted-with-pakistani-sabre-rattling-india-gears-up-to-meet-the-challenge-826299-1998-05-04. Accessed on 17 November 2020.

Vajpayee took a far more hawkish stance, when he told Parliament: 'Our party feels India should have the bomb since it will place the country in a strong position vis-à-vis the outside world, but other political parties apparently have a different view and therefore we have decided to keep the issue aside till a national consensus is reached.'[17] Even President K.R. Narayanan's address to the joint session of Parliament was conspicuously silent on nuclear-related issues.

However, this was really a game of smoke and mirrors. The Vajpayee government, as opposed to its public pose, was preparing the ground for Pokhran-II. Even though the top leadership of the BJP had reconciled itself to the compulsion of coalition politics by putting the incendiary issues of Ram Janmabhoomi, Article 370 and the Uniform Civil Code on the back-burner; the party chose to follow a vigorous line, albeit unobtrusively, with regard to the nuclear question.

The PM has virtually unrestricted discretion on the issue of nuclear tests, subject to expert counsel that he may receive or solicit. Vajpayee made full use of his powers and the tests were enveloped in complete confidentiality. In public, the government committed to a defence review, while preparations were given the go-ahead behind the curtain.

What was the inflection point that triggered the decision to test? Was it Vajpayee's desire to fulfil the long-standing commitment of the BJP, or did he want to crown his first 50-odd days in office with a major decision? There could be another reason, for the mind of a politician works in strange ways. Vajpayee had had a very long innings in politics before ascending to the office of prime minister. He must have known that the nuclear test would certainly get a disparate 24-party coalition to focus as never before. There would be a fallout that would consume the collective energy of the government to surmount. Subsequent events would establish this thesis to be correct.

---

[17]John Cherian, 'The BJP and the Bomb', *Frontline*, Print edition: 11 April 1998, https://frontline.thehindu.com/cover-story/article30161203.ece. Accessed on 15 March 2021.

As most of the dramatis personae are dead, it is impossible to accurately pinpoint the precise moment Vajpayee made up his mind, given that PM Narasimha Rao had handed his successor an option that was locked, if not fully loaded.

Going by publicly available facts, it seems that Vajpayee's mind was made up even as he assumed the mantle of PM. He was sworn in on 19 March 1998 and the next day, he had a discussion with Dr R. Chidambaram, secretary of the Department of Atomic Energy (DAE) and chairperson of the AEC. A fortnight and four days later, Vajpayee approved the tests in a meeting with Chidambaram and Dr A.P.J. Abdul Kalam, who was then head of the Defence Research and Development Organisation (DRDO). Brajesh Mishra, principal secretary to PM Vajpayee, was the designated point person to liaise with the scientists. The groundwork was carried out in complete secrecy, finally culminating in three nuclear tests on 11 May and two more on 13 May 1998.

Mishra had this to say on the first day of the tests:

As announced by the PM this afternoon today, India conducted three underground nuclear tests in the Pokhran range. ...These tests have established that India has a proven capability for a weaponised nuclear programme. ...These tests provide reassurance to the people of India that their national security interests are paramount and will be promoted and protected. Succeeding generations of Indians would also rest assured that contemporary technologies associated with the nuclear option have been passed on to them in this 50th year of Independence. We would like to reaffirm categorically that we will continue to exercise the most stringent control on the export of sensitive technologies, equipment and commodities—especially those related to weapons of mass destruction. Our track record has been impeccable in this regard. Therefore, we expect recognition of our responsible policy by the international community.

India remains committed to a speedy process of nuclear

disarmament leading to total and global elimination of nuclear weapons... In our neighbourhood we have many friends with whom relations of fruitful cooperation for mutual benefit have existed and deepened over a long period. .... For India, as for others, the prime need is for peaceful cooperation and economic development.[18]

He added that like the 1974 tests, the latest tests too were fully controlled with no release of radioactive substances into the atmosphere. He went on say that Indian scientists would benefit immensely as they explored nuclear capabilities. He reiterated India's commitment to the Partial Test Ban Treaty (PTBT) of 1963 and global disarmament. India would remain at the forefront of preventing environmental damage caused by nuclear-related activities.

The tests drew a swift reaction from Pakistan that had been just a few steps from exploding its own bomb. On 28 May, Islamabad conducted five tests in the Ras Koh hills in the Chagai district of Balochistan. 'We have settled the score,' declared Nawaz Sharif, the Pakistani prime minister.[19]

It cannot be said with any degree of certainty that had India not conducted nuclear tests in 1998, Pakistan would not have either. Analysts however believe that once India conducted its test, the option of not testing for Pakistan became a non sequitur. Anecdotal evidence suggests that there was a lack of willingness in the Sharif government to run the gauntlet. The decision was apparently taken by the military and presented as a fait accompli to the civilian government. Pakistan Railway Minister Sheikh Rasheed revealed in 2020 that Sharif and his

---

[18]'Indian Government Statement on Nuclear Tests', *Atomic Archive*, 11 May 1998, https://www.atomicarchive.com/resources/documents/deterrence/india-statement.html. Accessed on 15 March 2021.
[19]John Ward Anderson and Kamran Khan, 'Pakistan Sets-off Nuclear Blasts', *Washington Post*, 29 May 1998, https://www.washingtonpost.com/archive/politics/1998/05/29/pakistan-sets-off-nuclear-blasts/be94cba3-7ffc-4ecc-9f67-ac6ddfe2a94c/. Accessed on 15 March 2021.

entire cabinet, barring a few, were opposed to conducting nuclear tests. However, his brother, Shahbaz Sharif denied these claims and asserted that nuclear tests in Pakistan must be credited to Nawaz.

These nuclear tests were the finale of a quest that had begun in Multan, Pakistan, 31 days after the devastating defeat and humiliating surrender in the 1971 war that led to the creation of Bangladesh.

On Monday, 24 January 1972, President Zulfikar Ali Bhutto held a secret meeting in Multan where it was decided that Pakistan would acquire nuclear weapons. Bhutto set up the Multan meeting barely a month after assuming the office of president. Pakistan's nuclear decision was first broadcast by journalists Steve Weissman and Herbert Krosney on the BBC show *Panorama* in 1980, and later detailed in their book *The Islamic Bomb: The Nuclear Threat to Israel and the Middle East.*[20] The meeting was attended by the country's top scientists: Abdus Salam, who went on to win the Nobel Prize; Ishrat Usmani, head of the Pakistan Atomic Energy Commission and Munir Ahmad Khan, future chairman of the Pakistan Atomic Energy Commission. The meeting's objective was not to consult with scientists, but to have them commit to what Bhutto now considered an existential quest. Over a period of time, this would also result in A.Q. Khan's ubiquitous nuclear Walmart.

With the Pakistani nuclear tests, the fig leaf of nuclear deniability in South Asia was blown to smithereens and the power balance was now frozen into perpetuity. Whatever overt asymmetry, in conventional terms, India may have had earlier was lost forever. From now on, everything would operate under a nuclear overhang. In reality, however, it was a well-known fact that both Pakistan and India had developed nuclear weapons much earlier, and the events of May 1998 simply turned the de facto into a de jure. In fact, the reality of an existing nuclear template in

---

[20]Steve Weissman and Herbert Krosney, *The Islamic Bomb: The Nuclear Threat to Israel and the Middle East,* Crown Publishing Group, 1981.

both countries prior to the 1998 tests is confirmed by the stand-off during India's Operation Brasstacks (November 1986–March 1987) and the Robert Gates Mission (May 1990) that followed a second military gridlock resulting from an insurgency spike in Jammu and Kashmir (J&K).

DOWN THE NUCLEAR ROAD

More than two decades have passed since that fateful epoch in May 1998. Both nations, along with the Democratic People's Republic of Korea, and possibly Israel, are now referred to as powers of the second nuclear age. So how secure have nuclear weapons made India and Pakistan? If looked at from India's perspective, the answer is far from straightforward.

India's tests paved the way for a reset of its relationship with the US, a hyper power of the 1990s. This relationship has now reached a plateau of strategic stability. However, in the South Asian, or larger Asian context, strategic parity with Pakistan has not improved the India–Pakistan bilateral relationship. Disagreements have only gotten sharper. Both nations have attempted to test the threshold of the other's nuclear theology. Pakistan has done so through the increased usage of non-state actors. India has responded to these depredations by crafting retaliatory strikes, such as the ground strikes after the Pakistan-sponsored terror attack at the Uri army cantonment in September 2016 and the Balakot/Jaba Top air strike after the Pulwama terror attack of February 2019. Nuclear weaponization, envisioned as a way to bring strategic sanity to South Asia, has only resulted in escalating conflict.

China is the third leg of the region's nuclear triangle. George Fernandes, defence minister at the time of India's nuclear tests, stated that besides Pakistan, China was the potential threat number one. PM Vajpayee, in a letter to US President Bill Clinton immediately after the nuclear tests, declared,

I have been deeply concerned at the deteriorating security environment, especially the nuclear environment, faced by India for some years past. We have an overt nuclear weapon state on our borders, a state which committed armed aggression against India in 1962. Although our relations with that country have improved in the last decade or so, an atmosphere of distrust persists mainly due to the unresolved border problem...'[21]

Twenty-three years have passed since that prophetic observation. In 2020, India experienced one of the worst stand-offs with China in eastern Ladakh, and at other points along the Line of Actual Control (LAC). This has been the most alarming confrontation in close to six decades. China, like India, has a declared No First Use (NFU) nuclear policy. The country is not an irrational actor on the global stage, though it is a canny performer by all standards, with pretensions of returning the world to the Middle Kingdom template of the yesteryears. Even with the Chinese, Mutually Assured Destruction (MAD), the bedrock of nuclear theology, has not resulted in resolving outstanding issues. It can be concluded that nuclear tests have not brought a strategic windfall. There has been no moving on from deep-rooted conflicts for almost three billion people who call South Asia and China their home.

On 17 August 1999, buoyed by the Kargil victory about a month earlier, India released the draft report of the National Security Advisory Board (NSAB) on Indian nuclear doctrine. The intent was to provide clarity about the theological basis of India's nuclear thinking. Since the Vajpayee government had fallen short by a single vote and Lok Sabha elections were yet to be held, Brajesh Mishra, the PM's principal secretary and de facto national security advisor

---

[21]'Nuclear Anxiety: Indian's Letter to Clinton on the Nuclear Testing', *The New York Times*, 13 May 1998, https://www.nytimes.com/1998/05/13/world/nuclear-anxiety-indian-s-letter-to-clinton-on-the-nuclear-testing.html. Accessed on 17 November 2020.

(NSA), was keen to emphasize that the draft nuclear doctrine had to await approval of the new government.

Mishra's opening remarks make for some very interesting reading:

> A cardinal principle regarding the use of nuclear weapons is that of civilian control. Only the elected civilian leader of the country is empowered to authorize the use of nuclear weapons. As the recent operations in Kargil have demonstrated, our system and the political leadership believe with great responsibility and restraint, as you would expect from the largest democracy in the world. This sense of responsibility will also guide our actions with regard to nuclear weapons.[22]

The doctrine outlined,

> Autonomy of decision-making in the developmental process and in strategic matters is an inalienable democratic right of the Indian people. India will strenuously guard this right in a world where nuclear weapons for a select few are sought to be legitimized for an indefinite future, and where there is growing complexity and frequency in the use of force for political purposes.
>
> India shall pursue a doctrine of credible minimum nuclear deterrence. In this policy of 'retaliation only', the survivability of our arsenal is critical.
>
> The fundamental purpose of Indian nuclear weapons is to deter the use and threat of use of nuclear weapons by any State or entity against India and its forces. India will not be the first to initiate a nuclear strike, but will respond with punitive retaliation should deterrence fail.

---

[22]'Opening Remarks', MEA, 17 August 1999, https://www.mea.gov.in/in-focus-article.htm?18915/Opening+Remarks+by+National+Security+Adviser+Mr+Brajesh+Mishra+at+the+Release+of+Draft+Indian+Nuclear+Doctrine. Accessed on 15 March 2021.

Four clear principles emerge from the declarations of 17 August.

1. India's nuclear arsenal will be under rigorous civilian control.
2. The autonomy of nuclear decision-making clearly implies that India will not be a part of any inequitable nuclear regimes, like the NPT, that seek to perpetuate inherent arbitrariness by dividing the world into nuclear haves and have-nots.
3. Minimum credible deterrence is a dynamic concept— how the word minimum would operationally play out will depend on a number of variables. The size, means of deployment and platforms utilized will be subject to revisable imperatives, periodically revisited.
4. There will be NFU of nuclear weapons.

More than two decades later, this continues to form the bedrock of Indian nuclear thinking.

The question remains: why did a 'caretaker' NDA/BJP government not wait until the ensuing Lok Sabha elections had brought in a new government? An ostensible reason is that they wanted to complete the process they had kicked off in March 1999 by taking complete and total ownership of the second round of nuclear tests. They clearly wanted to demonstrate to the world that unlike the PNE of 1974, this was about India gatecrashing its way into the club of nuclear weapon states, albeit with a sense of responsibility. It was also a strong signal to the electorate that they would be back after the elections to follow through on their promise. By then, it was all but clear that the country was going to give another five years to the victor of Kargil.

On 4 January 2003, the Prime Minister's Office (PMO) put out a press release outlining India's nuclear doctrine. The terse statement, 'Cabinet Committee on Security Reviews Progress in Operationalizing

India's Nuclear Doctrine', deserves reproduction in full.[23]

1. The Cabinet Committee on Security (CCS) met today to review the progress in operationalizing of India's nuclear doctrine. The Committee decided that the following information, regarding the nuclear doctrine and operational arrangements governing India's nuclear assets, should be shared with the public.

2. India's nuclear doctrine can be summarized as follows:

    i.   Building and maintaining a credible minimum deterrent;

    ii. A posture of 'No First Use' nuclear weapons will only be used in retaliation against a nuclear attack on Indian territory or on Indian forces anywhere;

    iii. Nuclear retaliation to a first strike will be massive and designed to inflict unacceptable damage.

    iv. Nuclear retaliatory attacks can only be authorized by the civilian political leadership through the Nuclear Command Authority.

    v.   Non-use of nuclear weapons against non-nuclear weapon states;

    vi. However, in the event of a major attack against India, or Indian forces anywhere, by biological or chemical weapons, India will retain the option of retaliating with nuclear weapons;

    vii. A continuance of strict controls on export of nuclear and missile related materials and technologies, participation in the Fissile Material Cut-off Treaty negotiations, and continued observance of the moratorium on nuclear tests.

---

[23]'Cabinet Committee on Security Reviews Progress in Operationalizing India's Nuclear Doctrine', *Press Information Bureau Archives*, 4 January 2003, https://archive.pib.gov.in/archive/releases98/lyr2003/rjan2003/04012003/r040120033.html. Accessed on 15 March 2021.

viii. Continued commitment to the goal of a nuclear weapon free world, through global, verifiable and non-discriminatory nuclear disarmament.

3. The Nuclear Command Authority consists of the Political Council led by the Prime Minister and the Executive Council led by the National Security Advisor. The CCS approved existing command and control structures and alternate chains of command as well.

STIRRING THE CAULDRON

Strategists often comment on India's nuclear doctrine, particularly questioning its NFU policy. Security experts like Bharat Karnad believe that India is not positioned to sufficiently recover from a nuclear attack to retaliate and cause 'unacceptable' damage to the aggressor. Other analysts and members of the strategic fraternity point out that tactical nuclear weapons make it difficult to determine the threshold of an attack and therefore effectively nullify the first use clause.[24] India can be bombarded repeatedly without legitimately reaching a stage where it can hit back.

The NFU policy also underscores that India's reactive nuclear posture has allowed major powers to consider a favourable position, even special status, when it comes to export and import of sensitive material. Additionally, a change in NFU demands a sophisticated structure comprising intelligence, surveillance and reconnaissance systems. It would also deprive India of fighting conventional wars beneath the nuclear threshold if such a space realistically exists. For a first-use posture to be effectively operationalized, India will have to establish a precise intellectual and physical infrastructure that can prevent any possibility of an

---

[24]Harsh Pant and Yogesh Joshi, 'Why a rethink of India's nuclear doctrine may be necessary', Observer Research Foundation, 27 March 2017, https://www.orfonline.org/research/why-a-rethink-of-indias-nuclear-doctrine-may-be-necessary/. Accessed on 18 November 2020.

unintended and inadvertent launch. Whether India is in a position to nurture such an infrastructure in the short term, remains an open-ended question.[25] A review of NFU faces practical challenges.

A possible trigger for doing away with NFU is the active repositioning of foreign powers and their strategic interests in South Asia's nuclear environment which could lead to meddling and flaring up of tensions. However, shifting to a first-use policy could take India back to the sanctions era of 1998 and destroy all the diplomatic work done over the years. It has taken consistent efforts to convince India's allies of the country's peaceful nuclear posture. A change in that policy, especially when India is not economically well placed in the global landscape, could be quite hazardous. Adversaries like Pakistan, and now China, are sure to launch diplomatic attacks and vilify India.

From January 2003 to May 2014, across three different administrations, there was no ambiguity with regard to India's nuclear doctrine. This was primarily because both Vajpayee and Dr Manmohan Singh were cognizant that any other posture in such a volatile neighbourhood would have a destabilizing effect.

However, even before taking over the reins of the government in 2014, the BJP had hinted that it might review the NFU; while the Congress has always maintained that NFU is a credible policy for India's nuclear future which did not require immediate change unless faced with an emergency. In April 2014, Dr Singh called for a global NFU convention to prevent the domino effect of nuclear escalation.

When the BJP formulated its manifesto for the 2014 general elections, it incorporated a rather amorphous formulation with regard to nuclear weapons.

---

[25]Gurmeet Kanwal, 'India's Nuclear Doctrine: Need for a Review', *CSIS*, 5 December 2014, https://www.csis.org/analysis/india%E2%80%99s-nuclear-doctrine-need-review#:~:text=Criticism%20of%20the%20nuclear%20doctrine,forces%20on%20the%20adversary's%20own. Accessed on 15 September 2021.

The sub-paragraph on page 39 of its Manifesto states that regarding:[26] [27]

> 'Independent Strategic Nuclear Programme', BJP believes that the strategic gains acquired by India during the Atal Bihari Vajpayee regime on the nuclear programme have been frittered away by the Congress. Our emphasis was, and remains on, beginning of a new thrust on framing policies that would serve India's national interest in the twenty-first century. We will follow a two-pronged independent nuclear programme, unencumbered by foreign pressure and influence, for civilian and military purposes, especially as nuclear power is a major contributor to India's energy sector. BJP will:
>
> - Study in detail India's nuclear doctrine, and revise and update it, to make it relevant to challenges of current times.
> - Maintain a credible minimum deterrent that is in tune with changing geostatic realities.
> - Invest in India's indigenous Thorium Technology Programme.

The first sub-point set alarm bells ringing among the analyst community and the non-proliferation Ayatollahs across the world. Would the BJP/NDA government revisit its NFU doctrine? Responding to the concern, more out of anxiety of being labelled as an irresponsible political outfit, the BJP hurriedly clarified its position. Writing for *The Diplomat* on 15 April 2014, Ankit Panda reported:

> In an effort to clarify the statements made in the manifesto, BJP President Rajnath Singh told *The Hindustan Times* that 'the no first use policy for nuclear weapons was a well-thought-out

---

[26]'BJP Election Manifesto, 2014', *BJP Central Library*, http://library.bjp.org/jspui/bitstream/123456789/252/1/bjp_lection_manifesto_english_2014.pdf. Accessed on 15 March 2021.

[27]'Full Text: BJP Manifesto for 2014 Lok Sabha Elections', *News18*, 7 April 2014, https://www.news18.com/news/politics/full-text-bjp-manifesto-for-2014-lok-sabha-elections-679304.html. Accessed on 15 March 2021.

stand of the [former BJP-led coalition government].' He added that the BJP does not intend to reverse it in any way. According to the *Hindustan Times*, BJP 'party leaders say the policy has not only boosted India's standing in the international community but also gives a certain amount of leverage in foreign-policy matters.'[28]

It is evident to any discerning observer of Indian politics that the deliberately ambiguous formulation of India's nuclear doctrine was to inject an element of muscularity into its national security narrative. The target was the more hawkish constituency of Indian society who thrive on elevated levels of bellicosity.

However, the swirling debate on NFU did not end with the BJP/NDA government coming to power in 2014. The late Manohar Parrikar, former defence minister, a genteel soul from Goa but fairly out of his depth in New Delhi, mused aloud at a book release two-and-a-half years later, 'Why a lot of people say that India has No First Use policy. Why should I bind myself to a... I should say I am a responsible nuclear power and I will not use it irresponsibly. ... I am not saying that you have to use it first just because you don't decide that you don't use it first. The hoax can be called off.'[29]

The *Business Standard* quoted him as follows: 'If written down strategy exists or you take a stand on a nuclear aspect, I think you're actually giving away your strength in nuclear.'[30]

It is not expected of the defence minister to ruminate in public

[28]Ankit Panda, 'No, India Won't Abandon Its No First-Use Nuclear Doctrine', 15 April 2014, *The Diplomat*, https://thediplomat.com/2014/04/no-india-wont-abandon-its-no-first-use-nuclear-doctrine/. Accessed on 15 March 2021.

[29]Sushant Singh, 'Manohar Parrikar questions India's no-first-use nuclear policy', *The Indian Express*, 11 November 2016, https://indianexpress.com/article/india/india-news-india/manohar-parrikar-questions-no-first-use-nuclear-policy-adds-my-thinking-4369062/. Accessed on 21 November 2020.

[30]ANI, 'Defence Minister Parrikar questions "no first use" nuclear strike doctrine', *Business Standard*, 11 November 2016, https://www.business-standard.com/article/current-affairs/defence-minister-parrikar-questions-no-first-use-nuclear-strike-doctrine-116111001609_1.html. Accessed on 21 November 2020.

about such sensitive matters except if it is not deliberate. Politicians and policymakers often do float trial balloons in the public space subterfuging them as personal opinions. At times, it is because of the temptation to see their name making front-page headlines. In any case, it is a dangerous street to walk down.

Parrikar had to face the embarrassment of being contradicted by his own ministry barely hours later. This was a first of its kind—a union minister, and that too a member of the CCS, being contradicted by his own ministry. A spokesperson of the MoD clarified, 'What he (Defence Minister Parrikar) said was that India, being a responsible power, should not get into first use debate. But once again it is clarified that this was his (Parrikar's) personal opinion.'[31]

Was there a need for such a clarification when the defence minister himself had prefaced his remarks saying that he was speaking in an individual capacity? It was obvious that Parrikar's headline-hunting expedition had not gone down very well with his political bosses.

However, matters did not end there. In his 2016 book, *Choices: Inside the Making of India's Foreign Policy*, Shivshankar Menon, NSA to Prime Minister Manmohan Singh, and former foreign secretary, stated: 'There is a potential grey area as to when India would use nuclear weapons first against another nuclear weapons state (NWS). Circumstances are conceivable in which India might find it useful to strike first, for instance, against as NWS that had declared it would certainly use its weapons, and if India were certain that adversary's launch was imminent. But India's present nuclear doctrine is silent on this scenario.'[32]

---

[31]HT Correspondent, 'Parrikar questions "no first use" N-policy, MoD calls it his personal opinion,' *Hindustan Times*, 11 November 2016, https://www.hindustantimes.com/india-news/parrikar-questions-no-first-use-policy-mod-says-it-is-his-personal-opinion/story-BDtyPr5VPzd6AkjrfXlSLN.html. Accessed on 21 November 2020.
[32]Harsh V. Pant, 'India's nuclear debate has only just begun,' *ORF Online*, 31 March 2017, https://www.orfonline.org/research/indias-nuclear-debate-has-only-just-begun/. Accessed on 21 November 2020.

Menon makes a fair point of doctrinal silence. If hard, unimpeachable and irrefutable intelligence pointed to such a possibility, any decision maker would face a catch-22 situation. It would all boil down to his willingness to convince himself that he was indeed doing the right thing and there was no other option available. This is a gut-wrenching yet probable scenario. Again, the policy community went into a tizzy with many trying to catch their own tails. There is a distinction between the academics of nuclear weapons, and the dilemmas a decision maker faces, always perhaps silently praying that push would never come to shove.

On 16 August 2019, less than two weeks after the BJP-led NDA government amended Article 370 and abrogated Article 35A from the Constitution, Defence Minister Rajnath Singh stirred the nuclear cauldron again. He tweeted, 'Pokhran is the area which witnessed Atal Ji's [A.B. Vajpayee] firm resolve to make India a nuclear power and yet remain firmly committed to the doctrine of "No First Use". India has strictly adhered to this doctrine. What happens in future depends on the circumstances.'[33]

This was after his Pokhran visit to mark the first death anniversary of former prime minister Vajpayee, under whose government India had conducted the 1998 tests. Surprisingly, Rajnath was contradicting what he had said five years earlier as BJP president to quell the storm on NFU after the ambiguous formulation in the BJP's 2014 manifesto had set off a flurry of speculation.

Lieutenant General B.S. Nagal, former strategic forces commander, in his statement had expressed that while India maintained its NFU, decision makers could not sit back and watch when there is sufficient evidence to prove an impending nuclear attack by an adversary. Necessary action in that case must be taken.[34]

---

[33]Available at https://twitter.com/rajnathsingh/status/1162276901055893504?lang=en. Accessed on 15 March 2021.

[34]Ajai Shukla, 'Rajnath Singh says India could use nukes first if circumstances demand', Business Standard, 17 August 2019, https://www.business-standard.com/article/current-affairs/rajnath-singh-says-india-could-use-nukes-first-if-circumstances-demand-119081601939_1.html. Accessed on 15 March 2021.

All this clearly indicates two separate realities. A doctrine that outlines a stable, relaxed and even recessed nuclear posture, and a probable threat scenario under which difficult choices would have to be taken by the person in the hot seat. The statements divergent to the country's official nuclear doctrine by two CCS members in the recent past, Manohar Parrikar and Rajnath Singh, also serve as a reminder that a country's nuclear doctrine is too serious a matter to be the subject of casual remarks or kite-flying tweets.

NO WINNERS

When viewed from the outside, it has always been complicated to get a holistic view of India's nuclear power. Within the country, the popular wisdom, notwithstanding opposition from certain groups, leans towards India being more secure with nuclear weapons in its arsenal. The opposition to this attitude is healthy as it allows India's thinkers to study the subject's history and probable outcomes.

The nuclear tests of 1974 and 1998 have decidedly changed the way India is perceived abroad. They have elevated its status as a responsible power over the years because of the care taken in handling nuclear weapons and committing to peaceful use of nuclear power. India's nuclear status has had a profound impact on its relations with key western powers and their allies.

It is noteworthy that a one-time decision to go nuclear was perhaps not the only determinant of India's success in managing its nuclear weapons. It was what followed over the decades—consistent diplomacy and wise posturing which allowed the country to retain the weapons, mend relations with important allies, and even be viewed as a de facto player in global security. The onus is now on the current and succeeding Indian governments to maintain the equilibrium of its posture, and international trust that comes along with it.

These tests are also milestones that defined India as a second nuclear age power. To decide whether the nuclear option has made the country safer or not would be like drawing lines in black and white. Did stresses in India's neighbourhood exacerbate or lessen as a consequence of the decisions that India, Pakistan and China took with regard to their respective nuclear weapons programmes? The answer is squarely in the negative. This is notwithstanding the balance of power theory integral to the realist theory that governs much of global foreign policy. The tests have certainly not made India's security environment more benign than what it was before these tests. If anything, India's national security environment has only worsened in the last decade and continues to slide. It has become far more volatile with a two-pronged collusive front between China and Pakistan becoming a veritable reality.

Unfortunately, the issues that bedevil the respective bilateral relationships between India and Pakistan, and India and China cannot be surmounted merely because all three are now within the zone of MAD. These frictions stem from deep-rooted socio-political realities, the baggage of history and the broader insecurity that plagues the region.

India must rethink both its neighbourhood policy and pick up threads of the debate on universal, comprehensive and verifiable nuclear disarmament. The region's three billion people, and the entire world for that matter, will continue to live under the spectre of a probable nuclear Armageddon until every nation commits to universal and verifiable nuclear disarmament. Even the threat of weapons of mass destruction (WMD) should not be bandied about.

Unlikely as it may seem at the moment, the first and second age nuclear powers will have to sit together and work out a multilateral modus vivendi on the existential question that confronts humankind—is it ethically and morally defensible that a few countries have monopoly over such awesome destructive powers that threaten the very existence of planet earth? Has the time not come to roll back this destructive march that commenced in 1945? An invisible, odourless and un-feelable entity called coronavirus or COVID-19 brought the entire humankind to a standstill. Try and imagine what a nuclear launch could do. There are no winners in a nuclear war.

TWO

KARGIL: AN EYE-OPENER, SANS RECKONING

Kargil was a resounding military victory for India. It had a lasting effect on India's foreign and security policies, and it became a consequential catalyst for a slew of reforms in the national security infrastructure. Two decades after a hard-fought victory, questions linger: Why did the incursion occur in the first place? Why, like the recent Chinese infiltration, was the military and intelligence caught napping back then too? More importantly, were those lessons internalized? Is India better prepared to handle such a volatile situation today? To answer these questions, one must explore the events leading up to the Kargil War that lasted from May to July 1999.

The Vajpayee government had fallen by a solitary vote on 17 April 1999. The Opposition, led by the INC, failed to mobilize the numbers to form an alternative government. The Opposition was in an ambivalent mood. The failure to form an alternative government was laced with a quiet sense of jubilation that the second Vajpayee ministry had barely survived 13 months. The first one had lasted a record 13 days only. The country was on the brink of fresh elections as the Lok Sabha was dissolved on 26 April 1999.

Election groundwork was in full swing when initial reports of the Pakistani infiltration reached the wider citizenry. As the president of the Indian Youth Congress (IYC), I was knee-deep in mobilizing the organization for the upcoming electoral battle. Even the Opposition did not give the news much attention. We had been on the receiving end of Pakistan-sponsored terrorism for nearly two decades now, and there was a collective perception of this being yet another attempt to subvert the Lahore Spirit that was very much the flavour of the season.

THE NUCLEAR AFTERMATH: A BUS RIDE TO LAHORE

Prime Minister Vajpayee's oratory and eloquence went beyond him being just the quintessential wordsmith. His politics, much like his speeches, embraced grand gestures. One such significant initiative that occurred less than a year after the May 1998 nuclear tests was an outreach to Pakistan which culminated in a visit to Lahore on 19 February 1999.

Vajpayee—acutely aware of India's responsibility as a newly minted nuclear nation, and to set an example in the eyes of a rattled global strategic community—took a bus ride across the Attari-Wagah border into Lahore. Vajpayee visited the Minar-e-Pakistan, the symbol of Pakistani nationalism, and went on to sign the Lahore Declaration with PM Nawaz Sharif.

This declaration, hailed as a sequel to the 1972 Simla Agreement, resolved to explore a modus vivendi with regard to issues continuing to afflict the bilateral relationship, including the legacy issue of J&K. A concurrent Memorandum of Understanding (MoU), keeping the new-born nuclear reality of South Asia in view, was also signed by both foreign secretaries.

Point 3 of that MoU is rather instructive:

> The two sides are fully committed to undertaking national measures to reduce the risks of accidental or unauthorized use of nuclear weapons under their respective control. The two sides further undertake to notify each other immediately in the event of any accidental, unauthorized or unexplained incident that could create the risk of a fallout with adverse consequences for both sides, or an outbreak of a nuclear war between the two countries, as well as to adopt measures aimed

at diminishing the possibility of such actions, or such incidents being misinterpreted by the other. The two sides shall identify/ establish the appropriate communication mechanism for this purpose.[1]

Vajpayee's bus trip brought with it a new wave of hope and optimism. The incidents that, however, took place two months later proved to be a complete antithesis of the Lahore Declaration and all the promise it had held out.

Vajpayee and the Pakistani deep state drew paradoxical conclusions from the nuclearization of South Asia. Vajpayee envisioned much-needed tranquillity, while Pakistan's Inter-Services Intelligence (ISI) and the army probed for a limited conflict under a nuclear overhang. The legitimacy of nuclear deterrence was stretched to its limits multiple times after the 1998 nuclear tests; the first of which was the Kargil incursion.

Its origins could be traced back to a Pakistani war game from the 1980s. Captain Amarinder Singh points out in his book, *A Ridge Too Far*, that as a counter to Operation Brasstacks (1986–7), the Pakistani Army developed a war game called Operation Tupac (also known as Operation Topac), to look at different possibilities in case Pakistan invaded India.[2] A decade later, Gen. Pervez Musharraf, Pakistan's chief of army staff (COAS), decided to implement Operation Tupac. Only four army officers, including Musharraf, knew about this operation (code-named Operation Koh Paima), and together they came to be known as the 'Kargil Cabal.'[3]

---

[1]'Lahore Declaration 1999', MEA, 2 February 1999, https://mea.gov.in/in-focus-article.htm?18997/Lahore+Declaration+February+1999. Accessed on 15 March 2021.

[2]Srijan Shukla and Sajid Ali, 'How Indian Army's valour and Vajpayee's diplomacy won the Kargil War for India', *The Print*, 8 July 2019, https://theprint.in/past-forward/how-indian-armys-valour-and-vajpayees-diplomacy-won-the-kargil-war-for-india/259362/. Accessed on 15 March 2021.

[3]Ibid.

HEIGHTS OF FOLLY

Pakistan's Kargil incursion was premised on the belief that it could unilaterally alter the status quo on the Line of Control (LoC) by using stealth and surprise without inviting any significant counter-retaliation from India. This strategy was based on India's illusory restraint and the overt nuclear capabilities of both countries. Pakistan wrongly assumed that India would not use air power.[4] Pakistan had, in the past, employed this clandestine stratagem. They caught us by complete surprise in the mountainous terrain of J&K, in October 1947 and again in September 1965, also known as the Monsoon War.

The first report of Pakistani infiltrators having occupied Indian posts, routinely vacated during the winter months, was brought to the Army's attention by two local shepherds on 3 May 1999. But the full import of the situation was not known for another two weeks. By then, at least one Indian Army patrol had been fatally ambushed (4 May); another patrol had gone missing (14 May); and two Indian Air Force (IAF) aircrafts—comprising a helicopter (12 May) and a Canberra aircraft (21 May) on separate reconnaissance missions in the Kargil sector—had been damaged by Pakistani ground fire. It had become more than evident that Pakistani troops had occupied commanding heights up to nine kilometres on the Indian side of the LoC across a frontage of approximately 160 km.

It did not help that General Ved Prakash Malik, the COAS, was overseas (9–19 May); and Lt Gen. H.M. Khanna, the Northern Army commander, was in Pune for five days (14–19 May). Apart from the all-round failure of both Intelligence and Military appreciation, the situation was initially compounded by differences on the employment of air power between the Army and the IAF. The Army, ignorant about the limitations of the IAF's Soviet-origin attack helicopters, wanted the latter to evict the high-altitude intruders.

[4]Jayant Prasad, 'The Kargil War and India's Security Environment', *Journal of Defence Studies*, Vol. 13, No. 3, 2019.

India's three services recovered quickly from their initial coordination hiccups. Realizing the situation was far more serious than a trivial intrusion, the Indian Army concentrated on enhancing its deployments. Artillery-supported infantry physically evicted a well-entrenched enemy on a high-altitude rocky landscape of heights above 15,000 feet. After suffering initial casualties, comprising two fighter aircraft and a helicopter, the IAF revised its tactic of targeting small-sized hilltops. It went on to conduct air attacks at high-altitude terrain that have few parallels in military history. The software on Mirage aircrafts was tweaked to enable them to operate at those altitudes.[5]

The Indian Navy launched Operation Talwar that involved augmenting the Western Naval Command fleet with battleships from the Eastern Naval Command and deploying them on barrier patrols off the coast of Dwarka that bottled up the Karachi harbour.[6] The civil and military infrastructure responded effectively after a slow start.

The Vajpayee government's permissive attitude towards the press ensured that the conflict was televised live to every household, negating the adversary's propaganda efforts. This is in total contrast to the complete information blackout has been happening with regard to Chinese intrusions in eastern Ladakh. Information is provided on deep background and that too to select journalists who behave more like note takers and propagandists rather than members of the once respected fourth estate. The people are made to hear what the government wants them to hear.

It is also true that whenever tensions have arisen with China along the LAC, successive governments across all political dispensations have attempted to control the narrative but the extent of the paranoia of the government in the current stand-off with China is of another level altogether.

---

[5]Benjamin S. Lambeth, *Airpower at 18,000': The Indian Air Force in the Kargil War*, Carnegie Endowment for International Peace, 2012.
[6]Alok Deb, 'Kargil and Its Impact on India's National Security', *Journal of Defence Studies*, Vol. 13, No. 3, 2019.

It would have been far better if the NDA government had allowed journalists and academics well-versed in the reportage and analysis of national security access to the conflict areas. The narrative that would then have emerged of China's illegal transgressions into Indian territory would have had far greater resonance internationally. It would have put China squarely in the dock of international public opinion. The Chinese fig leaf and the myth of perception lines could have effectively been demolished by clearly demonstrating through facts on the ground that the Chinese were indeed ill-intentioned intruders into what clearly is not their territory even by their own interpretation.

THE OPPOSITION VIEW

The INC, like every other opposition party, was critical of the Pakistani intrusions. There was anxiety that the conflict was taking place while a caretaker government was at the helm in India. There was the additional concern of a looming general election and the fact that the party was dealing with internal turmoil as the leadership of Sonia Gandhi was challenged by certain senior leaders. On May 15 1999, Sharad Pawar, P.A. Sangma and Tariq Anwar had raised certain issues in a meeting of the Congress Working Committee (CWC). Five days later, they were expelled from the INC, and on 25 May they formed their own outfit, the Nationalist Congress Party (NCP).

The INC grappled with two contrasting responses to the Kargil incursion. On one hand, party apparatchiks were of the opinion that the government should be held directly responsible for allowing such a serious lapse. Others more grounded and well-versed in the realities of electoral politics, acutely aware of how the nation comes together as one in the face of an external threat, were of the opinion that an overly critical approach would not resonate well with the people. There were raging debates within the party about the merits of both approaches. However, no matter which side anybody took, nobody was just factoring in the electoral ramifications. From the grassroots to the All India Congress Committee (AICC), the undulating dilemma was to find the perfect balance i.e., how to hold the government accountable without sounding stridently critical.

Unfortunately, the hard-line view prevailed—the truth of the government's inability to prevent the transgression in Kargil must be put across to the people in a direct manner. The hardliners were oblivious to the spirit of nationalism that had pervaded the country. The people were in no mood to listen to criticism of the government when the country's most fiercely contested border had been encroached.

Most notably, however, the Kargil War once again underscored the absolute courage and valour of the Indian soldier. Once on the battlefield, they rapidly adapted to very adverse conditions and a hostile terrain. They fought the adversary with utter grit and determination. Another element that acquitted itself with aplomb during the conflict was the 155 mm FH77 Bofors howitzer. This piece of heavy artillery with a range of over 35 km in high-altitude terrain, capable of firing three rounds in 12 seconds, proved to be the nemesis of the enemy in Kargil. The towed howitzer could target enemy posts at close to a 90-degree angle, allowing the Indian army to attack Pakistani soldiers from under their very noses.

The Kargil War was very costly in terms of Army lives—527 soldier fatalities and 1,363 more injured, according to official figures. Since the Pakistani Army had captured all the heights, the Indian Army had to contend with topographical disadvantages. There was a rapid spike in hostilities about a fortnight into the war that further pressurized the defence establishment. It should not be forgotten that a caretaker government was running the country on the cusp of a general election. The Army's top brass has denied claims that they were asked by the government to complete the war and reclaim the heights but the context in which the conflict was unfolding was not lost on anyone.

Around mid-June, the Battle of Tololing turned the tide in India's favour. The capture of Tiger Hill was seen as *the* de facto victory for India. The performance of six battalions was especially sterling and paved the way for India's ultimate victory—2 Rajputana Rifles, 13 Jammu and Kashmir Rifles, 1/11 Gorkha Rifles, 13 Jat Regiment, 18 Grenadiers and 8 Sikh Regiment.[7] By 26 July, all Pakistani forces had been evicted and India emerged triumphant.

The outcome of the war proved that India was a responsible power and helped shape perceptions of the international strategic community in the decades that followed. It also exposed Pakistan for embarking on a dangerous adventure using semi-state actors, backed by elements of its regular armed forces, to alter the territorial status quo by the force of arms. This isolation of Pakistan was further intensified with President Clinton reading out the Riot Act to Prime Minister Nawaz Sharif on 4 July 1999, when the latter made an uninvited dash to Washington DC to seek mediation with India.[8] Though the Kargil intrusions were the handiwork of his Army Chief General Pervez Musharraf, it was Sharif who was overthrown by his army chief, paving the way for a new chapter in Pakistani politics that would dominate much of the first decade of the millennium.

Ironically, Sharif had appointed Musharraf as army chief superseding two people senior to him. Perhaps, he felt more comfortable with a Muhajir from India than the Punjabis who make up the bulk of the officers and men of the Pakistani Army.[9]

---

[7]Srijan Shukla and Sajid Ali, 'How Indian Army's valour and Vajpayee's diplomacy won the Kargil War for India', *The Print*, 8 July 2019, https://theprint.in/past-forward/how-indian-armys-valour-and-vajpayees-diplomacy-won-the-kargil-war-for-india/259362/. Accessed on 15 March 2021.

[8]Taylor Branch, *The Clinton Tapes: Wrestling History with the President*, Simon & Schuster, 2009.

[9]Usman Manzoor, 'Four of 13 Army Chiefs Were Senior-Most When Appointed', *The News International*, 27 November 2016, https://www.thenews.com.pk/print/168018-four-of-13-army-chiefs-were-senior-most-when-appointed. Accessed on 15 March 2021.

RECKONING: THE NEED FOR REFORMS

Kargil Review Committee

Three days after the limited war was declared over, the Kargil Review Committee (KRC) was appointed on 29 July 1999, to 'review the events leading up to the Pakistani aggression' and 'to recommend such measures as are considered necessary to safeguard national security against such armed intrusions.'[10] Led by one of India's better-known strategic thinkers, Krishnaswamy Subrahmanyam (Foreign Minister S. Jaishankar's father, the four-member committee also included Lt Gen. (retd) K.K. Hazari (former vice chief of the army), B.G. Verghese (senior journalist) and Satish Chandra (chairperson of the Joint Intelligence Committee [JIC]).

The KRC was noteworthy in at least two respects. First, it was not appointed pursuant to the Commissions of Inquiry Act, 1952 and thus, did not have the formal power to requisition records or summon witnesses. At the same time, 'it was given the widest possible access to all relevant documents, including those with the highest classification and to officials of the Union and Jammu and Kashmir governments.'[11] Second, the KRC covered, under its ambit, the entire political-bureaucratic-military dimension of India's national security,[12] the first such study in India's post-Independence history.

The Committee interviewed several serving and former government officials including presidents, prime ministers, civilian and military officers and defence ministers. It submitted its report to the Vajpayee government within five months (on 15 December 1999). To their credit, the government tabled the report in Parliament two months later on 23 February 2000, albeit with some redactions.

---

[10]Kargil Review Committee, *From Surprise to Reckoning: The Kargil Review Committee Report*, Sage Publications, 2000.

[11]Anit Mukherjee, 'Failing to Deliver: Post-Crises Defence Reforms in India', IDSA Occasional Paper No. 18, 2011.

[12]Ibid.

It was the first time in India's post-Independence history that a war-related report was released by the government and that too almost immediately after its submission.

The KRC received a fair amount of criticism, and perhaps rightly so, for not taking the investigative route. There was a clear reason why the committee was given a non-investigative remit. All stakeholders had a natural interest in air-brushing their lapses, lest they be held directly responsible for the events that led to Pakistan's intrusions.

The Committee argued that its focus was on the lessons the country and its security structures could learn from the Kargil experience and it was not interested in engaging in an 'inquisitional witch-hunt'. 'They also argued that this approach helped them to achieve full cooperation from key decision-makers and various agencies.'[13]

The KRC made a scathing indictment of the all-round intelligence failure of the national security apparatus. It stated:

> The Review Committee had before it overwhelming evidence that the Pakistani armed intrusion in the Kargil sector came as a complete and total surprise to the Indian government, Army and intelligence agencies as well as to the J&K state government and its agencies. The Committee did not come across any agency or individual who was able clearly to assess before the event the possibility of a large-scale Pakistani military intrusion across the Kargil heights.[14]

This, along with other such lapses, galvanized the government to look within, identify shortcomings and implement remedial measures, including the creation of new structures.

---

[13]Ibid.

[14]Manish Tewari, 'Parliament Oversight Key for Reforms in Intelligence Agencies', *Deccan Chronicle*, 20 July 2020, https://www.deccanchronicle.com/opinion/columnists/200720/manish-tewari-parliament-oversight-key-for-reforms-in-intelligence-a.html. Accessed on 15 March 2021.

The report stated that India was militarily underprepared and there were hard lessons to be learnt from the conflict. It argued that while the country had been lucky to have scraped through various national security threats, it could no longer afford to adopt an ad hoc attitude, and therefore the entire gamut of national security management needed to be comprehensively studied and reorganized.[15]

In making this judgement, the KRC pointed out several areas in the Indian defence system that were in dire need of reforms. Key recommendations made by the Committee included strengthening of the NSC, induction of Unmanned Aerial Vehicles (UAVs), reforming the command culture in the Indian military, publishing war histories, declassifying official documents to establish facts, jointness in all three services and creation of an integrated defence intelligence agency. For the most part, reforms that faced the least amount of political and bureaucratic resistance have been implemented.

One thing seems to be very clear from the observations made by the KRC: there had been 'continuity' and hardly any critical appraisal over five decades (from 1947 to 1999) in India's security philosophy and thinking. This was partly due to institutional inertia, inter-service rivalry and a generalized bureaucracy that exercised superintendence over the defence establishment and infrastructure. The recommendations of the KRC included the need for a comprehensive re-evaluation of the entire national security system. For this purpose, they envisioned the creation of a task force towards that end. However, the Vajpayee government set up a Group of Ministers (GoM) to take the process further.

Despite India's intense and eventful history of national security challenges and military engagements—starting from Partition-cum-Independence—a major problem is, and continues to be, the disjointed nature of the civil–military national security architecture, deliberately structured and siloed since Independence to act as

---

[15]Kargil Review Committee, *From Surprise to Reckoning: The Kargil Review Committee Report*, Sage Publications, 2000.

a bulwark to preserve democracy. Therefore, the Indian state's approach remains essentially reactive rather than proactive.

There is, however, a silver lining to this approach. Of all the countries in Asia, Africa and both South and Central America that attained liberation from colonial and imperialist tyranny, India is among the handful that did not have to suffer the jackboot of military dictatorship or even one-party rule. The nation has steadfastly remained a multiparty democracy despite its many flaws. As far back as the early 1960s, Samuel Huntington, a well-known American political scientist, had described India to be way ahead of even certain highly evolved western democracies.

In retrospect, more than two decades after Kargil and the KRC's recommendations, it is safe to surmise that India's higher defence management is more or less similar to what it was between 1947 and '99. The questions with regard to India's approach to national security remain. Can this be put down to continuity or sheer redundancy? The answer is a no-brainer. There still remains an unwillingness to accept even now, as it was then, that both the battlefield and modes of warfare would be enormously altered in the decades ahead.

Group of Ministers Report

The GoM, formed in April 2000, comprised Home Minister L.K. Advani, Defence Minister George Fernandes, External Affairs Minister Jaswant Singh and Finance Minister Yashwant Sinha. The GoM went on to create four task forces to examine different aspects of national security—Internal Security, Intelligence, Border Management and Management of Defence.[16] The task forces on Intelligence and Management of Defence, the two important task forces for this chapter, were headed by G.C. Saxena, a former chief of the Research and Analysis Wing (R&AW) and Arun Singh, former minister of state for defence during the erstwhile Rajiv Gandhi

---

[16]'Report of the Group of Ministers: Reforming the National Security System', Government of India, 2001.

government, respectively. According to their mandates, these task forces adopted a mix of site visits and interviews, and presented their reports to the GoM. As was the case with the KRC report, the combined reports of the task forces were released in the public domain with heavy security redactions.

In line with the KRC recommendations, members of the Arun Singh Committee for Defence Management or the Defence Task Force agreed on the need to restructure the national security institutions. However, there were differing opinions on the nature of these reforms—whether they should be incremental or revolutionary.[17] Fearing the rigidity and friction they could face from the political-bureaucratic nexus, they went ahead with slow and incremental reforms, which, incidentally, is the nature of decision-making of even successive Indian governments.

The centrepiece of the reforms suggested by the Defence Task Force was the creation of the post of Chief of Defence Service (CDS) to head the Integrated Defence Staff (IDS), the creation of a tri-service Andaman and Nicobar Command (ANC) for the strategically located archipelago, a tri-service Strategic Forces Command (SFC) and the integration of service headquarters with the MoD. The CCS in Vajpayee's government accepted and implemented all recommendations, except for one, i.e., the creation of a CDS, primarily because of:

i. opposition from the highest political authorities, who feared (but never explicitly stated) that India might face a military coup just like other post-colonial nations,

ii. lobbying by the civilian bureaucracy to preserve its position against what they perceived as encroachment by service headquarters on their turf and

iii. the fear within the services itself, that one service would have preeminence over the others. For example, the IAF

---

[17]Anit Mukherjee, 'Failing to Deliver Post-Crises Defence Reforms in India', IDSA Occasional Paper No. 18, 2011.

felt that it could possibly be at a relative disadvantage after the creation of CDS.[18] An apprehension increasingly being expressed now in public by former chiefs of the Air Force and the Navy in the public debate over the creation of theatre commands that is concurrently in play.

Certain reforms suggested by the Defence Task Force have failed to see the light of day, as was the case with a report prepared in 1990 by the Committee of Defence Expenditure that had also been headed by Arun Singh. However, the Defence Task Force must be commended for ushering in a number of changes—the creation of IDS, establishment of a tri-service Defence Intelligence Agency (DIA) and pushing the idea of an Indian National Defence University.

All in all, both Intelligence and Defence task forces played a crucial role in initiating the debate around restructuring the Indian military. Two decades later, partial implementation of their recommendations is an issue that is constantly raised by renowned security experts in the public sphere.

Naresh Chandra Task Force

Despite the new measures, as suggested by committee reports and approved by the CCS, many lacunae remained in the management of national security. Several developments took place 10 years after the CCS gave its approval. In addition to reviewing the progress made, there was a need to take stock of subsequent developments, especially post the terror strikes in Mumbai in 2008, and the worsening situation of the regional security situation in South Asia and qua a growingly assertive though not yet belligerent China. Under these circumstances, the Congress-led United Progressive Alliance (UPA) government appointed a Task Force on National Security in June 2011.

This 14-member task force was helmed by Naresh Chandra, a

---

[18]Manoj Joshi, *The Unending Quest to Reform India's National Security System*, S. Rajaratnam School of International Studies (RSIS), 2014.

seasoned bureaucrat who had been the cabinet secretary. The aim of the Naresh Chandra Committee or the National Security Task Force was to review the country's defence management and make suggestions for the implementation of major defence projects.

The Task Force submitted its report in May 2012, but its contents, given our paranoid approach to issues of national security, are yet to be made public, almost even a decade later. This is hardly surprising considering that declassifying reports, even after several decades, is a complete exception rather than the norm in India.

Various media reports and academic works[19] however point to how the Naresh Chandra Committee focused attention on the shallowness of the national security decision-making process while recommending urgent changes in the defence management system. Certain important recommendations of the committee were:

i.   framing a public document on a National Security Strategy;
ii. a special cadre of Defence to be introduced in the civil service to ensure knowledge accumulation in the Defence Secretariat;
iii. surmounting the key lacunae of silo mentality in the intelligence agencies and the issue of overlap in the functions of various agencies and
iv. the principal recommendation related to the appointment of a CDS-like figure, by creating a position of a Permanent Chairman of the Chiefs of Staff Committee.[20]

For the one year that it took to prepare its report, the committee consulted multiple governmental bodies. However, it does not appear that they consulted strategic/domain experts. Since the report of the Committee has not been made public (and may

---

[19]The leaks of the report have been referred from: Manoj Joshi, *The Unending Quest to Reform India's National Security System*, S. Rajaratnam School of International Studies (RSIS), 2014.

[20]Manoj Joshi, *The Unending Quest to Reform India's National Security System*, S. Rajaratnam School of International Studies (RSIS), 2014.

never be). However, going by media reports, the committee's recommendations are exhaustive and far reaching. If they are implemented, they will have a profound impact on the shortcomings in India's defence sector.[21]

THE DEAD LETTERS

Many reforms suggested by the KRC and the GoM have either been ignored or partially implemented. While a Press Information Bureau (PIB) of 2012 claimed that 63 of the 75 recommendations made by the GoM had been implemented, it ignored the fact that crucial suggestions pertaining to the integration of the three services and jointness of approach on questions of national security have not been implemented.[22]

Even the implemented reforms are considered 'benign' by many as they faced the least amount of bureaucratic resistance, making for easier execution. Any recommendation involving the creation of a new post or organization was quickly approved by bureaucrats, bringing in both budgetary support and increased bureaucratic control. For example, the creation of the IDS, DIA, ANC, etc., all of which were readily accepted. Softer recommendations like lowering of age profile and induction of UAVs were also accepted.[23]

However, a key recommendation was to create the post of CDS. The appointment finally took place on the penultimate day of 2019 with the appointment of General Bipin Rawat as the country's first CDS. The task of the CDS is two-fold—to head a newly created Department of Military Affairs (DMA) mandated to deal with the administrative functioning of the three wings of the armed forces

---

[21]Gurmeet Kanwal and Neha Kohli, *Defence Reforms, A National Imperative,* IDSA, 2018.

[22]Jayant Prasad, 'The Kargil War and India's Security Environment', *Journal of Defence Studies,* Vol. 13, No. 3, 2019.

[23]Anit Mukherjee, 'Failing to Deliver Post-Crises Defence Reforms in India', IDSA Occasional Paper No. 18, 2011.

and to function as the permanent chairman of the Chiefs of Staff Committee.[24]

While it is too soon to evaluate the functioning of the post of CDS, the other softer reforms have failed to bring about structural changes and have been termed 'merely cosmetic'[25] by former army chief, General Malik.

The system's inability to absorb even incremental reform and implement them in good faith has taken a toll on our military and national defence. In fact, Satish Chandra in a searing disquisition wrote that, 'the bureaucracy on its part has, in the implementation of security reforms approved at the highest level in government, been at best dilatory and at worst, obstructive. Turf battles have also taken their toll in slowing down or even completely blocking reform.'[26]

It is also important to understand reforms that were either bypassed or imperfectly implemented. These reforms have been divided into four broad headings: Intelligence, Integration, Transparency and Resource Allocation and Planning.

Intelligence

The truism 'Intelligence is the first line of defence' is only accepted when nations are confronted with unexpected or catastrophic scenarios. The intelligence failures during the Kargil War led to a much-needed review of India's intelligence architecture. The KRC observed, briefly, that, '...there is no institutionalized mechanism for coordination or objectives-oriented interaction between intelligence agencies and consumers at different levels.'[27] Later, the

---

[24]Manoj Joshi, 'CDS: The Long and Arduous Road Ahead', *ORF*, 31 December 2019, https://www.orfonline.org/expert-speak/cds-the-long-and-arduous-road-ahead-59717/. Accessed on 15 March 2021.

[25]General V.P. Malik, 'The Kargil War: Some Reflections', *Claws Journal*, 2009.

[26]Gurmeet Kanwal and Neha Kohli, *Defence Reforms, A National Imperative*, IDSA, 2018.

[27]Kargil Review Committee, *From Surprise to Reckoning: The Kargil Review Committee Report*, Sage Publications, 2000.

GoM appointed a Task Force on Intelligence Reforms, headed by a former R&AW chief, Gary Saxena. Their recommendations were incorporated in the GoM Report, and subsequently approved by the government. A pertinent question that should have been asked then: Should a former R&AW chief, a quintessential insider, have headed this task force or could an outsider—for example, a former home, defence minister or even a retired cabinet secretary—have been a better choice?

The wisdom of having an institutional insider heading such review committees is seriously debatable. Without casting any reflection, much less aspersions on the professional competence or institutional integrity of a particular individual, the fact remains that when such insiders form part of such committees or task forces, they are mentally conditioned to overlook institutional redundancies. If an 'outsider' who understands the business of intelligence were to have headed this task force, it would have brought both a detached perspective coupled with an objective appraisal, without the individual concerned having to ascend the learning curve or being completely blank about the subject at hand.

The Saxena task force helped establish several key institutions in the intelligence infrastructure such as the tri-service DIA and the National Technical Research Organisation (NTRO). These were going to be specialized agencies to procure all forms of technical intelligence (TECHINT). This would ease the burdened R&AW with both human intelligence (HUMINT) and TECHINT responsibilities.[28] The NSC and the NSAB were also established for the macro-management of intelligence collected from various agencies.[29]

However, the establishment of these institutions did little to alleviate core issues plaguing India's intelligence infrastructure. Overlapping responsibilities and poor management led to agencies

---

[28]'Report of the Group of Ministers: Reforming the National Security System', Government of India, 2001.
[29]Gurmeet Kanwal and Neha Kohli, *Defence Reforms: A National Imperative*, IDSA, 2018.

both over-exceeding their capabilities and being unable to execute tasks to achieve targets. For instance, NTRO's main task was to procure and provide all forms of TECHINT, but all these assets were controlled by the DIA.[30]

Owing to this, there have been issues between the DIA and the NTRO over asset management and control. A similar tension exists between NTRO and the Aviation Research Centre (ARC), the TECHINT wing of the R&AW. While NTRO controls high-resolution satellites and is responsible for space- and ground-based communication intelligence (COMINT), the ARC is responsible for collecting image intelligence (IMINT) and COMINT through aircraft-mounted sensors.[31] This has resulted in friction between the two agencies on whether NTRO's task is to merely collate data or provide clear analysis as well. Therefore, NTRO's mandate created quite a storm, since it was given tasks already being done by other intelligence services. Strangely enough, these problems were neither anticipated nor addressed by the government. There is an urgent need for a proper articulation of individual agency mandates, only then will they be able to yield maximum output and work efficaciously.

The DIA faces considerable opposition from intelligence directorates that have been unwilling to part with their intelligence assets which has resulted in duplication of work and excessive bureaucratization.[32] Therefore, much more needs to be done to ensure that the DIA is able to meet its chartered responsibilities. The DIA must be given a statutory backing and be made the single-point contact for all defence-related aspects of intelligence to solve this problem.

---

[30]Manoj Joshi and Pushan Das, 'India's Intelligence Agencies: In Need of Reform and Oversight', *ORF Issued Brief 98*, 2015.
[31]Ibid.
[32]Anit Mukherjee, 'Failing to Deliver Post-Crises Defence Reforms in India', IDSA Occasional Paper No. 18, 2011.

ISSUES OF ANALYSIS, RECRUITMENT AND LEGISLATIVE OVERSIGHT

Analysis is another vulnerability in India's intelligence system. The way in which the JIC was subsumed into the National Security Council Secretariat (NSCS) in 2001 and then resurrected in 2006 has only made things worse.[33] There is a need for the system to differentiate between intelligence collection and analysis while improving each of these roles.

There is another problem pointed out by the KRC regarding the issue of specialized recruitment in the national defence architecture. Intelligence agencies like R&AW, Intelligence Bureau (IB) and NTRO lack specialized personnel with considerable military and intelligence expertise. Recruitment to the R&AW depends heavily on other central agencies especially the Indian Police Service (IPS).[34] This problem was also highlighted by the Arun Singh Committee and the N.N. Vohra-headed Task Force on Internal Security. There has, therefore, been a demand for the government to create a separate cadre like the Indian Intelligence Service and tailor the entrance exams to attract the brightest minds in the country. After common basic training, they can be distributed among the NTRO, the R&AW and the IB. There is also need for lateral entry to fill up specialist positions, especially on the analysis desks.[35] Simultaneously, HUMINT skills must be fostered and sharpened, especially in areas where covert operations need to be mounted.

The final problem with the current intelligence infrastructure is the lack of legislative oversight. This supervision is required to act as a guarantee, a check against the misuse of the immense powers

---

[33]Manoj Joshi, *The Unending Quest to Reform India's National Security System*, S. Rajaratnam School of International Studies (RSIS), 2014.
[34]Manoj Joshi and Pushan Das, 'India's Intelligence Agencies: In Need of Reform and Oversight', *ORF Issue Brief 98*, 2015.
[35]Subir Bhaumik, 'A Case for Intelligence Reforms', *The Telegraph*, 29 January 2020, https://www.telegraphindia.com/opinion/a-case-for-intelligence-reforms/cid/1740566. Accessed on 15 March 2021.

available to such agencies. It is important to spell out, in clear terms, their duties, responsibilities and authority.

In this context, I introduced a Private Members' Bill in the Lok Sabha, first in 2011 and then again in 2020, seeking to regulate the functioning and exercise of powers of the Indian Intelligence Service.[36] As I had mentioned in my article in 2016,[37] the proposed bill is divided into eight parts, dealing first and foremost with the task of putting the R&AW, IB and NTRO on a proper legal footing and defining the scope and mandate of their remit. The next part of the bill dealt with authorization processes, including warrants, procedure for both physical surveillance and electronic interception of communication, including an estoppel on taking action on any intelligence that is obtained without specific authorization.

For the first time, it talks about a legal authorization for the R&AW and NTRO to undertake activities outside India. An Indian authorization would not make an individual immune from breaking law in a foreign country. It, nonetheless, would still make an arguable case for deportation or exfiltration if they become an undeclared though prospectively acknowledged intelligence asset.

Moreover, if they were to be arrested, tortured, murdered or executed in a foreign country for being an alleged spy, i.e., for discharging their assigned national duty, at least their next of kin would have access to some compensation for them if there is a paper trail that shows the person in question was an intelligence asset. There are reports galore in the public domain as to how intelligence assets have been simply abandoned by their handlers, God forbid if they get arrested in the country that they have been infiltrated into illegally or legally.[38]

---

[36]Manish Tewari, 'State of the Union: Time for Intelligence Reforms?' *Deccan Chronicle*, 19 March 2016, https://www.deccanchronicle.com/opinion/op-ed/190316/state-of-the-union-time-for-intelligence-reforms.html. Accessed on 15 March 2021.
[37]Ibid.
[38]Rohit Prasad, 'The Hapless Fate of an Alleged Spy', *LiveMint*, 20 April 2017, https://www.livemint.com/Opinion/U0eysVQGgTb9Z93Iiz9BlK/The-hapless-fate-of-an-alleged-spy.html. Accessed on 15 March 2021.

The Bill also provided for the constitution of a 'national intelligence and security oversight committee'. This was perhaps the most contentious part of the entire scheme of the bill. In detailed consultations with retired senior officials, repeated apprehensions were expressed that the members of the oversight committee would not be able to restrain themselves from examining the conduct of intelligence operations.

A special provision has specifically been engrafted, prohibiting the oversight of current or past intelligence operations. Even the membership of the committee was pegged at the highest level with the chairperson of the council of states, Lok Sabha speaker, prime minister, the leaders of the Opposition in both the Houses and one member each from both the Houses to be nominated by their respective presiding offices.

The Bill also talked about an intelligence ombudsman and a national intelligence tribunal. The former is necessary because, in the recent past, a number of officers have knocked the doors of various constitutional courts to get their grievances addressed. In the process, a lot of dirty linen gets washed in public. There are many such cases that require sensitive handling as the people who work in these organizations do so in an atmosphere of great stress, secrecy and are privy to matters that should not find their way into the public domain in circumstances that are less than dignified and honourable.

An ombudsman, who has been the head of the IB, R&AW or the NTRO and is well versed in the culture and working imperatives of these organizations, would provide a much-needed ventilation mechanism for a quiet and efficient redressal of grievances.

Similarly, a specialized national intelligence tribunal, headed by a retired Supreme Court judge and consisting of a retired high court judge and the head of the IB and R&AW alternatively, is required to go into complaints by any individual who has reasons to believe that any intelligence organization has done something wrong to him or his property. The Bill laid down a detailed procedure for doing so.

By no means is the proposed legislation perfect. However, it is a developed template which has gone through a detailed consultation process with not only former officers of these organizations, but with a host of lawyers, civil liberty activists, journalists and parliamentarians who take an interest in strategic affairs and issues pertaining to national security. Primarily, the reason I chose to delve, at some length, into the salient aspects of the said bill is because this is an idea whose time has come.

Integration

War requires complete synergy among all agencies and institutions of the national security structure. All post-Kargil reform committees have been of the opinion that such a strategic structural transformation calls for a change in the collective mindset of the military establishment.

However, the cold reality is that the Indian military is among the least integrated major militaries in the world. It took independent India 50 years and the Kargil War to ring the alarm bells of integrated military structures in the defence corridors of the country. The British Armed Forces were restructured in 1964; the US, under the Goldwater–Nichols Act of 1986; and, China most recently, reformed its military structures to create five theatre commands.[39]

The GoM had put the onus of the suboptimal outcomes of India's security infrastructure on the lack of overall integration and jointness within the Indian armed forces. Despite the issue being flagged by the GoM, the reforms proposed by the KRC remain imperfectly implemented. However, in October 2020, the media reported that India would be restructuring its 17 single-service commands into five theatre commands.

First, let us take the case of the Integrated Headquarters (IHQ) of the MoD, seen by many as a key reform in the sphere of integration and jointness. The IDS aimed at integration through the re-designation

---

[39]Satish Dua, 'HQ Integrated Defence Staff in the National Security Structure', *Journal of Defence Studies*, Vol. 13, No. 3, 2019.

of service HQs from 'Attached Offices' to 'Integrated HQs of MoD'.[40] While the IDS has played a pivotal role in capability development, the fact that it continues to be merely 'attached offices' of the IHQ of the MoD (Army/Air Force/Navy), with inadequate influence over policy formation, has severely hampered its true potential.

While the DMA, within the MoD and under the CDS, has been created to tackle this old lacuna, the problem of integration still looms large. There is an urgent need to reform both the MoD and its structures, like DRDO, Ordnance Factory Board (OFB) and Defence Public Sector Undertakings (DPSUs); integration of services has to be the most immediate reform to prevent the Ministry from functioning in silos.[41]

Second, the ANC was established with the expectation that it would lead to geographically delineated joint commands in the future. But even the ANC has failed to realize its true potential. The first unified command is facing major operational and administrative issues. For instance, the commander-in-chief of the ANC has little to no influence in the allotment of resources to his command as this is done by the respective services.[42] Additional joint commands and theatre commands have been resisted by all three services. But this is now expected to change by 2022.

Finally, the absence of integration creates an overlapping problem. There are, as of 2021, 14 intelligence agencies operating in India with overlapping mandates. Former home minister P. Chidambaram aptly sums it up by stating:

> ...Intelligence elements are spread over different ministries: there is the IB which reports to the Home Minister; there is Research and Analysis Wing which falls under the Cabinet Secretariat and hence, reports to the Prime Minister; there

[40]Gurmeet Kanwal and Neha Kohli, *Defence Reforms, A National Imperative*, IDSA, 2018.

[41]Ibid.

[42]Anit Mukherjee, 'Failing to Deliver Post-Crises Defence Reforms in India', IDSA Occasional Paper No. 18, 2011.

are organizations such as JIC, NTRO and ARC which report to the NSA; and there is the NSC Secretariat (NSCS) under the NSA which serves the NSC. The armed forces have their own intelligence agencies, one each under the Army, Navy and Air Force and an umbrella body called the Defence Intelligence Agency.[43]

This absence of integration creates three main problems. First, it hampers operationalization of strategies within the Indian military. A prime example is the Indian Army's Cold Start Doctrine (more on this in the next chapter)[44]. Second, is the problem of logistical duplication and separate procurement channels. Third, the socio-cultural divide between the services—a consequence of single-service thinking.

While the CDS may be a step in the right direction towards integration and jointness of the national security structure, there is still a lot to be done. The MoD should break from these self-contained silos. A restructured MoD with the IHQ of all three services (like the Pentagon) should be the aim of these reforms. Stakeholders should work towards a common integration and jointness objective.

However, the ongoing debate in the media suggests that there is still no consensus within the services about the need, efficacy and even the structure of the proposed theatre commands. It would also be instructive to examine how other nations have brought about this jointness or integration.

Lately, there has been quite a bit of commentary in the public space about the proposed reorganization of the armed forces into theatre commands. A large number of retired defence officers including former chiefs of the Air Force and Navy have written profound opinion pieces expressing apprehensions and reservations

---

[43]Manoj Shrivastava, *Re-energising Indian Intelligence*. Vij Books Pvt. Ltd, 2013.
[44]Anit Mukherjee, 'Failing to Deliver Post-Crises Defence Reforms in India', IDSA Occasional Paper No. 18, 2011.

about the process and the fact that it is being rushed through rather impulsively.

Let us first understand what is being attempted. On 24 December 2019, the government announced the creation of a Chief of Defence Staff (CDS) and a new DMA in the MoD. This was followed by the appointment of the outgoing Army Chief General Bipin Rawat as the first CDS on 31 December 2019. This new paradigm brought into sharp relief the question of the proposed institution of Theatre Commands for the Indian Armed Forces.

The fundamental concept underpinning the Theatre Commands paradigm is achieving jointness. Jointness means the synergy and synchronization of different branches of the fighting arms into one cohesive and integrated organization.

The idea is neither new nor novel. Over three dozen countries in the world have evolved and adopted a combined services template for their militaries. Major powers like the US, Russia, China and even the UK from where we have inherited our military ethos are all tasked on this jointness archetype now, as mentioned earlier.

In the US, prior to 1986, each Service had its own chief. The service chiefs together stood constituted as joint chiefs of staff. Its elected chairperson reported to the defense secretary. The defense secretary in turn was accountable to the president.

The above arrangement was analogous to India before the appointment of the chairman of Joint Chiefs of Staff in the US as the principal military advisor to the president, NSC, Homeland Security Council and the defense secretary, post the implementation of the Gold Water–Nichols Act of 1986. He assists the president and the defense secretary, both civilians, in giving strategic direction to the armed forces. He proffers advice with regard to force structures and budgetary practices. When rendering counsel, he is obligated by law to confabulate with the service chiefs who act as secondary military advisors.

This Act, promulgated in 1986, transformed both the character and configuration of the US Defense Forces. The important thing to mark is that the reorganization came through legislation and not via an executive fiat.

The Act provided the latitude for both joint- and single-service commands. It ordained that a unified combatant command means a military command that comprises personnel from two or more military realms. The command hierarchy of a unified or specified combatant command travels from the president downwards to the secretary of defense, and from there directly to the theatre or the combatant commander. The president only selects an officer to lead a combatant command, if the officer concerned has diverse experience and has served in at least one joint responsibility role in a senior command position.

Democratic nations must be extremely vigilant about excess centralization of authority in any one defence official. The US arrangement guarantees this by mandating the chain of operational command runs from the president to the defense secretary—a cabinet-level position in the US and then directly to the Theatre Commander. The chairperson of the joint chiefs of staff, therefore, has no operational command authority.

Even in the UK, a new epoch for the British Armed Forces is emerging. On 22 March 2021, the government officially released its Integrated Review of Security, Defence, Development and Foreign Policy. It delineates the government's visualization of the UK's role in the world over the next decade and thus provides a clear road map to the armed forces in terms of what the policy priorities of the State are over the medium term.

Thus, whatever operational concepts the defence establishment wants to evolve need to be clearly fine-pointed to cater to the tactical, diplomatic and foreign policy priorities of the UK's civilian government. What is noteworthy is that defence reform is a part of a larger strategic horizon and not merely an act of internal reorganization.

That is why in India, strategic experts, specialists and researchers across the board have been arguing for transparency and openness on the specificities of the proposed theatre commands in India. Even among the services, the opinion seems to be split. It is not a mere coincidence that retired Air Force and Navy officers are forcefully arguing against theatre commands. Even the proxy views of these two services are being aired in the public space and social media, suggesting that there is trouble in paradise.

The fundamental decision that must be taken even now is that if we are headed in the direction of Theatre Commands, this transition must be carried out through legislation like in the US and not by mere executive instructions of the DMA in the MoD.

Moreover, politicians who understand India's strategic imperatives, especially the two-front challenge that the country confronts, must proactively guide this transition.

They need to be assisted by foreign policy and strategic affairs professionals who never lose sight of the big picture. A generic bureaucracy where an officer serves in the Department of Animal Husbandry one day, the Department of Cooperation the next day and the MoD the third day will never measure up to the task of guiding the defence forces through the single biggest transformative change attempted by them ever since their inception. Neither should this task be left to the CDS and a bunch of military officers to superintend this makeover as just another internal reorganization process unique to the armed forces being implemented in a strategic vacuum.

When this osmosis of the defence establishment played itself out in the US, politicians, defence professionals, strategic thinkers, foreign policy practitioners, and most vitally, the media absorbed themselves in five years of knowledgeable and cogent public discussions before the US Congress finally passed the Goldwater–Nichols Defence Reorganization Act of 1986.

Since India's military reform process will be equally intricate, protracted and even complicated, with competing and conflicting demands, claims, issues and even turf battles that would have to be reconciled, the legislature needs to play a far more proactive role. It must seriously apply itself to the establishment of a Dedicated

Standing Committee of Parliament staffed with military advisors and other professionals to independently monitor this transition very minutely.[45] The bottom line being that while jointness and integration are vital given the ecosystem that has evolved over the past couple of decades, proper conceptualization, calibration and consensus building among the services are key for the successful fructification of any such initiative.

Transparency

Both the KRC and the GoM had made an important recommendation regarding the publication of war histories and declassification. Although ostensibly a minor matter, the lack of declassification has produced two major problems. First, within these ministries itself there is an 'absence of history' in most organizations. Many of India's wars, for example, are mired in conflicting perceptions that can evidently be settled by opening up files. More portentously, there is no introspection and transmission of learnings, culminating in experiences having to be re-learnt. There will always be the likelihood that even these official accounts will be heavily sanitized and may not tell the full story. Notwithstanding this apprehension, war accounts must still be declassified.

Ironically, the very reports that made these recommendations had several portions redacted. The Naresh Chandra Task Force report has not even been made public. In contrast, the National Commission on Terrorist Attacks Upon the United States, created after the 9/11 terror attacks in the US, was a 10-member bipartisan commission created through legislation passed by the US Congress. The commission included politicians, lawyers and academics. National security professionals, especially from the intelligence and law-enforcement agencies were conspicuous by their absence.[46] The

---

[45]Manish Tewari, 'Does India Need Theatre Commands?', *Deccan Chronicle*, 1 August 2021, https://www.deccanchronicle.com/opinion/columnists/310721/manish-tewari-does-india-need-theatre-commands.html. Accessed on 15 March 2021.

[46]'About the Commission', *The National Commission on Terrorist Attacks Upon the*

585-page report released in the public domain had none or probably hardly any redactions whatsoever.[47]

Not making the reports of the KRC, GoM and even the Naresh Chandra Committee public in their entirety, save where extremely sensitive national security considerations are at play, triggers myriad complications. First and foremost, institutional parables and chronicles are seldom tested. Second, officials in these organizations, agencies and departments (specifically Defence and Home) do not have the comprehension or the skill sets to assay the reasoning and assessments arrived at by the armed and paramilitary forces. Finally, there is, and will remain, an abyss between the realms of scholarship and policy formulation.[48]

There is, therefore, an urgent need for creating an open and transparent ecosystem to transcend the problems caused by this opaque security culture.

Resource Allocation and Planning

Indian planning, especially defence and foreign policy, has been retrospective instead of proactive, with a knee-jerk approach to problem-solving. This is the reason the GoM recommended a Long Term Integrated Perspective Plan (LTIPP) and national security doctrine.

While the LTIPPs have been formulated, they are rarely given approval by the government. The 10th Defence Plan (2002–7) and 11th Defence Plan (2007–12) met the same fate and were running on ad hoc basis. Neither are these ad hoc measures future proof, nor do they help in combating sustained conflicts. The policy paralysis

---

United States, https://govinfo.library.unt.edu/911/about/index.htm. Accessed on 15 March 2021.

[47]Manish Tewari, 'Parliament oversight key for reforms in intelligence agencies' *Deccan Chronicle*, 20 July 2020, 20 July 2020, https://www.deccanchronicle.com/opinion/columnists/200720/manish-tewari-parliament-oversight-key-for-reforms-in-intelligence-a.html. Accessed on 15 March 2021.

[48]Anit Mukherjee, 'Failing to Deliver Post-Crises Defence Reforms in India', IDSA Occasional Paper No. 18, 2011.

in the defence sector becomes a serious lacuna and needs to be addressed effectively. Budgetary support on the lines of the UK's Defence Capital Expenditure Plan (DCEP) is needed to prevent these plans from turning into academic dissertations.[49]

TIME FOR A FRESH THINKING HAT

Two decades after the limited war of 1999, questions still remain. Are we tactically, strategically, organizationally and logistically better prepared as a nation to deal with a similar or an analogous situation? Is India's security environment more stable than it was in 1999? The answer, unfortunately, is squarely in the negative.

A Kargil-like situation replayed itself in Eastern Ladakh in April 2020 where the Chinese militarily occupied significant areas that fall within the Indian perception of an un-delineated and un-demarcated LAC. India's response has been similarly reactive, as it was two decades ago. The defence and national security establishment notwithstanding, the myriad reviews and incremental reforms remain where they were in terms of both their decision-making paradigms and lack of dexterity in preempting and preventing almost a Kargil redux.

The capacity of the intelligence structures is again in question. Either they failed to detect the Chinese build-up or if they did, they were then unable to get a correct read on the Chinese intentions. If they did end up getting a correct fix, as some reports in the public space do tend to suggest, then even graver questions arise as to why their assessments or advisories were not given the attention that they deserved.

It again underscores the fact that the capacity of the intelligence apparatus has still not been fully optimized. The silos seem to be where they were two decades back. Moreover, the political and military leadership continues to display either little or very

---

[49]Satish Dua, 'HQ Integrated Defence Staff in the National Security Structure', *Journal of Defence Studies,* Vol. 13, No. 3, 2019.

incremental preemptive capability.

To compound the situation further, successive reports prepared by innumerable Parliamentary Committees, including the Estimates Committee, Standing Committee on Defence and even the Comptroller and Auditor General (CAG) continue to reveal, with monotonous regularity, the serious equipment deficiencies that plague the Indian armed forces.

Since the 1999 war in Kargil, the nature of warfare has also changed substantially in the past two decades. There has been a veritable revolution in military affairs. We are in an era of unrestricted warfare as enunciated by two Chinese colonels, Qiao Liang and Wang Xiangsui, in their seminal treatise published in February 1999.[50] No longer is the battlefield earthbound; it is multidimensional now. The means of warfare range from financial warfare to environmental conflicts encompassing smuggling warfare, cultural warfare, drug warfare, international law warfare, and the like. Technological advancement has ensured that the goalposts with regard to weaponry have also changed.

The growing hybridity between the battlefield and the way in which a war is conducted in today's highly sophisticated digital environment and across all domains that were not traditional areas of warfare earlier, are serious issues that still remain outside the thinking arenas of our national security establishment.

The Kargil reviews mainly devoted themselves to try and reform the existing structures without really looking at the larger canvas outside. Now with the spectre of drones, unmanned air and naval assets, the apparition of super soldiers and autonomous weapons coupled with the marriage of Artificial Intelligence (AI) to the conduct of warfare, the challenge that India faces requires that a fresh thinking hat be worn by its strategic planners.

---

[50]Qiao Liang and Wang Xiangsui, *Unrestricted Warfare*, PLA Literature and Arts Publishing House, Beijing, February 1999. Available at https://www.c4i.org/unrestricted.pdf. Accessed on 15 March 2021.

THREE

OPERATION PARAKRAM: A LOST OPPORTUNITY

Pakistan's rout in the limited war in Kargil in July 1999 proved to be, at best, a temporary hiatus in its proxy war against India. The hijacking of IC-814 en route from Kathmandu to Delhi just six months later illustrated that fairly clearly.

Let me begin with a personal recollection of the events around that unfortunate and tragic episode. Sudhir Chandra, a close friend from Chandigarh, who was with the Taj Group of Hotels back then, called me on the evening of 24 December 1999. It was Christmas Eve. I still recall sitting in the coffee shop of Ashok Hotel, having just finished a workout at their health club. I was then the national president of the IYC.

'Where's Naaznin?' asked Sudhir.

'She's on a flight,' I replied. I could almost hear the uneasy silence on the other end of the line.

'An Indian Airlines flight from Kathmandu to Delhi has been hijacked,' Sudhir said, very slowly.

'I don't know where she is today. Let me find out,' I said, saying a silent prayer as the conversation ended.

Naaznin, my wife, works with Air India. She used to fly with the erstwhile Indian Airlines then. Since both of us used to travel frequently even in those days, we would track each other's schedules to the extent that one of us was always in Delhi to look after Ineka, our two-and-a-half-year-old daughter. I called Naaznin, aware that she only uses her phone when she wants to get in touch. After a couple of rings, she answered, much to my relief.

Like all wives, she could sense something was not right even before I uttered a word. I told her about the hijacking of IC-814. There was a slight tremor in her voice, but she remained steady, 'We're trained to handle such situations.' I asked her when was she coming back. '10 p.m. tonight,' she replied.

During our courtship, there were innumerable occasions when I picked her up from Delhi Airport whenever she would come from Mumbai to Delhi on a flight. However, 24 December 1999 stands out because I had never been more relieved to see her walk out of the airport as I was that evening. For families that have loved ones in the aviation industry, a hijacking is as close as it can get to an air crash.

Naaznin was among those who responded when the call went out for volunteers to take a relief aircraft to Kandahar. When she was flannelled that no women were being taken, she tried to convince and cajole the airline to let her go by telling them she could speak Dari. Pashto and Dari are the two main languages spoken in Afghanistan. A Parsi born in India, Naaznin's ancestors hailed from the city of Zahedan in south-eastern Iran. The city is the capital of Sistan and Baluchestan Province on the tri-junction of Iran, Afghanistan and Pakistan. Her grandfather had immigrated to India at the turn of the twentieth century. Dari is therefore her ancestral language. The next seven days were traumatic, to say the least, as we watched the catastrophe unfold.

SURRENDER AND RELIEF

The NDA-BJP government was basking in the lingering glow of the Kargil victory. Having just won a mandate for another five years, it was settling into the groove of governance. The world was preparing for the millennium. The Y2K glitch had digital nerds on edge. In the middle of all this, Pakistan-backed terrorists had commandeered this Indian passenger aircraft.

After landing in Amritsar, Lahore and Dubai, the desperados finally ordered the aircraft to Taliban-controlled Kandahar. After tense negotiations that went on for over six days, the NDA-BJP government finally agreed to release three dreaded terrorists: Mushtaq Ahmed Zargar, Ahmed Omar Saeed Sheikh and Maulana Masood Azhar, in exchange for the hostages. The Indian negotiating team in Kandahar included NSA Ajit Doval, who was then additional director with the IB, C.D. Sahay of the R&AW, Vivek Katju from the Ministry of External Affairs (MEA) and A.R. Ghanshyam from the Indian High Commission in Islamabad, who was the first to reach Kandahar.

India had to suffer the added ignominy of its External Affairs Minister Jaswant Singh having to chaperone the trio to Kandahar by way of securing the release of passengers. The hijacking and its aftermath were a national humiliation. One cannot help but admire and praise the late Jaswant Singh's sense of duty. He was well aware of the political cost of becoming the public face of this capitulation, but he did not flinch when asked, or as some reports suggest, volunteered to perform this unpleasant task.

I had always been intrigued by what must have gone through the mind of this soldier-turned-scholar politician when he agreed, or was asked, to fly the three terrorists to Kandahar. While serving on the Joint Parliamentary Committee (JPC)—the ubiquitous Parliamentary Committee that examined the presumptive and eventually bogus loss report of ₹1.76 lakh crore to the state exchequer authored by the then CAG Vinod Rai—examining matters relating to allocation and pricing of telecom licences and spectrum, I noticed that Jaswant Singh would always arrive at least half an hour before a meeting, invariably bearing a copy of *The Washington Post* under his arm.

Mustering the courage, I popped the question: 'why did you agree to go to Kandahar?' He looked at me, raising his bushy eyebrows, a sardonic smile on his lips, and replied in his classic baritone, 'What I'm going to tell you, I do not want to hear it on the 9 o'clock news tonight.' I gave him my word. After a drawn-out pause, he said, 'There was but no option. We had no diplomatic relations with the Taliban regime and once the terrorists were in Kandahar, what if they reneged on their commitment to release the passengers and the plane? Someone had to ensure that there was no slip between the cup and the lip.'

Emboldened by the response, I asked him, 'Was any ransom paid for the release of the passengers by the Government of India, or by certain private individuals, as has been speculated?'

'It is all propaganda; nothing was paid by the Government of India,' he replied, and then reiterated, 'Nothing was paid by the Government of India.'

I did not press him on the latter part of my question.

There was a lot of talk in the aftermath of the hijack that the terrorists had demanded $200 million in cash, in addition to a laundry list of terrorists to be released. I wrote his answer down in my JPC notebook for the sake of posterity. The reason I choose to mention this conversation here is because while researching this book I realized that Jaswant Singh had said more or less the same thing publicly on numerous occasions earlier.[1]

Two decades after the IC-814 hijack, if a similar situation were to manifest itself again, would India's response be any different? I doubt it. We may just end up walking the same path again.

BLEEDING INDIA THROUGH A THOUSAND CUTS

Twenty-four months later, another terror strike would unleash the largest mobilization of the Indian Army since the 1971 war. That year, 1971, is of seminal importance in the Indo–Pak relationship because whatever is happening today in the form of cross-border

---

[1]PTI, 'Advani Knew about My Going to Kandahar with Terrorists: Jaswant Singh', *The Economic Times*, 31 October 2013, https://economictimes.indiatimes.com/news/politics-and-nation/advani-knew-about-my-going-to-kandahar-with-terrorists-jaswant-singh/articleshow/24999471.cms. Accessed on 15 March 2021.

terrorism has its genesis in the ignominious rout of the Pakistani armed forces, and the subsequent cleaving up of that nation. It is an institutional scar on the collective psyche of the Pakistani military establishment. Even today, the lust to avenge that humiliation is what drives their anti-India posture.

The third war between India and Pakistan took place in 1971. The first two, that were fought over Kashmir, could be located both in the imperatives of domestic Pakistani politics and their enduring rhetoric on Kashmir.

However, 1971 was different. It was a ghastly genocide perpetrated by the Pakistani Army and its collaborators, the Razakars. The political divide between the Pakistan People's Party and the Awami League, after the December 1970 elections, and the subsequent demand for autonomy from East Pakistan, led to the Punjabi-dominated Pakistani military embarking on a vicious onslaught. The violence that followed resulted in several million people fleeing the country and seeking refuge in various Indian border states. By May 1971, the refugee influx had reached nearly 10 million.[2]

This influx turned into a massive humanitarian problem for India. It was left with no other option but to extend political support to the leaders and people opposing this brutal crackdown. Unable to quell the internal uprising sparked by the reign of terror unleashed by the West Pakistan army, aided and abetted by the Razakar militias, the Pakistan Air Force attacked India's northern air bases on 3 December 1971. Nevertheless, this assault proved largely ineffective and provided India with the official casus belli to invade East Pakistan.

In the 1971 war, India was able to gain a preeminent position as a regional power, transforming Pakistan into a revisionist one. The map of South Asia was once again redrawn and a new nation called Bangladesh emerged. The Multan conference in West Pakistan, or

---

[2]Sumit Ganguly, *Deadly Impasse: Indo-Pakistani Relations at the Dawn of a New Century*, Cambridge University Press, 2016.

what remained of Pakistan—five weeks after their defeat in the winter war of 24 January 1972—was a by-product of this revisionism.

It was the Multan conference that crystallized PM Bhutto's two-pronged strategy. The first one had taken shape earlier in 1965 when PM Bhutto pompously stated that 'if India builds the bomb, we will eat grass or leaves, even go hungry, but we will get one of our own.'[3] At Multan, the country's nuclear establishment received a directive to build a nuclear device within three years. The second was the beginning of Pakistan's new strategy to 'bleed India with a thousand cuts.'[4] Pakistan operationalized this approach, and by the late 1970s, commenced a revisionist proxy war in Punjab, and then upscaled it to J&K in the late 1980s.

Punjab became the first frontier for the policy of bleeding India with a thousand cuts. By the mid-1970s, Pakistan became heavily involved in laying the groundwork for a terrorist insurgency in Punjab, and provided sanctuary for training and military assistance to insurgents. There were well-established ties between certain Punjabi separatist groups and Pakistan's intelligence agencies. Taking full advantage of India's internal contradictions, Pakistan tried to draw India into an expansive counter-insurgency operation. They supplemented it with a shrill international campaign that underscored the ambivalence of India towards those regions with large minority populations.

The second frontier originated as a result of a distant crisis in Afghanistan when the Soviet Union withdrew over the Amu Darya River. The US in the early 1980s had acquiesced to an arrangement whereby military assistance to the jihadis from Afghanistan, fighting the USSR, would be routed through Pakistan's ISI. 'In practice, this meant that while the US would pay for the Islamist kite flying in

---

[3]Robert Hathaway, 'India Transformed: Parsing India's "New" Foreign Policy', *India Review*, 2003.

[4]Sumit Ganguly, *Deadly Impasse: Indo-Pakistani Relations at the Dawn of a New Century*, Cambridge University Press, 2016.

Afghanistan, Pakistan would hold the strings.'[5] Pakistan had trained a force of 80,000 mujahideens by the late '80s.[6] Once the Soviets withdrew, the focus of these militants turned to Kashmir. The Soviet withdrawal and the victory of the mujahideens was the key to the Kashmiri turmoil that followed subsequently. A confident Pakistan believed that it could replicate Afghan's victory in Kashmir too.

Therefore, in December 1989 when the state of J&K erupted—largely enthused by the transformative changes taking place in Europe due to the collapse of totalitarian communist states—Pakistan worked assiduously to transform it from a people's movement into a properly synchronized, religiously underpinned and externally funded armed proxy conflict. It waged a proxy war to annex Kashmir from India, a turmoil that has lasted for three decades and is still ongoing—the outcome of which is the complete destruction of normal life in J&K, and the death of thousands of innocent people and personnel from security forces.

The tactical blunder in Kargil and relentless attempts to internationalize the Kashmir issue were all elements of the doctrine: to bleed India through a thousand cuts. It undermined the limited trust that the Lahore Peace Process had engendered, and showed that the Pakistani Army will always be the defining factor in Pakistan's national strategy qua India, until the time the civilian leadership in Pakistan is able to come into its own.

THE WAR THAT WASN'T

The twentieth century ended with the Kandahar hijack which set the stage for the twin attacks—the first on the J&K legislative assembly on 1 October 2001 and the second on India's Parliament on 13 December 2001. India retaliated with Operation Parakram.

---

[5]Praveen Swami, 'Lessons from a Lost War', *The Hindu*, 12 September 2016, https://www.thehindu.com/opinion/lead/lessons-from-a-lost-war/article5747040.ece. Accessed on 15 March 2021.
[6]Ibid.

Even while the world was recovering from the 9/11 attacks, Pakistani terrorists targeted the J&K Legislative Assembly in October 2001. An explosive-laden Tata Sumo slammed the assembly's main entrance, while militants with guns and explosives tried to enter the complex. They were eventually killed in a fierce encounter with security forces. Forty bystanders lost their lives.

At the time, PM Vajpayee wrote a letter to President Bush that India would be compelled to take matters in its hands if Pakistan refuses to mend its ways.[7] There were demands to term Pakistan-based extremist group Jaish-e-Mohammed (JeM), which was behind the attack, a terrorist outfit.

While the casualties in the attack on the J&K Legislative Assembly were higher, the events of 13 December, attacking the temple of Indian democracy, proved to be the last straw that broke the camel's back. It could well have provided the casus belli for a 'just war'.

On that fateful day in 2001, five fully armed terrorists drove a stolen white Ambassador into the campus of India's Parliament, attempting to enter the building complex. The car had a Ministry of Home Affairs label and was therefore allowed to pass through the security barricades.

Coincidentally, at about 11:30 a.m. that morning, I had been travelling from South Delhi to meet my predecessor as the IYC president, Sardar Maninderjit Singh Bitta. Bitta used to live on 14 Talkatora Road, which is a stone's throw away from Parliament. Those days, Red Cross Road used to merge into Talkatora Road and it used to be left open for public traffic. Now, a part of Red Cross Road is closed as it has been subsumed into the Parliament House Complex.

Barely had I entered Bitta's heavily guarded house that news came that Parliament was under a terror attack. We went out into his front garden and could hear gunfire in the distance. By then

---

[7]Polly Nayak and Michael Krepon, 'U.S. Crisis Management in South Asia's Twin Peaks Crisis,' in Zachary S. Davis (ed.), *The India-Pakistan Military Standoff*, Palgrave Macmillan, 2011.

Bitta had taken out his personal weapon and his NSG commandoes were urging us to go back into the house. We spent a tense one hour inside his home watching the attack unfold on live TV. Once his NSG commandoes gave the all clear I made my way to the Supreme Court and Bitta headed for K.P.S. Gill's place that was right opposite his on 11 Talkatora Road.

Later, my driver told me that at the Red Cross Road–Talkatora Road roundabout, a white Ambassador car had almost sidewinded us as it turned into Parliament House. I often wonder if it was the same white Ambassador that was carrying the terrorists.

As an aside, Bitta continues to be heavily protected by the Indian state for he was injured in two bomb blasts carried out by Khalistani terrorists. The first in Amritsar on 9 May 1992 and the next at the national HQ of the IYC on 11 September 1993.[8]

The terrorists had planned to kill and hold Parliamentarians hostage during the morning session of Parliament that was to be attended by senior leaders, including the prime minister. The plot failed because of sheer luck, as the House had adjourned before the attack began.[9] One of the militants blew himself up outside Gate No. 1, the main entrance of Parliament. The remaining four died in the resulting gun battle. The heroism of the Parliament watch-and-ward staff who shut Gate No. 11 and 12 of the Parliament building, thereby saving countless lives, was sterling to say the least. The attack was immediately linked to the Pakistan-based Lashkar-e-Taiba (LeT) and JeM militant organizations.

The national mood was pugnacious. Home Minister L.K. Advani described the attack as the most heinous and audacious attack

[8]R. Pathak, 'Youth Congress(I) President Maninderjit Singh Bitta Escapes Another Assassination Attempt', *India Today*, 30 September 1993, https://www.indiatoday.in/magazine/indiascope/story/19930930-youth-congressi-president-maninderjit-singh-bitta-escapes-another-assassination-attempt-811568-1993-09-30. Accessed on 15 March 2021.

[9]Polly Nayak and Michael Krepon, 'U.S. Crisis Management in South Asia's Twin Peaks Crisis,' in Zachary S. Davis (ed.), *The India-Pakistan Military Standoff*, Palgrave Macmillan, 2011.

originating from Pakistani soil.[10] 'Nothing will harm India more than inaction at this moment,' declared Brahma Chellaney, a defence analyst.[11] Six days later, on 19 December, India launched Operation Parakram against Pakistan.

On the political front, the BJP-led NDA government launched a coercive diplomatic offensive against Pakistan. It recalled its high commissioner from Pakistan on 22 December, broke off all road and rail links, and put forth the following four demands:

i)   The handover of 20 criminals and terrorists residing in Pakistan.

ii) Putting a stop to cross-border infiltration of terrorists.

iii) The closure of facilities, training camps, funding channels and all other means of assistance provided to terrorists operating from Pakistani soil.

iv) A 'categorical, and unambiguous renunciation' of terrorism in all its manifestations.[12]

While specific demands were placed, there was no time limit for compliance which was indicated. Subsequently, Pakistani civilian aircrafts were prohibited from flying over Indian territory. The US concurrently chose to place the LeT and the JeM on the US Department of State's Foreign Terrorist list.[13]

Action had to be taken on the military front for this threat

[10]'Statement Made by Shri L.K. Advani, Union Home Minister on Tuesday, the 18th December, 2001 in Lok Sabha in Connection with the Terrorist Attack on Parliament House', *Ministry of External Affairs*, https://www.mea.gov.in/articles-in-indian-media.htm?dtl/16856/Statement+made+by+Shri+LK+Advani+Union+Home+Minis ter+on+Tuesday+the+18th+December+2001+In+Lok+Sabha+in+Connection+with+ the+terrorist+attack+on+Parliament+House. Accessed on 15 March 2021.

[11]Sumit Ganguly, *Deadly Impasse: Indo-Pakistani Relations at the Dawn of a New Century*, Cambridge University Press, 2016.

[12]S. Kalyanaraman, 'Operation Parakram: An Indian Exercise in Coercive Diplomacy', *Strategic Analysis*, 26:4, 478–492, 2002.

[13]Sumit Ganguly, *Deadly Impasse: Indo-Pakistani Relations at the Dawn of a New Century*, Cambridge University Press, 2016.

of coercive diplomacy to be seen as both potent and credible by Pakistan. Operation Parakram was thus set in motion. It was marked by two distinct peaks. The first peak, immediately after the Parliament attack, occurred in December 2001–January 2002. The second peak, in May-June 2002, followed another assault, this time at Kaluchak near the town of Jammu. War appeared to loom large, as a million soldiers stood along the IB and LoC, prepared for battle.

The First Peak

In the first week of January 2002, the CCS met with the three chiefs in attendance to discuss the plan of action. While politicians favoured limited action restricted to J&K, the military insisted on full-scale mobilization. In the beginning, there were also strident calls for air strikes against terrorist camps located in Pakistan. However, as early as 17 December, the service chiefs argued before the CCS that such strikes would be of limited efficacy in tackling the insurrectionist threat. These camps that apparently amounted to little more than 'drill squares and firing ranges,' could be easily reconstituted.[14]

As an aside, this institutional wisdom that terror training camps were limited value targets and an attack on them would not be an efficacious solution in dismantling terrorist networks seems to have been given a short shrift 18 years later in February 2019, when a successor NDA government decided to launch air strikes on Balakot and Jabba Top situated in the Khyber Pakhtunkhwa province of Pakistan. It was evident that these strikes caused limited or no damage as a number of international reports and independent ground reporting underscored.[15] The government seemed to have been interested in creating an optical illusion for electoral considerations rather than any serious retaliatory or

---

[14]S. Kalyanaraman, 'Operation Parakram: An Indian Exercise in Coercive Diplomacy,' *Strategic Analysis*, 26:4, 478–492, 2002.

[15] Michael Sheldon@DFRLab, 'Surgical Strike in Pakistan a Botched Operation?' *Medium*, 1 March 2019, https://medium.com/dfrlab/surgical-strike-in-pakistan-a-botched-operation-7f6cda834b24. Accessed on 15 March 2021.

punitive action. Furthermore, such attacks increased the prospect of military escalation.

After a brief discussion, it was decided that mobilization must be completed within two weeks, while the final decision to go to war would be taken by the government.[16] The chiefs held their in-house consultations. The Air Force and Navy said that they would be able to mobilize within a week's time, while the Army had serious difficulties and the three strike corps took almost three weeks to complete their mobilization.[17]

As a consequence, the strategy operationalized and predicated upon the swift deployment of a substantial portion of the Indian Army along the western border, with the goal of inducing Pakistan to comply with India's demands getting severely undercut. It was not until 11 January 2002 that Indian forces were in a sufficient state of mobilization for the scheduled operations against Pakistan to be carried out. Pakistan got ample opportunity to also mobilize and, therefore, any element of surprise was effectively lost. As a matter of fact, no strategic aims or end state were debated or set down in terms of either the territories to be captured, or any other form of capacity degradation. Admiral Sushil Kumar, the naval chief up to 31 December 2001, has stated, on record, that no political-military aims were articulated. When he sought the rules of engagement post-mobilization, the PM replied: 'Mobilize for the present, the rest will follow.'[18]

The mobilization was substantially different from the military position India had in the preceding three decades. It was the first time that troops from India's Eastern Command were mobilized and moved to the Western Sector to deal with a contingency involving

---

[16]Lt Gen. H.S. Panag (Retd), 'Operation Parakram: The War That Wasn't but Could Have Reined in Pakistan', *The Print*, 3 January 2019, https://theprint.in/opinion/operation-parakram-the-war-that-wasnt-but-could-have-reined-in-pakistan/172471/. Accessed on 15 March 2021.
[17]Ibid.
[18]Ibid.

Pakistan. Salient provisions of the Union War Book (UWB) were invoked,[19] the Border Security Force (BSF) was placed under command of the Indian Army and provisions of the UWB pertaining to expenditure for mobilization were promulgated.[20]

The military then set about laying mines: we must keep in mind that this was not done even in the 1971 and the Kargil wars.[21] There were also full dress rehearsals of strategies for counter operations predicated on Pakistani retaliation. All this was done maintaining both secrecy as well as what was left of the element of surprise. In the first week of January 2002, tensions steadily mounted in the subcontinent, while troops awaited orders. However, no war was waged.

This was perhaps a given since a general war was impossible. An important reason for this state of play was the US intervention and repeated calls for restraint. These demands for restraint were criticized by many as evidence of Washington's 'double standards' on terrorism, considering the hard position it took post the 9/11 attacks.

The US needed Pakistan's cooperation for operations against both the Taliban and al-Qaeda in neighbouring Afghanistan. With India gnashing its teeth, US officials were apprehensive that the two Pakistani army corps deployed along the Tora Bora Mountains to intercept fleeing al-Qaeda elements, would get redeployed along the LoC to help block an Indian advance. To secure its own interests, the US sent out a series of cabinet-level officials at various junctures in an effort to neutralize the possibility of an Indo-Pak conflict.[22]

The US government's diplomatic manoeuvres did yield an ashen-faced address by General Musharraf. He vowed to crackdown

---

[19]The Union War Book documents the role of each ministry at the time of war.
[20]G. Kanwal, 'Military Dimensions of the 2002 India-Pakistan Stand-off—Planning and Preparation for Land Operations', in Zachary S. Davis (ed.), *The India-Pakistan Military Standoff*, Palgrave Macmillan, 2011.
[21]Ibid.
[22]Rajesh Basrur, 'India's Pakistan Problem: Operation Parakram Revisited', *India Review*, 18:5, 503-519, 2019.

on the terrorists and also said that, in respect of Pakistan's stance on Kashmir, he would not tolerate any terrorist acts.[23] New Delhi still remained deeply sceptical and rightly so. The approach was 'wait and watch' till April–May, when there was generally a surge in infiltration. In the meantime, troops were ordered to remain in place in their respective deployment areas.

A most unusual incident took place that underscored the severe international constraints that India was operating under because of western involvement in Afghanistan. It perhaps also brought out, very early into the mobilization, that India did not have any clearly quantified or delineated war aims and therefore had not gamed the entire deployment, especially the calibration of pressure that it wanted to impose on Pakistan.

On 21 January 2002, when the Strike Corps had just about completed their mobilization, Lt Gen. Kapil Vij, commander of 2 Strike Corps, was suddenly stripped of his command, after the US expressed 'disquiet'[24] over the forward deployment of the strike formations under his command.[25] General Vij was a 'highly accomplished officer'. The Ambala-based 2 Corps is India's principal strike corps capable of delivering the strongest punch. It holds almost 50 per cent of Indian strike capabilities, and although based at Ambala, its domain extends over a 400 km frontage, thereby providing it with operational and tactical flexibility.

The 2 Corps is skilled, outfitted and charged with the remit to launch invasive forays deep into the adversary's territory. For

---

[23]S. Kalyanaraman, 'Operation Parakram: An Indian Exercise in Coercive Diplomacy', *Strategic Analysis*, 26:4, 478–492, 2002.

[24]Shishir Gupta, 'Controversial Transfer of Key Corps Commander Fuels Speculation about India-Pakistan War', *India Today*, 5 September 2012, https://www.indiatoday.in/magazine/defence/story/20020204-controversial-transfer-of-key-corps-commander-fuels-speculation-about-india-pakistan-war-795824-2002-02-04. Accessed on 15 March 2021.

[25]Special Correspondent, 'Transfer Tag on Army Officer "Removal"', *The Telegraph*, 23 January 2002, https://www.telegraphindia.com/india/transfer-tag-on-army-officer-removal/cid/904881. Accessed on 15 March 2021.

any contemplated, planned and war-gamed coercive cross border thrust, the 2 Corps is the key element. A strike corps has a sizeable armour (tank) constituent and strategic capacity.[26] All three strike corps—including the Mathura-headquartered 1 Corps and the Bhopal-positioned 21 Corps—had been deployed during Operation Parakram.

General Vij had ostensibly commenced a deployment drill along the International Border that was perceived as the precursor to an armoured thrust across the border. A significant number of 2 Corps' battle tanks strayed either deliberately, or inadvertently, very close to the International Border, that caused panic among the Pakistanis.

In pursuance of an unofficial and unwritten arrangement, the Indian Armed Forces deploy their tactical assets, including heavy armour, east of the Indira Gandhi Canal, that by and large runs analogous to the International border. Pakistani armoured elements stay at a comparable distance from their edge of the dividing line. The 2 Corps elements deeply lanced this non formal bulwark, positioning themselves scarcely two kilometres away from the International border.[27]

In normal circumstances, this would have been dismissed as an unusual but not alarming military strut. Nevertheless, in the light of an already aggravated situation, this artifice of the strike corps was interpreted as a clear inclination to go across the border.

US satellite imagery detected this forward deployment of 2 Corps heavy armour. Satellite images evidently revealed that some tanks belonging to the 2 Corps had congregated at their preordained strike positions, moving up from their usual concentration zones, that are invariably at a benign distance away from the boundary line. Frontward positioning of a strike corps

---

[26]'Key Commander Was Shifted at US Behest', *Samar IAF*, https://samariaf0.tripod.com/parakram23.html. Accessed on 15 March 2021.
[27]Ibid.

is always decoded as an ominous posture.[28]

Given the active military to military cooperation between the US and Pakistan going back decades, the US obviously would have shared the satellite imagery with Pakistan thus further reinforcing their paranoia. The US then articulated its apprehensions to India, a proxy pitch on behalf of Pakistan. Despite all the stresses in the US-Pakistani relationship especially post 9/11, what keeps the relationship going are the institutional ties between the Pentagon and the Pakistani defence establishment.

US interlocutors, armed with those satellite images, had purportedly quizzed their Indian counterparts. Consequently, the PMO issued a rather unusual but direct diktat stripping General Vij of the command of the 2 Corps. Supplanting him was Lt Gen. B.S. Thakur, the then chief of staff posted with the Army Training Command at Shimla.[29] [30]

Nonetheless, it appears fairly 'implausible' that a responsible officer heading the most vital strike corps of the Indian Army had decided to unilaterally forge ahead without first clearing it with the Western Army Command and the Army headquarters in Delhi. In fact, such a crucial call that would have definitely sparked an all-out conflict could not perhaps have been possible without the knowledge, if not concurrence of the then Defence Minister.

Given that the 2 Corps, or the Kharga Corps as it is also known, is the hammerhead if an operation to cross the border is ever green lighted, the Western Army Command, Army Headquarters and even the MoD would quickly proscribe any unusual or unsanctioned proclivity in real time. Such would or at least should be the level of oversight.

The Pakistanis must have obviously interpreted a strike force

---

[28]Ibid.

[29]Ibid.

[30]'Lt-Gen Vij Moved Forces "Too Close"' to Border', *Times of India*, https://timesofindia.indiatimes.com/india/lt-gen-vij-moved-forces-too-close-to-border/articleshow/1970101322.cms. Accessed on 15 March 2021.

commander being asked to 'proceed on leave' and that too after the US flagged the movement of his strike assets as a signal that India did not want to cross the rubicon, notwithstanding the massive mobilization of its armed forces. The obvious inference they would have drawn would have been that India was merely posturing for domestic purposes, otherwise who in their right minds would remove a well-regarded Strike Force Commander on the cusp of a battle?

A number of retired Pakistani defence and foreign policy elites that I have spoken to over the years at various Indo-Pakistan Track One and a Half and Track Two engagements, also confirm the above assessment that post Lt Gen. Vij being relieved of his command, the Pakistani military establishment assessed that India was not willing to push the envelope beyond a point, despite the self-assurance displayed during the Kargil War.

Lt Gen. Vij was not the first military commander to be substituted by another. Nor will he be the last. But the timing and optics were all wrong if the intent was to get India's demands enforced through the coercive mobilization of its armed forces.

Around this time, the topmost leadership in Pakistan reached out to an 'American expert on South Asian affairs'. Revered as the presiding deity of the South Asian strategic community, he was asked for his readout on India's intentions. He opined, much to the disbelief of the Pakistani apex leadership, that India would do nothing. When pressed for the basis of his assessment, he philosophically pontificated, 'Based upon my profound study of the Indian psyche, I have come to believe that India fights over territory, it does not fight over loss of people for it has just too many'. Prophetic, some might say, at least at that point in time.

The government should never have shifted Lt Gen. Vij at that juncture even if it was a routine transfer, as the government officially claimed in a PIB press release.[31] For the entire attempt at coercive

---

[31]'Move of Lt Gen Kapil Vij', 22 January 2002, https://archive.pib.gov.in/archive/releases98/lyr2002/rjan2002/22012002/r220120029.html. Accessed on 15 March 2021.

diplomacy gets undermined when your principal strike force commander stands replaced for perhaps pushing the envelope to a limit where intent does not only look real but becomes real. Could it have provoked an all-out war with Pakistan? Perhaps so. However, that possibility should have been weighed by the government when the entire army was mobilized in the manner it was for the first time post 1971.

Another way could have been found to express concerns arising out of the purported forward deployment, including telling Pakistan to walk the talk on dialling back its state-sponsored depredations. The lesson is to stand firm in such situations as Prime Minister Indira Gandhi did when the US sent the Seventh Fleet and Britain its own naval armada into the Bay of Bengal and Arabian Sea to thwart the liberation of East Pakistan in December 1971.

By late January 2002, Pakistani officials detained members of the LeT and JeM who stood implicated in the various attacks on India. A pleased Indian government claimed that our 'coercive strategy' had worked. However, celebrations began too soon. In fact, Pakistan had become cockier and more brazen when it realized that the unprecedented mobilization was only for domestic consumption, and perhaps nothing more. It therefore planned and executed another terrorist attack on 14 May 2002. This is often referred to as the second peak of the 2002 crisis.

The Second Peak

The second opportunity for India to take decisive action, if it ever intended to, presented itself after an attack at the Indian Army garrison at Kaluchak in Jammu on 14 May.[32] This was another dastardly attack by militants that killed 22 people, including several children and wives of Indian Army personnel. People's expectation

---

[32]Polly Nayak and Michael Krepon, 'U.S. Crisis Management in South Asia's Twin Peaks Crisis', in Zachary S. Davis (ed.), *The India-Pakistan Military Standoff*, Palgrave Macmillan, 2011.

for retribution had reached a fever pitch. Two days later, PM Vajpayee visited the frontlines in Jammu, delivering a chilling message to the troops that 'the time has come for a decisive battle, and we will have a sure victory in this battle.'[33]

The IAF moved several squadrons of fighter aircraft to forward military bases, the Navy moved five of its vessels to the western fleet; and its only operational aircraft carrier, INS Viraat, was taken out of dry dock and placed on alert near the coast of Mumbai.[34] The Indian military's actual plans reportedly were 'so daring they had never been war-gamed before.'[35]

Summer climes in the Kashmir valley were conducive to offensive activity around the LoC. However, in Punjab and Rajasthan, the temperature often soars above 40°C making it difficult for both man and machine, but the disadvantage was equally shared by both India and Pakistan.[36] Consequently, despite the fact that the Pakistan Army was already mobilized and defensively positioned, a significant offensive action was within the realm of possibility.

An *India Today* article affirmed that after the Kaluchak massacre, India had come close to declaring war.[37][38] The report went on to say that on 18 May, a CCS meeting agreed on military intervention, but there was a lot of disagreement about whether to go for a small

[33]Patrick Bratton, 'Signals and Orchestration: India's Use of Compellence in the 2001–02 Crisis', *Strategic Analysis*, 34:4, 594-610, 2010.

[34]Sumit Ganguly, 'Toward Nuclear Stability in South Asia', *Strategic Analysis*, 2009.

[35]Polly Nayak and Michael Krepon, 'U.S. Crisis Management in South Asia's Twin Peaks Crisis,' in Zachary S. Davis (ed.), *The India-Pakistan Military Standoff*, Palgrave Macmillan, 2011.

[36]G. Kanwal, 'Military Dimensions of the 2002 India-Pakistan Stand-off—Planning and Preparation for Land Operations', in Zachary S. Davis (ed.), *The India-Pakistan Military Standoff*, Palgrave Macmillan, 2011.

[37]Rajesh Basrur, 'India's Pakistan Problem: Operation Parakram Revisited', *India Review*, 18:5, 503-519, 2019.

[38]Shishir Gupta, 'Twice in 2002, India Was on the Verge of Striking against Pakistan. Here's Why It Didn't', *India Today*, 23 December 2002, https://www.indiatoday.in/magazine/cover-story/story/20021223-twice-in-2002-india-was-on-the-verge-of-striking-against-pakistan-793809-2002-12-23. Accessed on 15 March 2021.

attack or a massive operation. While the CCS endorsed the military alternative, it was not operationalized either due to international pressure or because ballistic missiles were tested by Islamabad between 25 and 28 May, or both. The intended or contemplated action therefore never took place, notwithstanding high-pitched rhetoric and intense sabre-rattling.

India's inability to at least carry out even token attacks against targets across the LoC in Kashmir remains puzzling. It becomes all the more perplexing that there were no punitive reprisals whatsoever, considering Indian military capabilities stood fully mobilized and had been battle ready for five months.

On 21 May, Abdul Ghani Lone, a long-standing Kashmiri politician of comparatively moderate disposition, was assassinated.[39] In fact, the assassination of Ghani Lone was an inflection point that began to redefine Vajpayee's political approach to the 'Masla-e-Kashmir' (Kashmir imbroglio).

Shortly after Lone's death, Musharraf gave yet another public address on 27 May, in which he reaffirmed his willingness to end infiltration into Kashmir. Despite his reaffirmation, the Bush administration felt compelled to intervene in the ongoing crisis.

Both Deputy Secretary of State Richard Armitage and Defense Secretary Donald Rumsfeld were dispatched to Islamabad and New Delhi.[40] They told the Pakistani regime that intrusion into Kashmir must come to an end and reportedly asked New Delhi for a drawdown of Indian forces along the Indo-Pak frontier.

The crisis began winding down in the aftermath of these visits. Both Indian and Pakistani forces began staggered withdrawals from their forward deployments. The chances of a confrontation, however, still remained reasonably high. It eventually concluded on 16 October 2002, when the CCS realized that economics of diminishing returns had been in place for several months.

---

[39]Sumit Ganguly, *Deadly Impasse: Indo-Pakistani Relations at the Dawn of a New Century*, Cambridge University Press, 2016.
[40]Ibid.

As Lt Gen. (Retd) H.S. Panag puts it, 'we probably lost the last opportunity for a decisive conventional war to achieve our political aims.'[41]

THE OUTCOMES: COERCIVE DIPLOMACY OR A GRAND BLUFF

What did Operation Parakram accomplish? Some Indian analysts have argued that it achieved its goals because Pakistan-sponsored terrorism tapered off in the autumn of 2002. As Lt Gen. (Retd) Ashok Mehta put it, the political outcomes of the crisis are under appreciated: 'CBMs (confidence building measures) and peace process were a direct outcome of Parakram.'[42] He was of the view that Operation Parakram demonstrated that 'if pushed beyond a point, India is prepared in its national interest to go to the brink of war despite attendant nuclear risks to deter Pakistan from its policy of jihad.'[43] It is also argued that it was successful as it made the global community aware of Pakistan's constant use of terror as an instrument of state policy. Others, however, argue that the Indian strategy of coercive diplomacy failed to accomplish most of the stated objectives, for not one, but myriad reasons.

The cost of sustaining Operation Parakram, as per what the Defence Minister George Fernandes told Parliament, was ₹8,000 crore (₹7 crore a day as per the NSAB). This is without even a single bullet being fired.

Decisive conventional dominance was evidently absent. General V. P. Malik, former COAS, pointed to the detrimental results

---

[41]Lt Gen. H.S. Panag (Retd), 'Operation Parakram: The War That Wasn't but Could Have Reined in Pakistan', *The Print*, 3 January 2019, https://theprint.in/opinion/operation-parakram-the-war-that-wasnt-but-could-have-reined-in-pakistan/172471/. Accessed on 15 March 2021.
[42]Ali Ahmed, 'India's Limited War Doctrine: The Structural Factor', *IDSA Monograph Series No. 10*, IDSA, 2012.
[43]Ibid.

of the fall in defence spending.[44] Between 1990 and 1996 it came down from 3.5 per cent to 2.5 per cent and has not looked up since. It came down to 2.10 per cent in 2020, almost at the level it was in 1961.[45] [46] However, according to a 2018 report by the Estimates Committee of Parliament, headed by the former BJP President Murli Manohar Joshi, defence spending as a percentage of GDP dropped from 1.96 per cent in 2012–13 to 1.56 per cent in 2017–18. This was the lowest since 1962, when China and India fought a bruising border war that did not end well for India, notwithstanding some heroic last stands like the battle of Rezang La.

Since India has been tied down by a proxy war, it costs the army 'one Kargil every 16 months'. The reduction in the defence budget and the consequential commitments had resulted in a 'reduced conventional advantage qua Pakistan from 1:1.7 in 1971 to 1:1.2 at the time of Operation Parakram.'[47]

Rear Admiral Raja Menon (Retd) wrote: 'India does not have the surgical capability and is reluctant to mount a cross-border operation because our strategy, our weapon systems don't give us the capability to "prevent" the operation from turning horribly messy.'[48]

In that 10-month period, the frontline equipment of the army was exposed to high levels of attrition. The sands of Rajasthan and

[44]G. Kanwal, 'Military Dimensions of the 2002 India-Pakistan Stand-off—Planning and Preparation for Land Operations', in Zachary S. Davis (ed.), *The India-Pakistan Military Standoff*. Palgrave Macmillan, 2011.

[45]Armaan Bhatnagar, 'India's Defence Spending in 7 Charts', *The Times of India*, 30 January 2021, https://timesofindia.indiatimes.com/india/indias-defence-spending-in-7-charts/ articleshow/80600625.cms. Accessed on 15 March 2021.

[46]Committee on Estimates, 'Twenty-Ninth Report', Ministry of Defence, 25 July 2018, https://eparlib.nic.in/bitstream/123456789/764418/1/16_Estimates_29.pdf. Accessed on 15 March 2021.

[47]Ali Ahmed, 'India's Limited War Doctrine: The Structural Factor', *IDSA Monograph Series No. 10*, IDSA, 2012, https://www.idsa.in/monograph/ IndiasLimitedWarDoctrine_aahmed. Accessed on 15 March 2021.

[48]Ibid. G. Kanwal, 'Military Dimensions of the 2002 India-Pakistan Stand-off—Planning and Preparation for Land Operations', in Zachary S. Davis (ed.), *The India-Pakistan Military Standoff*. Palgrave Macmillan, 2011.

the dust of Punjab caused significant damage to gun barrels, vehicle motors, auxiliary propulsion units (APUs) and moving objects. Everyday equipment with a short lifespan had been completely run down. To put things in context, when Operation Parakram commenced, the equipment and ammunition consumed during the Kargil conflict was still being produced.[49]

There were serious training inadequacies. For a professional army like India's, there were unacceptably large numbers of mine-laying accidents. It was officially stated that as of 15 March 2002, 'the army had lost 176 men in Operation Parakram as a result of mishaps with minefields, mishandling of ammunition and explosives and traffic accidents'.[50] The *Times of India* quoting the Defence Minister's statement in Parliament reported: 'During Operation Parakram up to July 2003, a total number of 798 army personnel suffered casualties'.[51] This was a heavy cost when compared to the death of 527 soldiers during the intense action in Kargil.

Terrorist infiltration, albeit numerically reduced, persisted across the LoC. Pakistan did not detain the leaders of LeT and JeM or close their training camps and other establishments. They did not proscribe their finances or hand over even one of the 20 terrorists demanded by the Indian government. President Musharraf and the military continued in power, and no further efforts were made by the Pakistani government to arrive at a rapprochement with India.

The goal of Operation Parakram was thus only partly accomplished. On balance, it did significantly weaken the efficacy of coercive diplomacy attempted by India. In fact, when one looks at the events of 2002 with the benefit of hindsight, analysts opine

---

[49]Ibid.

[50]G. Kanwal, 'Lost Opportunities in Operation Parakram, Indian Defence Review,' http://www.indiandefencereview.com/spotlights/lost-opportunities-in-operation-parakram/#:~:text=There%20were%20unacceptably%20large%20casualties,and%20 explosives%20and%20traffic%20accidents. Accessed on 15 March 2021.

[51]G. Kanwal, 'Military Dimensions of the 2002 India-Pakistan Stand-off—Planning and Preparation for Land Operations', in Zachary S. Davis (ed.), *The India-Pakistan Military Standoff.* Palgrave Macmillan, 2011.

that the Indian exercise was not even an exercise in coercive diplomacy; it was only an attempt to intimidate Islamabad to mend its ways.

All diplomatic channels had been clogged and there was no attempt to arrive at any form of a modus vivendi with Pakistan. Cutting off all contact was in fact counterproductive. Chellaney was more forthright:

> The harsh truth is that the government played a game of bluff not just with Pakistan but also with its own military...When a nation enjoys credibility, it can usually achieve its objectives with a mere threat to use force. However, when there are serious credibility problems, even modest objectives are difficult to accomplish. Vajpayee ended up practicing coercive non-diplomacy.[52]

In my estimation, Operation Parakram underscored the limits of coercive diplomacy under a nuclear overhang. It also exposed the limitation, if not the handicap or the asymmetry, of dealing with the depredations of semi-state actors using conventional means. Hypothetically, if the attack on Parliament had succeeded, India would have been left with no other option but to respond with overwhelming force. The psychological impact on the country would have been far worse than 26/11. The consequences of such an all-out conflict are hard to even fathom, and the costs, perhaps, impossible to calculate.

Moreover, it once again highlighted the truism that every country, in the ultimate analysis, more often than not, prioritizes its own national interest above the common good. The perspective of the western powers, especially the US then engaged in Afghanistan, underwent a complete metamorphosis when its own interests stood in juxtaposition to the interests of another 'friendly nation' also reeling from the scourge of terror. Its abandonment of Afghanistan in August 2021 may be for entirely valid reasons from the US political

---

[52]Ibid.

and public opinion, but certainly not from a strategic standpoint which only underscores the fact that the defining inflection point characterizing national security decision-making is national interest and not global good. This is as true about Iraq as it is about Afghanistan today, both places where the US has sought to bring a quietus to its military engagement.

The subsequent initiative that Vajpayee took, qua both Jammu and Kashmir, in April 2003, by articulating the doctrine of 'Insaniyat (humanity), Jamhuriyat (democracy) and Kashmiriyat (identity of the Kashmir people)', followed by the renewed outreach to Pakistan demonstrated that the author of Parakram had realized that a sustained political dialogue was the only way forward for enduring peace in J&K and the subcontinent.

COLD START: THE WHISPERED GHOST

The inability of India's armed forces to carry out cost imposing punitive strikes against select targets had underscored the limits of deterrence capabilities. Therefore, there was a search to develop a military strategy to transcend Pakistan's doctrine of 'bleeding India with a thousand cuts.' This was the genesis of the Cold Start Doctrine.

Cold Start is all about quick and substantial damage, the theology or idea being that the strike corps would be broken into eight division-sized integrated battle groups (IBGs) with the Air Force and Navy acting in aid and support of the ground action. This required a complete transformation of the force structure of the Armed Forces.[53]

At its heart, the doctrine is the army's attempt to develop a useable, conventional, retaliatory operation without blowing the trumpet of war. The doctrine emphasizes the achievement of limited

---

[53]Gurmeet Kanwal, 'Army Doctrine Undergoes Change in Nuclear Era', *ORF*, 29 June 2006, https://www.orfonline.org/research/army-doctrine-undergoes-change-in-nuclear-era/. Accessed on 15 March 2021.

objectives on short notice while simultaneously denying Islamabad the justification to escalate the conflict by opening additional conventional fronts or employing nuclear weapons.

However, Cold Start has remained but a whispered ghost. Although debated in think tanks and strategic circles, the idea and its implementation have remained, at best, ambiguous, with no formal acceptance of the doctrine by the Indian government.

In fact, there is a fair amount of informed speculation whether India even possesses such a doctrine. While former Army Chief Gen. V.K. Singh publicly disowned this doctrine,[54] Gen. Bipin Rawat in a 2017 interview to *India Today*, stated that, 'The Cold Start doctrine exists for conventional military operations.'[55]

While the Cold Start doctrine remains in the realm of ambiguity, the implications of such abstruseness have significantly moulded the security debate in India. A handful of thinkers in the Indian strategic circles do believe that Cold Start had generated enough uncertainty in the mind of Pakistani decision-makers so as to deter them from green lighting militant attacks in the Indian hinterland. However, this myth was conclusively busted by the 2008 Mumbai attacks.

The Pakistani state never gets tired of citing the threat posed by 'the doctrine' as justification for enhancing both the size and capacity of their nuclear forces as well as the tacticalization and miniaturization of their weaponry. There are reports that suggest that the Pakistani side is developing, and possibly has developed, low-yield tactical nuclear weapons to specifically counter the eight division-sized IBGs.

Nonetheless, Gen. Rawat's statement did inject some much-

---

[54]Manu Pubby, 'No Cold Start Doctrine, India Tells US', *The Indian Express*, 9 September 2010, http://archive.indianexpress.com/news/no--cold-start--doctrine-india-tells-us/679273/. Accessed on 15 March 2021.
[55]Sandeep Unnithan, 'We Will Cross Again', *India Today*, 4 January 2017, https://www.indiatoday.in/magazine/interview/story/20170116-lt-general-bipin-rawat-surgical-strikes-indian-army-985527-2017-01-04. Accessed on 15 March 2021.

needed realism into the long-shrouded doctrine. While some view the public assertions about its existence as mere semantics, others believe that the Indian Army has, in fact, secretly reorganized its formations into aggressive and offensive platforms quietly and without any attendant fuss. At the end of the day, the lack of an answer is an answer itself.

So did Operation Parakram fail to meet its intended objectives? Or can it be said that it never had any clearly defined military objectives in the first place? The latter would be a fairer assessment. In hindsight, it is now quite evident that the mobilization of India's military power was completely bereft of a grand strategy. It is here that civil–military relations play a cardinal role. The armed forces should have insisted that the CCS clearly lay down the aim and objects of this mobilization. Was it to be limited to enforcing the demands that India had set forth, as outlined earlier, with concrete compliance timelines? Or was there supposed to be an actionable and defined plan in place to then inflict punishment on Pakistan for its recalcitrance or failure to do so?

At best, it can be claimed that what Operation Parakram did achieve was greater acknowledgement from around the world that the turmoil in J&K is a consequence of Pakistan's state-sponsored terrorism.

The Operation was a defining moment in India's national security trajectory for it circumscribed the efficacy of coercive diplomacy. The fact that its gains were, at best, tactical or transitory and Pakistan did not wind up its infrastructure of terror should have made us reflect if the cost-benefit analysis added up. It turned out to be a high risk-low reward strategy. It has also now provided Pakistan with a historic reference point, if such an exigency were to manifest itself again. It shows how far India went the last time and what its push points are when push comes to shove.

It was also a lesson with regard to the need for long-term planning for the successful execution of our strategic and tactical imperatives under a nuclear overhang. Subsequently, a unified nuclear command and control structure was established in 2003.

The operation also laid bare the inadequacy of critical war fighting material and reserves.

Post Operation Parakram, India's national security system was defined both by these chronic shortcomings and their half-hearted rectification. For the Pakistani state, the lesson was simple; it requires economic growth to sustain a proxy war. Pakistan, therefore, redoubled its efforts to diversify sources of economic sustenance. In short, it began moving from being an American ally to a China lackey.

Musharraf perhaps began having second thoughts about the zero-sum game that Pakistan had been playing with India since the late 1970s. He began displaying greater flexibility about possible negotiations when he publicly stated that he was willing to set aside the UN Resolutions of 1948 and '49 on J&K to resolve the dispute with India. To that end, he also to restarted the 'back-channel' in 2003.

In conclusion, it can be said that Operation Parakram unfortunately ended up blunting the sword arm of India's coercive diplomacy template because of the manner in which it was implemented.

FOUR

INDIA'S NUCLEAR SHANGRI-LA

In the twenty-first century, India and the US have discovered various convergences in their foreign policy and national security interests. Not too long ago, this bilateral relationship was marked by distrust, animosity and diverging perceptions. A major reason being the Cold War and India's high-wire trapeze act of balancing the two superpowers—the US and the erstwhile USSR. This began to change in 1991 when India embraced the Washington consensus.

India began liberalizing and globalizing its economy. The burgeoning middle class was aggressively marketed as a tempting prize to the 'ayatollahs' of the neoliberal economic order. India's constant import of foreign arms made it an attractive mark for western military-industrial complexes. It did not take long for the US and its band of merrymen to realize that India had greater value than just a transactional destination. They understood that China's aggressive rise could only be countered by maintaining a balance of power in the larger Asian region, beyond North and East Asia, and India was in the best position to play that role.

However, the joker in the pack was still the legacy relationship that the Western Alliance had with Pakistan. The Soviet's withdrawal from Afghanistan diminished Pakistan's value as a frontline state in the Afghan Jihad. Coupled with the transformed global paradigm post 1989, many new vistas manifested themselves in a global order that, till then, seemed frozen in permanence.

The Indo–US relationship has long orbited around a shared anti-imperial and anti-colonial past. It is grounded in the values of democracy, liberalism, an independent judiciary, free press and a rules-based international order. On the strategic side, there is a convergence of interests in the larger Indo-Pacific region. Despite all these positives, the relationship has been challenged by a mutual trust deficit going all the way back to 1947.

India had always been important in the US's scheme of things to maintain stability in the region. However, the Cold War dynamic saw both nations on different sides of the Iron Curtain. India, though non-aligned, was ideologically and polemically tilted towards the erstwhile Soviet Union. The two democracies gradually warmed to each other after the collapse of the Soviet Union and Eastern Europe in 1991, with the US becoming the only axis in an increasingly unipolar world.

Of late, the China factor has become another important constant in the Indo–US equation. China has created a system of dependencies not only with the US, but with many other major players in the Asia-Pacific region including Japan, Australia, Association of Southeast Asian Nations (ASEAN) and even India. It is far from easy for any of these countries to independently tackle China's not too peaceful rise. The China-backed Regional Comprehensive Economic Partnership (RCEP) is the latest manifestation of this reliance, notwithstanding that even the majority who have signed onto this compact are wary of China's growing belligerence in the greater ASEAN and North Asian region. Even those who are members of the Quadrilateral Security Dialogue (QSD, also known as the Quad), namely Japan and Australia, have signed on the dotted line. The Indo–US relationship, therefore, remains the stoutest yoke in creating a sustainable balance of power in the region.

INDIA'S INHERENT ANTI-AMERICANISM

The Cold War period was particularly rough for Indo–US bilateral relations, as India leaned towards the USSR from the late 1950s due to its deteriorating relationship with China. Despite India warming up to the USSR, it winked, nudged and looked the other way, and essentially green-lighted the Chinese aggression into India in 1962, so that the Chinese did not break ranks with the broader communist bloc over the Cuban Missile Crisis.[1]

This compelled India to reach out to the US for military assistance and the latter was prompt in its response. However, before the assistance could become entirely fungible, the Chinese unilaterally declared a ceasefire on 21 November 1962.

The ceasefire declaration stated,

> Beginning from 21 November 1962, the Chinese frontier guards will cease fire along the entire Sino-Indian border. Beginning from 1 December 1962, the Chinese frontier guards will withdraw to positions 20 kilometres (12 miles) behind the line of actual control which existed between China and India on 7 November 1959.

For his proactive support during those critical times, President John F. Kennedy became a popular figure in India after 1962 and his photograph was displayed at paan (betel nut) shops across the country—a reliable benchmark of a leader's popularity.[2]

President Roosevelt had once notably told Churchill, 'I can't believe that we can fight a war against fascist slavery, and at the same time not work to free people all over the world from a backward colonial policy.'[3] Despite Roosevelt being a passionate supporter of Indian independence even during World War II (WWII), the

---

[1]Manish Tewari, 'Talk Ties Mindfully, Do Not Squander Options', *The Asian Age*, 27 October 2020, https://asianage.com/opinion/columnists/271020/manish-tewari-talk-ties-mindfully-do-not-squander-options.html. Accessed on 15 March 2021.

[2]Manish Tewari, 'China's Seizure of Territory in Ladakh Reinforces its Sharp Political Messages', *Outlook*, 13 July 2020, http://live.outlookindia.com/website/story/opinion-chinas-seizure-of-territory-in-ladakh-reinforces-its-sharp-political-messages/356596/?next=. Accessed on 15 March 2021.

[3]Khemta H. Jose, 'When Roosevelt Took on Churchill to End British Rule in India', *The Quint*, 30 January 2021, https://www.thequint.com/news/world/franklin-roosevelt-role-in-india-independence-british-rule-churchill. Accessed on 15 March 2021.

roots of Indo–US mistrust predates the above-mentioned period of collaboration in 1962.

This mistrust had everything to do with Pakistan. There was a substantial body of opinion in India from the late '40s, that the creation of Pakistan had less to do with the Choudhary Rahmat Ali, Muhammad Iqbal and Mohammed Ali Jinnah combine, but more to do with the Anglo-American alliance looking for a reliable buffer in West and Central Asia against Soviet expansionism after WWII. This theory would gain more traction when Pakistan would sign the Mutual Defense Assistance Agreement with the US in May 1954. Later that year, Pakistan also became a member of the Southeast Asian Treaty Organization (SEATO) along with Britain, the US, France, Philippines, Australia, New Zealand and Thailand.

On 24 February 1955, Pakistan joined the Central Treaty Organization (CENTO), formerly the Baghdad Pact, another key defence alliance, along with Britain, Turkey, Iran and Iraq. The US and the UK were the lynchpins of this arrangement. Early in 1959, Pakistan signed a bilateral Agreement of Cooperation with the US along with Turkey and Iran, which was designed to further reinforce CENTO. This was necessitated because Iraq withdrew from this defence arrangement after the 14 July Revolution of 1958 that overthrew the Hashemite monarchy that had been ruling Iraq since 1921. The new regime of free officers and civilian movement, led by Abd al-Karim Qasim, forged an alliance with the Soviet Union and other left-leaning nations. This also led to changing the name of the alliance from the Baghdad Pact to CENTO.

As the genocide in the then East Pakistan made the 1971 Indo-Pak conflict inevitable, US President Richard Nixon and his NSA Henry Kissinger decided that if push came to shove, they would stand behind West Pakistan. This was despite US administration's knowledge of the grave human rights violations being perpetrated by the Pakistani Army in East Pakistan. According to the plan in November 1971, Deputy NSA General Alexander Haig would instruct the US Navy, on Kissinger's advice, to keep an aircraft-carrier-led task force ready for deployment in the Indian Ocean.[4]

The tide of war turned against Pakistan and expectantly the US Navy's Task Force-74 of the Seventh Fleet led by the aircraft carrier USS Enterprise was ordered to sail at battle speed into the Bay of Bengal from the Gulf of Tonkin where it was then deployed for operations in the Vietnam War. At the same time, the British Navy also dispatched a naval group led by the aircraft carrier HMS *Eagle* comprising commando carrier HMS *Albion*, and several destroyers, towards India's west coast.

An audacious and coordinated 'grand bluff' to intimidate India was thus operationalized. British ships in the Arabian Sea were to draw away Indian naval assets, thereby providing a distraction for the US Task Force-74 to make a dash for the coast of East Pakistan and reinforce the Pakistani positions. The intent was to force an immediate ceasefire and prevent Dhaka from falling into Indian hands.

Obviously, this development escalated New Delhi's concerns. Articulating India's position, Defence Minister Jagjivan Ram thundered: 'Even if the US were to send the 70th fleet, we would still not be deterred.' However, the situation on the ground was not promising. The Indian Navy's Eastern Fleet, commanded by its aircraft carrier INS *Vikrant*, with barely 20 light fighter aircrafts, was being challenged by the British and the American Armada. The IAF was supposed to provide the rest of the muscle.

India invoked the Indo-Soviet Treaty of Peace, Friendship and Cooperation signed on 9 August 1971, and requested the Soviet Union for help to call out the Nixon-Kissinger chicanery. Moscow responded with alacrity and dispatched a nuclear-armed flotilla, the 10th Operative Battle Group (Pacific Fleet) from Vladivostok, under the command of Admiral Vladimir Kruglyakov. The Soviet Union also deployed two task groups consisting of six submarines,

[4]Manish Tewari, 'US Naval Fleet's Defiance of Indian Law Is Not Unprecedented. India Must Heed the Message', *The Indian Express*, 14 April 2021, https://indianexpress.com/article/opinion/columns/us-navy-fleet-warship-india-eez-area-7272626/. Accessed on 15 March 2021.

two cruisers, two destroyers and support vessels. Additional support was provided by a group of Ilyushin Il-38 anti-submarine warfare aircraft from Aden air base in Yemen. The Soviets stared down the Anglo-American flotilla and the rest is history.[5] This hostile attempt by the US is deeply ingrained in the collective psyche of the Indian people, though half a century down the line many are not conversant with these foundational facts of history.

The war of 1971 was the very pinnacle of rancour between the US and India. In many recollections of that time, it is often pointed out that even though efforts were made by President Nixon and Kissinger to convince Prime Minister Indira Gandhi not to undertake hostilities against Pakistan, especially during her visit to Washington DC in early November 1971, she did lead India to war upon her return to the country.[6] The creation of Bangladesh was the highest point of Indira Gandhi's career as she redrew the political map of South Asia again 25 years after the bloody partition of the subcontinent in 1947—albeit for all the right reasons.

This, however, did make her the prime target of the unadulterated hostility of the Western powers. It contributed greatly to the instability that India witnessed during 1972–5. The machinations of the ubiquitous 'foreign hand', as Indira Gandhi would describe it, were never researched in great detail by academics either in India or elsewhere. It may partly be due to the apprehension that if something substantive was unearthed in the research, it may validate or provide part justification for the unfortunate and utterly avoidable decision to impose Emergency in June 1975.

Indira Gandhi visited Washington after more than a decade, in 1982, upon an invitation by President Ronald Reagan.[7] The Indian

[5]Ibid

[6]'IANS, "This woman suckered us," said Nixon of Indira Gandhi', *Hindustan Times*, 2 March 2010, https://www.hindustantimes.com/delhi/this-woman-suckered-us-said-nixon-of-indira-gandhi/story-WGR773bfTnuAsEffYYvq5O.html. Accessed on 15 March 2021.

[7]Michael T. Kaufman, 'Mrs Ghandi (sic) Making the Most of Foreign Policy Openings', *The New York Times*, 6 June 1982, https://www.nytimes.com/1982/06/06/

leadership would, however, continue to view the US as closer to Pakistan, and the Soviet Union was India's all-weather time-tested friend. The equation largely remained the same until the disintegration of the USSR on 25 December 1991. It is only after the USSR finally collapsed, India, like many other nations, was then compelled to undertake a strategic reset with the only remaining hyper-power in the world—the US. India's relationship with the two superpowers had thus traversed the whole nine yards in the nine years between 1962 and 1971.

CLOSER DEFENCE ENGAGEMENT

The Agreed Minute on Defense Relations between India and the US in 1995 was a vital beginning. It opened a new chapter that carried the Indo–US bilateral relationship into many areas of strategic, economic and technological cooperation. There was a slow fading of the residual trust deficit from the Cold War. The 1995 agreement saw the setting up of three new bodies—Defence Policy Group, Joint Technical Group and Joint Steering Committee.[8] It could be seen as the culmination of efforts that had begun since 1991 when Lt Gen. Claude M. Kicklighter, the commander of the US Army Pacific, proposed a set of comprehensive exchanges between the defence establishments of both countries. In 1992 and '93, both navies undertook joint exercises and also participated in the Malabar exercise.

The growing synergy in foreign policy and security objectives between the two powers went into a temporary deepfreeze in 1998, when India, followed by Pakistan, decided to conduct nuclear tests.[9] Washington saw this as a step towards a potential nuclear

weekinreview/mrs-ghandi-making-the-most-of-foreign-policy-openings.html. Accessed on 15 March 2021.
[8]C. Samuel, 'Indo–US Defence Cooperation and the Emerging Strategic Relationship', *Strategic Analysis*, 31 (2): 209-236, 2007.
[9]K.P. Vijayalakshmi, 'India–US Strategic Partnership: Shifting American Perspectives on Engaging India', *International Studies*, 54 (1-4): 42-61, 2017.

flashpoint and an arms race in South Asia. It imposed a number of sanctions on India related to procurement of raw materials required for nuclear fission. It is noteworthy that American antagonism for India's nuclear capability development also meant hostility from many American allies, like Japan and Australia, key centres of politics and economics in the Indo-Pacific. Both these countries condemned India's 1998 nuclear tests.[10][11]

The thaw commenced as a consequence of conversations between Jaswant Singh and Strobe Talbott. Both of whom eventually struck up a friendship also. However, the expansive, multi-continent Singh-Talbott dialogue, followed by the 9/11 terrorist attack, changed America's approach to India that till then had been affected by the nuclear tests, notwithstanding President Clinton's visit to New Delhi in March 2000.

In December 2001, *CNN* reported that the US would lift sanctions imposed on India as a result of 'strengthened bilateral cooperation to combat terrorism.'[12] The US recognized India's importance for fighting terrorism and ensuring stability in South Asia. A change in American attitude also naturally allowed its allies to build better bilateral relations with India.

The Indo–US relationship, therefore, is not a stand-alone construct, but a pillar upon which many of India's crucial relationships in Asia-Pacific are dependent. While Indian foreign policy has been fiercely autonomous of any pressure with regard to security interests, synchronization of goals with the US has certainly been helpful.

---

[10]Ankit Panda, 'The Nuclear Problem in India-Japan Relations', *The Diplomat*, 31 October 2013, https://thediplomat.com/2013/10/the-nuclear-problem-in-india-japan-relations/. Accessed on 15 March 2021.

[11]'Australia's response to nuclear tests in South Asia', *Parliament of Australia*, https://www.aph.gov.au/Parliamentary_Business/Committees/Senate/Foreign_Affairs_Defence_and_Trade/Completed_inquiries/1999-02/nuclear/report/c06. Accessed on 15 March 2021.

[12]'U.S. Lifts Sanctions against India', *CNN*, 5 December 2001, https://edition.cnn.com/2001/WORLD/asiapcf/south/12/04/india.us.defense/index.html. Accessed on 15 March 2021.

A 2001 *New York Times* report stated that lifting of sanctions will allow for greater control and monitoring of India's nuclear material production.[13] This was almost a prophecy as India and the US signed the Civil Nuclear Deal seven years later, which did give the international community access to India's civil nuclear programme.

Prior to the Nuclear Deal, the relationship received a much-needed impetus with the New Framework for the US–India Defence Relationship, signed in 2005, that brought the countries closer in terms of both security cooperation and intelligence sharing. It is often seen as the base upon which many of the later agreements have been signed, including the Indo–US Basic Exchange and Cooperation Agreement (BECA) for Geo-Spatial Cooperation in 2020.

By January 2004, India and the US agreed upon the Next Steps in Strategic Partnership (NSSP) between the two nations. Speaking on 12 January, President George W. Bush stated,

> In November 2001, Prime Minister Vajpayee and I committed our countries to a strategic partnership. Since then, our two countries have strengthened bilateral cooperation significantly in several areas. Today we announce the next steps in implementing our shared vision. The United States and India agree to expand cooperation in three specific areas: civilian nuclear activities, civilian space programs, and high-technology trade. In addition, we agree to expand our dialog on missile defense. Cooperation in these areas will deepen the ties of commerce and friendship between our two nations and will increase stability in Asia and beyond. ... We are working together to promote global peace and prosperity. We are partners in the war on terrorism, and we are partners in controlling the proliferation of weapons of mass destruction and the means to deliver them. The vision of U.S.-

---

[13]Jane Perlez, 'U.S. Ready to End Sanctions on India to Build Alliance', *The New York Times*, 27 August 2001, https://www.nytimes.com/2001/08/27/world/us-ready-to-end-sanctions-on-india-to-build-alliance.html. Accessed on 15 March 2021.

India strategic partnership that Prime Minister Vajpayee and I share is now becoming a reality.[14]

This paved the way, in 2005, for a Defense Framework Agreement. It is noteworthy that while the NSSP was initialled by the Vajpayee government, the Defense Framework Agreement was signed by the Manmohan Singh government. This reflects a rare bi-partisanship in India's approach to the US. However, it proved to be short-lived. In July 2008, the BJP, that had embarked on the NSSP while in government, brought a no-confidence motion in the Lok Sabha against its successor UPA government accusing them of allegedly betraying 'national interest' on the nuclear deal.

The Defense Framework Agreement would be fundamental in boosting defence business between the two countries, and signing of some major logistics and intelligence-sharing agreements over the next 15 years. In more ways than one, the agreement laid important groundwork in India's push to secure a larger footprint in the global strategic space.

BANGING THE GAVEL: NUCLEAR COOPERATION AGREEMENT, 2008

The foundation for the landmark 2008 deal between the two countries, to a large extent, was the New Framework for the US-India Defense Relationship (NFDR). It was signed in 2005 between US Defense Secretary Donald Rumsfeld and Indian Defence Minister Pranab Mukherjee, and laid out a 10-year plan to enhance defence ties between India and the US. It opened up 13 specific areas of cooperation between the two countries. While clauses such as joint exercises and defence exchanges were the expected inclusions and formed the backbone of the framework, other clauses like collaboration in peacekeeping and multilateral

---

[14]'Next Steps in Strategic Partnership with India', *US Department of State Archive*, https://2001-2009.state.gov/p/sca/rls/pr/28109.htm. Accessed on 15 March 2021.

operations were important in strengthening military-to-military cooperation. Combating terrorism and proliferation was also an important part of the framework, which included technology transfer, defence trade and collaboration on missile technology, many areas of defence cooperation like joint weapons production, military exercises, missile defence cooperation, among others.[15] The agreement was renewed in 2015, highlighting its success and the intention of the leadership to maintain strategic engagement between the two countries.

In a joint statement, US President Bush and Indian PM Manmohan Singh announced that Bush would consult the Congress and request to adjust American laws and policies in India's favour, and also work with allies and friends to ensure that India has full cooperation in civil nuclear energy. The Henry J. Hyde US-India Atomic Energy Cooperation Act was passed in 2006, which was vital to reforming the American approach to India with regard to the harnessing of nuclear energy. It allowed the US to waive many requirements from the Atomic Energy Act of 1954 for India. Both countries announced in 2007 that they had reached an agreement on the text for the cooperation deal.

WHEN SINGH BECAME KING

Soon enough, the politics of the Indo–US nuclear deal began heating up. This was barely four months into my tenure as the national spokesperson of the INC.

In June 2008, I was in London to attend the Tehelka conference. The plan was to combine it with a brief vacation at a friend's castle in Scotland. Tarun Tejpal, his brother, Minty, and Tarun's wife, Geetan Batra and I had gone to college together in Chandigarh. Tarun and Geetan were about three years senior to us, while Minty and I were classmates.

---

[15]V. Mishra, 'India–US Defence Cooperation: Assessing Strategic Imperatives', *Strategic Analysis*, 42 (1): 1-14, 2018.

On 19 June, I left London to spend a week in Scotland, since the Tehelka conference was scheduled later on 26 and 27 June 2008. A day before leaving for Scotland, a London-based think tank invited me to deliver a talk. After the talk one of the attendees, I think from the press, told me that a senior functionary of the government had stopped over in London on the way back from Washington DC. During an informal interaction 'with a select group of people', he ostensibly expressed a view that the nuclear deal with the US would be signed in a month's time.

I was quite surprised. In fact, the previous October, Manmohan Singh had informed a media summit rather wistfully that there is life beyond the nuclear deal. Coming as I was from New Delhi only a day earlier, there was complete quietus on the deal. I just shrugged off the information. However, by the time I came back to London to attend the Tehelka Summit, all hell had broken loose in Delhi. The prime minister had given an ultimatum to the most trenchant opponents of the deepening engagement with the US, with the Indo–US nuclear deal being the cherry on the cake: my way or the highway.

Not surprisingly, there was considerable opposition from several political organizations, mainly from left-wing parties. These parties expressed dissatisfaction even over India's first nuclear tests and maintained that India did not face any external threat large enough to develop nuclear weapons as deterrence. The general secretary of the Communist Party of India (Marxist-Leninist) (CPI-ML), Vinod Mishra, had said in Parliament, 'We oppose the nuclear tests conducted by the Indian government because it will trigger an arms race in South Asia and will destabilize peace in the region.'[16] There was the additional argument of diverting financial resources away from economic development and social emancipation in the country.

---

[16]'Indian Communists Condemn Nuclear Tests', *Green Left*, Issue No. 321, 17 June 1998, https://www.greenleft.org.au/content/indian-communists-condemn-nuclear-tests. Accessed on 15 March 2021.

The communist party, staunchly opposed to the 2008 Civil Nuclear Agreement with the US, believed that any strategic alliance with the US was not in India's national interest, and wrongly felt that through this deal, America would be able to dictate India's foreign policy. Prakash Karat, then general secretary of the Communist Party of India (Marxist) (CPI-M), accused the government of compromising India's independent foreign policy and called the arrangement 'tragic.' He also added that the Left parties will continue their struggle against American imperialism.[17] The support of the Left parties at that time was crucial to the UPA government, and the CPI-M hinted at withdrawing support and thus risking the fall of the government if the deal went ahead. External Affairs Minister Pranab Mukherjee met with Left leaders to bring them on-board, but remained largely unsuccessful. The Left parties rejected any kind of reassurance by the panel constituted to review the progress of safeguards agreements.

In *The Long Game: How the Chinese Negotiate with India*, India's former foreign secretary Vijay Gokhale has put forth an interesting thesis that the Left opposition to the nuclear deal was at the behest of China or that China leveraged the intrinsic disquiet among the left wingers in India to the growing proximity between the US and India.

He writes, 'Instead, the Chinese appeared to operate through the Left parties and the left-leaning media in India that had an ideological problem with regard to nuclear weapons, in an effort to build domestic opposition to the Indo–US deal. This might have been the first instance for China to operate politically in Indian domestic politics. China is becoming more sophisticated in its manipulation of Indian interest groups.'[18]

---

[17]PTI, 'Left Refuses to Relent, Toughens Its Stand against Nuclear Deal', *LiveMint*, 22 August 2007, https://www.livemint.com/Politics/I1Siu0NzSpaHU9iHfKUuuL/Left-refuses-to-relent-toughens-its-stand-against-nuclear-d.html. Accessed on 15 March 2021.

[18]Shubhajit Roy, 'China Tried to Use Left to Scuttle N-Deal: Former Foreign Secretary Vijay Gokhale', *The Indian Express*, 3 August 2021, https://indianexpress.com/article/india/indo-us-nuclear-deal-china-opposition-vijay-gokhale-book-7435411/.

Karat, one of the key opponents of the Indo–US Nuclear engagement in 2008, has however denied having any discussions with the Chinese on this issue. He stated, 'We have had no discussions whatsoever.'[19]

Within a month, the UPA government was facing a vote of confidence on the issue. The national spokespersons had their job cut out for them.

Before moving to the vote of confidence, I would like to give a brief description of how the media outreach of the Congress functioned in those days under Veerappa Moily, the chairperson of the media department of the AICC and former CM of Karnataka. Traditionally, the Congress used to hold briefings at 4:15 p.m. every Monday, Wednesday and Friday. Sometime in the past, given that the Congress was the historical party of governance, a decision must have been taken to hold the briefing as late as possible, in order to answer all issues that had been raised throughout the day. Moreover, it seems that after 5 p.m., the wire services would get busy those days with stock market trade data flowing back and forth. This premise does not hold good in today's day and age.

Moily used to have a very collegial system of working. Every afternoon at 1 p.m. over idli, dosa, upma and coffee, he would brainstorm with the spokespersons about the party line at the afternoon briefing. The meeting was fixed at that time to accommodate everybody's schedules. The spokesperson of the day would present his thoughts and others would weigh in. The discussions were frank, free-flowing and nobody had the last word. The party line would be decided by consensus. Even if there were a diktat from the top, Moily would allow us to amend it if he was convinced by the logic of our summation.

It was an open and democratic forum where candour was both encouraged and appreciated. Moily would encourage the spokespersons to be aggressive and on the front foot. He asked us

---

Accessed on 15 March 2021.
[19]Ibid.

not to be worried about making mistakes since it was all part of the learning process. At times, he would even take the rap for our indiscretions.

However, everyone had to do their own research. There was no centralized assistance at that point in time. Often, Moily would brief the press himself both on briefing and non-briefing days, i.e., Tuesday, Thursday and Saturday. Never shy of controversy, he has rare leadership ability and goodness of heart. Spokespersons were encouraged to keep their briefings to 22 minutes. Two to three minutes for the suo motu and 19 minutes for question and answers. This duration had been arrived at based on some weird research. The rationale was that the media is fickle and their attention span does not last for more than 22 minutes, after which they start getting fidgety. This is complete hogwash. I found the women and men of the national media to be bright and engaged. Some of my briefings would go on for an hour or even an hour and a half as I enjoyed the cut and thrust. The national media does not suffer fools easily.

On 27 June, while addressing a rally in Kanpur, the prime minister-designate of the BJP, L.K. Advani, launched a frontal attack on the UPA government. He termed the Manmohan Singh government as critically ill and counting its last breaths in the ICU.[20] The press asked me for a reaction. I said something that came across as flippant and Advani was reportedly upset.

On 8 July 2008, after supporting the UPA government for four years or more, the Left finally withdrew its support, while the PM was in Japan attending the G-8 summit. The trigger was the PM's announcement in Tokyo that India would approach the Board of Governors of the International Atomic Energy Agency (IAEA) to take the nuclear deal forward.

The die had been cast for the next act. Soon another actor

---

[20]Shekhar Iyer, 'Govt in ICU, says BJP's PM Candidate', Hindustan Times, 23 June 2008, https://www.hindustantimes.com/india/govt-in-icu-says-bjp-s-pm-candidate/story-Sw9SL0f8wEBJfS0tH1QZwO.html. Accessed on 15 March 2021.

emerged on the Delhi scene, the general secretary of the Samajwadi Party, the irrepressible Amar Singh.

Amar Singh soon became the man about town. However, the real numbers were being counted elsewhere. Like a well-oiled machine, the Congress party burnt the midnight oil to get the numbers together. Contrary to all the irresponsible canards about money having played a role in swinging the confidence vote, it was really political skills that finally carried the day.

Since spokespersons were on the frontlines of this battle attacking, defending and jousting, we were very susceptible to red herrings. One late evening, a couple of days before the confidence vote, a guest coordinator from a leading news channel called me up and claimed that there were certain MPs from Punjab who were willing to switch loyalties if the price was right. I rebuffed him immediately and told him that in such ventures, going by the earlier Jharkhand Mukti Morcha experience, the alleged bribe giver goes scot-free, the bribe-taker also walks, but the intermediary gets his posterior whacked by the law-enforcement machinery. It sounds far more amusing in Punjabi. I could sense that the media was on a fishing expedition for a story.

My suspicions were confirmed when, on the morning of the trust vote, the same channel wanted me to do a live-from-home interview for their 9 a.m. bulletin. After a few inane questions, the anchor suddenly asked me if I could look into the camera, put my hand on my heart and swear that the Congress party had not bribed any MPs. I found that a bit odd, but since I had scrupulously and deliberately kept myself away from the counting of heads, I told him that while I would not put my hand on my heart, I would look into the camera (which I was doing anyway), and affirm that the Congress party does not indulge in such petty horse-trading. However, my antenna was up. There was something nasty going on and that particular channel seemed to be the vehicle of choice for the person who had planned it all.

On the day the Left withdrew support, it was decided that it was now time to take our gloves off qua the Left parties also. For years, Congress spokespersons had been gnashing their teeth as Left leaders flaunted their intellectual pretensions. They had to be treated with kid gloves and be allowed to walk all over us. After all, the survival of the government was at their mercy. They were exercising power without responsibility. It was party time for the Congress spokespersons. The heavy howitzers could fire at will across the spectrum. No mercy was asked for and none extended over the next 10 days. Friends and allies had turned foes overnight.

22 JULY 2008

Finally, the day of the confidence motion had arrived. The scene outside Parliament was a cross between a circus and a carnival. The media had invaded the beautifully manicured lawns outside the Parliament building, setting up little tents and makeshift studios. It resembled a school fête with a hundred different stalls, all selling the same kind of candy.

At about 3 p.m., as I wrapped up an appearance at the *Times Now* studios in Mandi House, and was headed for another one on the lawns outside Parliament, the penny dropped. Suddenly, a group of BJP MPs rushed into the well of the House brandishing wads of currency notes. Initially, it was not clear what they were trying to say, but soon it emerged that they were claiming that someone had ostensibly tried to bribe them for their vote. It was a dramatic yet disgusting moment. Parliament had been plummeted to the depths of defilement.

I quickly made my way back to a hotel room that was a temporary resting place to watch the events unfold. Just as Arvind Chowdhary (my media coordinator) and I entered the room and switched on the TV, one of the channels started announcing that they had decided to delay the broadcast of a 'sting operation to bribe MPs'. As events would later pan out, all those who were accused of allegedly trying to bribe lawmakers to vote for the nuclear deal were acquitted by the court for lack of evidence. In retrospect, it appeared more of an orchestrated attempt to sully the confidence vote.

Later in the evening, Dr Singh's government won the confidence vote with 275 members voting in favour of the motion, 256 against, and 10 members abstaining. The media started running 'Singh Is King' after a popular Bollywood movie that was showing in theatres those days.

The saddest part of this whole drill was the expulsion of the speaker of the House, Somnath Chatterjee, an eminent lawyer and a veteran Parliamentarian, from the CPI-M for courageously disregarding the diktats of his party to resign and vote against the UPA government in the no-confidence motion.

Many years later, I asked Dr Singh how he managed to swing the nuclear deal. He smiled and replied, 'I will write about it one day. However, all those who are claiming credit do not even know a bit about how it happened. It is I who requested the former president, Dr A.P.J. Abdul Kalam, an eminent atomic scientist, to persuade Mulayam Singh Yadav that this agreement is in national interest.'[21] He left it at that. The Indo–US nuclear deal was indeed Dr Singh's baby.

However, with all those shenanigans, the Opposition had managed to taint the victory. For days after the trust vote, the media kept trying to beat the bogey of money changing hands. I recall a particular morning, when I had gone to NDTV India, their Hindi channel, at the request of one of their brightest anchors, Vijay Trivedi, whose subtlety cloaked a sharp political mind. He had the Akali MP Sukhdev Singh Libra with him on the outdoor broadcast van connection. Trivedi asked him why he had abstained from voting in defiance of the party whip. Libra, whom I later got to know quite intimately as we represented my adjoining Parliamentary constituency in the 15th Lok Sabha, replied in Punjabi, a language

[21]IANS, 'Kalam Endorsed Nuclear Deal: Manmohan Singh', *Business Standard*, 29 July 2015, https://www.business-standard.com/article/news-ians/kalam-endorsed-nuclear-deal-manmohan-singh-115072901320_1.html. Accessed on 15 March 2021.

the anchor was unable to understand. But the thrust of Trivedi's questioning was to insinuate that Libra had been bought over. I interjected and translated Libra's explanation, and was promptly accused of being his lawyer. More evidence of alleged complicity. There were other MPs on the show who had cross-voted. They were subjected to the same 'tender treatment'. The short point being that there was a mental block in the media. They refused to believe that someone could have voted according to their conscience.

A couple of years later, while travelling to Ludhiana from New Delhi, I asked Libra sahib about his decision not to vote with the Akali Dal. Now you must understand that the late Mr Libra was a quintessential Sikh and a dyed-in-the-wool old-school Akali for whom politics was an extension of preserving the Sikh faith. He would wake up at 2:30 a.m., take a bath, pray till 5 and begin meeting people at 5:15 a.m. He ended his day at 6 p.m. and was in bed by 7:30–8 p.m. Libra explained that one day, Parkash Singh Badal, who had by then become the Punjab CM, took all the Akali Dal MPs to meet Dr Manmohan Singh and assured him of their support on the nuclear deal. The moment they stepped out, Badal got a call from Advani. In a matter of seconds, Badal did a volte-face and told the MPs that they would rethink their support for Dr Singh. Libra told me that he had made up his mind right then that if a Sikh prime minister required his support, then as a Sikh he was duty bound to support him. For him, it was not about the merits of the nuclear engagement or national interest. In his simple black-and-white world, it was about helping another Sikh at a time of need.

The battle for the nuclear deal was not over yet. At around 11 p.m. on 6 September 2008, I received a call from *Times Now* requesting a phono on the decision of the NSG to grant India a clean waiver from its existing rules which forbade nuclear trade with a country that had not signed the NPT. As they connected me to the studio, I could hear Rajiv Pratap Rudy, the spokesperson of the BJP, an old college friend from our Chandigarh days, prattling along about how this was a coup and that the NSG had taken this covert action in the dead of the night under the cover of darkness. I was mightily amused by how the BJP had allowed their paranoia to get ahead of them. After Rudy finished his diatribe, I laughingly said that the NSG was meeting in Vienna and not Delhi, where it would be 7:30 p.m., according to summer time—'Not a very unearthly hour, ol' chap.' When the anchor tried to go back to Rudy, he had disconnected. A clever spokesperson must know when to cut and run.

Again, on 19 September, at about 6:30 p.m. (that would be rather early in Washington DC), *Times Now* called saying they were breaking a big story that top US officials had just told the Senate Foreign Relations Committee that the nuclear fuel supply agreements to New Delhi were only 'a political commitment and the government cannot legally compel US firms to sell a given product to India.'[22] They wanted a phono and Arnab Goswami, then editor-in-chief, was anchoring.

As I was connected to the studio, Arnab said that the US had pulled a fast one on us and that the fuel supply commitments were not worth the paper they were written on. I replied, 'Mr Goswami, before you jump to these extreme positions, please refer to the text of the 123 Agreement dated 3 August 2007, and the IAEA and the NSG process.' When an agreement is negotiated between two countries, both are bound by the terms of the obligations they undertake. This is much like saying that India cannot 'compel its nuclear establishment to segregate their civil and military programme that is the essence of the deal.'

The UPA government faced stiff headwinds of such magnitude that initially it felt impelled to notify their counterparts in Washington that domestic difficulties were preventing a smooth go-ahead.[23] But that was not to be.

On 10 October 2008, Condoleezza Rice, the US secretary of state,

---

[22]Ibid.

[23]Sharad Joshi, 'A Pause in the Indo–US Nuclear Agreement', *Nuclear Threat Initiative*, 2 May 2008, https://www.nti.org/analysis/articles/pause-indo-us-nuclear-agreement/. Accessed on 15 March 2021.

and Pranab Mukherjee, India's then-external affairs minister, signed the agreement.[24] India became the only country in the world that was not part of the NPT, and continues to maintain a disinterest in signing it in the future too, to receive privileges of trade in nuclear material. By virtue of the deal signed with the US, India is free to buy nuclear material from other countries, including the US. It is, however, bound to accept regular monitoring checks on its nuclear reactors by the IAEA, except ones that it considers 'strategic'.

Subsequent NPT conferences have urged all non-nuclear weapon states to accept safeguards for all their nuclear material in a bid to prevent development of nuclear weapons. India is a non-signatory to the NPT and does not accept these safeguards but has been increasing its nuclear cooperation with other countries. It has become a de facto nuclear weapons state. The deal has allowed India not only to freely harness nuclear energy, but also get rid of its exclusion from the nuclear club. It has certainly bolstered its military strength and international standing. Prior to the sanctions, India could not import nuclear material from 45 countries across the world for over three decades, and its nuclear scientists could not travel to many countries in Europe. The agreement has allowed India to establish nuclear cooperation after a long period of alienation and assiduous attempts over the decades to establish its benign credentials. As non-threatening as it can possibly be when one is talking about technology that has the potential to devastate planet Earth as we know it.

DEMOLISHING THE ARCHITECTURE OF NUCLEAR APARTHEID

Why did the Indo–US bilateral relationship suddenly focus on India's nuclear dilemma? In part, it could be that Dr Manmohan Singh, during his illustrious career, served both as member (finance) in the

---

[24]Paul K. Kerr, 'U.S. Nuclear Cooperation with India: Issues for Congress', *Congressional Research Service*, 26 June 2012, https://fas.org/sgp/crs/nuke/RL33016.pdf. Accessed on 15 March 2021.

AEC and the Space Commission, respectively, while being secretary in the Department of Economic Affairs in the Ministry of Finance from 1976–80. This position would have provided him a unique perspective about the challenges that India's atomic establishment faced due to sanctions and other restrictions since 1974. The fact that it became the overriding public policy priority of his first term as prime minister, even though it put the future of his government at stake, very clearly demonstrates that breaking India's nuclear apartheid was an article of credo for him.

Many analysts, both within and outside India, had raised doubts over who would really benefit from the deal, and whether it would compromise India's strategic autonomy. Subsequent events have demonstrated that those fears were largely unfounded.

While India's foreign policy has not displayed any overt expression of antagonism towards China, the relations have remained largely adversarial due to unresolved issues, primarily the border question. Would India not assent, if the US were to engage more constructively in South Asia (as it does in North and East Asia), thereby balancing China's burgeoning power and influence in the larger Asian region? Under this overarching rubric, nuclear cooperation with the US was but the natural trajectory to evolve a closer relationship that would be a counterweight to rising Chinese belligerence that finally reached a zenith a decade later in April 2020 with the intrusions across the LAC with India.

However, post the US's ignominious exit in Afghanistan and their facilitation of the return of the Taliban in Afghanistan, the implications of the US's role or engagement and its attendant implications need to be seriously examined. The debris the US exit leaves in its wake and the centrifugal tendencies it unleashes need to be earnestly appraised.

The Indo–US nuclear deal did not compromise India's strategic autonomy because eight of its 22 reactors are not subject to safeguards and monitoring by the IAEA.[25] It therefore preserves

---

[25]P. Hosur, 'The Indo–US Civilian Nuclear Agreement: What's the Big Deal?' *International Journal*, 65 (2): 435-448, 2010.

India's autonomy to develop weapons. India has also maintained that it seeks minimum credible deterrence and does not wish to be involved in any kind of nuclear arms race. Its intensified production of nuclear fissile material, after the nuclear tests, was only aimed at developing credible deterrence before any international pressure could have prevented India from reaching that 'minimum threshold' it deems vital. Although the agreement does not prevent the US administration from cutting off supplies if India were to conduct nuclear tests again, it also does not explicitly delineate a specific US response if India did in fact conduct further tests.[26] Such events and actions therefore have been left ambiguous and dependent upon the bilateral relations of the two countries at that time and the wisdom of their respective governments.

The deal has been beneficial to India because its own nuclear material would be insufficient to develop nuclear energy, and at some point, it would need uranium imports. The deal allowed that to happen as many countries are now involved in nuclear cooperation with India: France, Canada, Russia and Australia. A few of these key supplier countries are strong US allies, and have recalibrated their approach to India's nuclear program only after the 2008 deal with the US.

The US and India have also agreed to maintain a minimum amount of nuclear fuel reserve to keep the energy production going even in the face of deficient supplies.

The Indo–US deal has allowed India to improve its foreign relations with certain key suppliers of nuclear fuel and sign nuclear cooperation agreements. India and France signed a nuclear cooperation agreement in September 2008 which included provisions for nuclear reactors and nuclear fuel. Later in December, a French company, AREVA, signed an agreement with India's DAE to supply Nuclear Power Corporation of India Ltd (NPCIL) with

---

[26]Paul K. Kerr, 'U.S. Nuclear Cooperation with India: Issues for Congress', *Congressional Research Service*, 26 June 2012, https://fas.org/sgp/crs/nuke/RL33016.pdf. Accessed on 15 March 2021.

300 metric tons of uranium. Russia and India also signed a nuclear cooperation agreement in 2008. Russia's TVEL Corporation signed an agreement in February 2009 with the DAE for research and development in nuclear energy, construction of nuclear power plants and supply of nuclear fuel. India and Namibia signed a nuclear deal in August 2009 for peaceful harnessing of nuclear energy. In June 2010, India and Canada signed an agreement for peaceful utilization of nuclear energy covering areas, design and construction of nuclear reactors and supply of uranium.

India's nuclear ambitions have been compared to other regional players like Pakistan. At one point, it was widely believed that India's fetish for nuclear technology will kick-start a nuclear arms race in Asia and impel countries like Iran and others to develop their own nuclear arsenals. However, such sensationalism was never backed by either reason or a keen appreciation of India's unique security situation. It is perverse to compare India with Iran, Pakistan or North Korea to flag concerns of nuclear proliferation. India has had an excellent record of non-proliferation as opposed to Pakistan, where the notorious A.Q. Khan opened his own private nuclear trading platform. The nature of the regime both in North Korea and Iran respectively has ensured that the world remains on tenterhooks insofar as their dalliance with nuclear armaments is concerned.

India is a functioning democracy, a trait not shared by any of these countries in question. The nuclear deal made it clear that the global community finds India's nuclear status more reassuring than that of others in the region. Ironically, it is the NPT signatories that have a murky record. Iran is a member of the treaty but is perpetually suspected of developing nuclear weapons. This has led to a major roadblock in the US-Iran relationship. Iran has been under heavy American sanctions for a long time. North Korea was also a member of the treaty but left it to develop nuclear weapons. It was allegedly assisted by Pakistan and supported by China. This indicates that India's record of non-proliferation carries more weight to qualify for nuclear cooperation than simply being an NPT signatory. India has signed biological and chemical weapons agreements reflecting its intent towards and support for mitigating and eventually rolling back WMD. Its nuclear program, however, constitutes a core defence capability that simply cannot be relinquished unless there is comprehensive, globally universal and verifiable disarmament.

Pakistan-sponsored terrorism is a constant irritant between the two countries, going back to the late '70s. Tensions between India and Pakistan are because of legacy issues and not their respective nuclear programs. While Pakistan's development of nuclear weapons can clearly be linked to its dismemberment in 1971, there is no empirical evidence to suggest that Pakistan would not have done so even if East Pakistan would have continued to exist as it did prior to 1971. A nuclear Pakistan therefore, with the prospect of being a serial proliferator, will always be a challenge, and would require international cooperation to keep it under check and subject its military nuclear programme and establishment to a far more robust internationally mandated and monitored safeguards regime. It is, however, assessed that due to its preoccupation with internal problems, Pakistan will not engage in a debilitating and long-drawn-out arms race with India as that would drain both its financial resources and erode whatever little credibility it has left after the A.Q. Khan saga.

In short, with the Indo–US Civil Nuclear Deal, India demolished the architecture of nuclear apartheid carefully constructed by the international community after India's first PNE on 18 May 1974. The PNE had led to the creation of the London Club, the precursor to the NSG, and other similar structures over the decades to cap and roll back India's nuclear capacity, albeit unsuccessfully.

NUCLEAR ENERGY: (NOT) SO RESOURCEFUL

While the self-defence aspect of India's nuclear program has so far been successful, its energy augmenting ability does not have a golden story yet. Nuclear energy has become increasingly ostracized around the world due to the risk associated with reactors. Unfortunate accidents like the Three Mile Island, Chernobyl and Fukushima have added to the unease of constructing nuclear power facilities. Even the US did not issue licences for nuclear reactors between 1975 and 2012. The country has over 100,000 MWe capacities for nuclear energy, but over the years, 34 nuclear reactors have been shut down. America's Westinghouse, which has been awarded the contract to help build six nuclear reactors for India in Andhra Pradesh, has emerged from a Chapter 11 bankruptcy settlement with regard to the building of similar reactors in Georgia and South Carolina in the US.

India's 22 nuclear reactors produce energy sufficient to meet less than 3 per cent of the country's energy needs. Considering the capital invested in the nuclear program to harness energy over decades, the return has been surprisingly low. Even in 2018, the total nuclear energy capacity amounted to 7,000 MWe, even though India had planned a target of 10,000 MWe by 2000.[27] India's performance in the renewable energy sector has been far better, but has not received the kind of attention and capital as the nuclear program.

The massive investments in nuclear energy appear to be delivering unsatisfactory results. According to Bhabha's plan to use India's large reserves of thorium to develop nuclear energy, it had to adopt a three-stage process. The first stage involved installing multiple 'pressurized heavy water reactors' which would be used to produce plutonium from the limited uranium resources. The second stage involved the installation of 'fast breeder reactors' that could produce large amounts of plutonium over a few decades to be used in the third stage. The third stage would involve special reactors where thorium could be converted to uranium-233, by using the uranium-233 from the previous stage. India has been stuck at the first stage. Its prototype fast breeder reactor has never seen the light of day and has been under construction since 2004.

---

[27]Manoj Joshi, 'India Is Waking Up from Nuclear Energy Dream', *FirstPost*, 29 March 2019, https://www.firstpost.com/india/india-is-waking-up-from-nuclear-energy-dream-6350851.html. Accessed on 15 March 2021.

The Civil Liability for Nuclear Damage Act of 2010 that places high degree of liability on foreign suppliers or plant contractors has prevented foreign interest in the sector. The commercial viability of nuclear power for electricity generation has also been moot. Reportedly, the cost of setting up new plants is in the range of about ₹15–20 crore per MW, and the electricity generated would be as high as ₹7 per unit.[28] It is simply too expensive given the current state of play in the Indian energy markets.

Certain core reasons behind the mismatch between target of nuclear energy and delivery allegedly includes technologically unsound plans of the DAE and local opposition to nuclear power plants.[29] The Kudankulam Plant in Tamil Nadu had taken about 30 years to start producing electricity and reactors would frequently shut down. The estimated cost of Unit 1 and 2 of the Kudankulam project was ₹13,171 crore, but increased to as much as ₹22,462 crore by 2014. The large gaps in estimated and realized costs reflect bad financial planning and it also impacts regular flow of funds. Strong local opposition to nuclear projects has often marred the progress in energy production. Large capacity plants at Kudankulam in Tamil Nadu and Jaitapur in Maharashtra have been the centre of sustained local protests. Proposed plants for Kovvada in Andhra Pradesh, Gorakhpur in Haryana, Chutka in Madhya Pradesh and Mithivirdi in Gujarat, have all met with local opposition. The core concerns include loss of land and livelihood, insufficient compensation, alleged fabrication of environment assessment reports and lack of transparency and accountability in India's nuclear establishment.

These concerns are not completely misplaced given India's poor track record of dealing with the Bhopal gas tragedy, an incident deep-rooted in the mind of the common Indian. Moreover, public

---

[28]M. Ramesh, 'Why Nuclear When India Has an "Ocean" of Energy', *The Hindu*, 30 June 2019, https://www.thehindu.com/business/Industry/why-nuclear-when-india-has-an-ocean-of-energy/article28230036.ece. Accessed on 15 March 2021.
[29]A. Khan, 'India Needs to Wake Up from Its Nuclear Fantasy', *Economic and Political Weekly*, 54 (41), 2019.

engagement about all things nuclear is almost non-existent. It is naive on the part of the Government of India to imagine that people would accept nuclear plants without having been taken into confidence or informed about the risks. Community participation is vital in such cases but government efforts have been totally unsatisfactory.

Instead, the government has strong-armed the protesting public, imposing sedition charges or accusations of waging war against the state on protestors. The police have been used to unjustly crackdown on protestors. Several protestors have died in the process and certain women demonstrators have spent months in jail. India's plans to proceed with nuclear energy and power plant development, without the approval of its communities and ground-level stakeholders, seems illogical and, therefore, bound to be counterproductive. A large amount of political will must be generated to effectively make nuclear energy a public issue and streamline processes of energy production. All in all, the energy aspect of the Indo–US nuclear deal has been a non-starter.

STRATEGIC ALIGNMENT OF INDIA AND THE US

Experts and South Asia watchers believe that the strategic alignment between India and the US are dependent on a couple of basic tenets. These include instability and terrorism under a nuclear shield mainly emanating from Pakistan, India's Iran policy, enhanced defence procurement and a stout ballast qua China.[30] India has been more than willing to show its commitment to these tenets except a hesitant approach to Iran. Even though India has reduced its oil imports from Iran over the years in a bid to show solidarity with the US, its own strategic interest lies in maintaining economic and diplomatic ties with Iran and balancing both relationships.

---

[30]Sameer Lalwani and Heather Byrne, 'Great Expectations: Asking Too Much of the US-India Strategic Partnership', *Stimson Center*, 21 October 2019, https://www.stimson.org/2019/great-expectations-asking-too-much-us-india-strategic-partnership/. Accessed on 15 March 2021.

India's Iran policy includes the balancing of Pakistan and access to Afghanistan through Chabahar Port.

Post the expansive 25-year China–Iran strategic cooperation agreement signed on 27 March 2021 and India being dropped from the Chabahar-Zahedan Railway project, how much access to Afghanistan would India really get? India has invested economic and human capital in Afghanistan, and given its animosity with Pakistan, Iran could have been a viable link to maintain perennial access to Afghanistan. However, post the Iran–China deal and the Taliban takeover, how much this hypothesis remains relevant any longer would have to be comprehended in the fullness of time.

The US administration has rather high expectations from India in the defence arena. For instance, India's participation in military exercises is still limited. The US has much deeper defence engagements in Asia all the way from Japan in the north to Australia in the Southern Ocean. These can in fact be successfully leveraged to counter Chinese influence in South Asia and the Indo-Pacific. Greater engagement without being either labelled as an ally or a client state is a fine-line that India needs to skilfully tread.

There is also exasperation in Washington over India's slow procurement of defence items, or to put it another way, its disinclination to put all its eggs in the US basket. Losing out to France's Dassault Aviation for Rafale jets and India's frequent purchase of arms including the S-400s from Russia, have been irritants for successive American administrations. However, India's appreciation of its own national interests naturally influences its defence purchases. New Delhi has not been too pleased with Washington's strategic relationship with Islamabad or its hesitation in transfer of technology to India, notwithstanding the fact that Pakistan has run circles around the US during the war on terror and now again recently in Afghanistan.

India has also been criticized both by the hawks in India and the South Asian strategic community in the US for not doing enough to project power beyond its borders, as is expected of a net security provider. There may be pressure in the future to fill the security void in Afghanistan that has manifested itself post the withdrawal of American troops and the takeover of Afghanistan by the Taliban. India would do well to weigh its options carefully and perhaps demur on the side of discretion.

INDIA'S HEDGING IN THE NEW WORLD

The Indo–US relationship remains a strategic planner's best bet to counter China's increasing influence in the Indo-Pacific. The foundational agreements that had been in the pipeline for about a decade and a half have finally been clinched.

The first Logistics Exchange Memorandum of Agreement (LEMOA), was signed in 2016. It allows both countries to replenish from each other's military facilities, including items such as food, water, transportation, oil, medical services, maintenance services, etc. The second agreement, Communications Compatibility and Security Agreement (COMCASA), was signed in 2018. It deals with secure military communication. In 2002, India had signed the lesser version of this pact called the General Security of Military Information Agreement (GSOMIA) that covered a lesser number of items. The COMCASA is more advanced and allows secure exchange of information between the militaries of two countries during joint exercises, therefore adding to interoperability. It also enables India to easily and safely communicate with US-made equipment used by foreign militaries such as Japan and Australia. The last of the three pacts, BECA, relates to sharing of all kinds of information useful to militaries like geomagnetic and gravity data, maps and aeronautical charts. Classified data like sensitive satellite information will also be shared between the forces by virtue of this agreement. The three agreements bring together Indian and American militaries in their operations.[31] However, the recent strategic alliance between

---

[31]Snehesh Alex Philip, 'The 3 foundational agreements with US and what they mean for India's military growth', *The Print*, 27 October 2020, https://theprint.in/defence/

Australia, the UK and the US (AUKUS) will not be limited to providing nuclear technology to Australia. It will have implications on the Quad between the US, Japan, India and Australia that in turn would impact the US–India dynamic also. India needs to tread with caution by not putting all its eggs in one basket, for others are hedging their bets.

India's development of nuclear weapons has been a strong determinant of its national security. With a nuclear-armed China as its neighbour, the nuclear option for India was more about when India was going to do it rather than whether it was going to do it at all. Although the development of nuclear weapons attracted strong censure from many western countries, including the nuclear powers, over the years, India has been accepted as a responsible nuclear-armed state. The role of the US has been substantial in this gradual change of attitude towards a nuclear India and should be acknowledged unequivocally. From being a nuclear outlier in the 1990s and early 2000s, India today is more or less integrated into the global nuclear order, able to engage in nuclear commerce and not be pushed around to give up its nuclear weapons. India has, however, not been able to invest in the production of massive amounts of nuclear energy despite the best efforts of Dr Singh's government.

Has the overt nuclearization of South Asia made it any safer? The answer as elucidated in Chapter 1 is a 'no'. As second age nuclear powers, both India and Pakistan, as well as other second age nuclear powers acknowledged or otherwise, must sit down with the first age nuclear powers to move the theological needle beyond the doctrine of MAD. The deteriorating security situation in South Asia makes it all the more imperative.

the-3-foundational-agreements-with-us-and-what-they-mean-for-indias-military-growth/531795/. Accessed on 15 March 2021.

FIVE

26/11 AND THE LACK OF OVERT MILITARY ACTION

26 November 2008. India's financial capital, Mumbai, was attacked by 10 Kalashnikov-wielding terrorists who had come ashore at Colaba, on the southern tip of the Mumbai peninsula. They had embarked from the port city of Karachi on a merchant ship and had subsequently hijacked an Indian fishing vessel to avoid detection by the Indian Coast Guard.

The terrorists struck a number of key locations including the iconic Taj Mahal Hotel near the Gateway of India, the Oberoi Hotel, the Leopold Cafe (a popular tourist watering hole), the sprawling Chhatrapati Shivaji Railway Terminus, Chabad House (a Jewish cultural centre) and even the Cama and Albless Hospital. The terrorists seemed at war not just with India, but with the whole world itself. The toll would finally include 26 foreigners—Americans, Britons, Australians, Singaporeans and Israelis.[1] More than 166 people were mercilessly butchered and over 300 wounded. Meticulously planned and ruthlessly executed, it evidenced that the terrorists were both physically optimized and mentally indoctrinated to perpetrate this macabre orgy of violence. The element of surprise that created confusion thereby paralysing the initial response was the sine qua non of this operation.

---

[1]Shivshankar Menon, *Choices: Inside the Making of Indian Foreign Policy*. Penguin Random House, 2016.

One of the deadliest attacks that came to be known as India's 9/11 had some nasty surprises for me too. On that fateful evening, I had a drink with Ambassador K.C. Singh, India's former ambassador to Iran, then recently retired as secretary in the MEA after several decades of distinguished service. He is now a prominent columnist and commentator on international affairs.

I returned home at about 9:30 p.m., put my phone on silent as I had to rise by 5 a.m. to catch the morning train to Ludhiana, where I had to meet with the Radha Soami—an influential spiritual movement with its headquarters at Beas in Punjab.

When I woke up the next morning, on 27 November, there were over a hundred missed calls from one number. The number belonged to Tom Vadakkan, then media secretary of the INC. Tom is now with the BJP. With trepidation, I called him back. He picked up on the third ring.

'What's wrong?' I asked him.

'Where have you been?' came his reply.

'Sleeping at home in my bed alone; isn't that what you are supposed to be doing at night,' I replied rather jocularly.

He did not find the riposte amusing at all. 'Mumbai has been taken over by an army of terrorists,' he shrieked.

'Hope you haven't been drinking the whole night?' I asked him.

Bemused, he told me, 'For God's sake, turn on the TV'.

I tiptoed into the living room, switched on the television and there it was, the carnage in Mumbai playing out live. I asked Tom why he had not called my residence if I wasn't answering my phone.

He mumbled something to the effect: 'It slipped my mind'.

I asked him if there were any instructions, and he said, 'None at all'.

RECOUNTING THE HORROR

The reason I have narrated this conversation in detail is because at that point in time, I was the national spokesperson of the Congress.

For all intents and purposes, party spokespersons were de facto government spokespersons because the government (UPA-I) would rarely speak on political issues. Over time, even governance matters fell to our remit to articulate and defend the decisions taken by the government. Despite having extremely articulate ministers in government, there was a strange reluctance to communicate even in UPA-I. It only got further compounded in UPA-II.

As there was nothing to be done, I got dressed and boarded the morning Shatabdi Express to Ludhiana that departed at its scheduled time, 7:20 a.m. Surprisingly, there was hardly any conversation about the continuing Mumbai massacre in the train. Possibly because Punjab had seen so much of innocent blood spilled at the hands of terrorists between 1980 and 1995, that maybe as a people we had become inured, if not numb, to the vicissitudes of wanton violence.

The journey from Delhi to Ludhiana takes exactly four hours. For me, it was a journey back in time to a fateful day twenty-four years earlier—3 April 1984—when three men masquerading as students had barged into our Sector 24 residence early in the morning and assassinated my father Dr V.N. Tewari. An academic by profession, he was a professor of Comparative Modern Indian Literature at the Panjab University, Chandigarh. He was also a nominated member of the Rajya Sabha. They even took a shot at my mother, also a medical professor at the PGI Chandigarh when she rushed to shield her husband. Luckily for her, the pistol was out of bullets. They had already emptied the magazine into my dad.

The events of that morning and the succeeding days played out, frame by frame, in my mind, alternating with prayers for those who were at the receiving end of the terrorists in Mumbai.

The train reached Ludhiana. I was received by my friend and trusted colleague, the redoubtable Pawan Dewan. Again, neither he nor anyone else raised the Mumbai incident that was continuing to unfold, perhaps out of sensitivity to my personal brush with terror.

We went to the meeting with the Radha Soamis. It was held in one of their prayer halls. Again, throughout the four hours that I spent with them from 12 noon to 3 p.m., nobody even mentioned the unfolding events in Mumbai.

I met some other political colleagues and reached the railway station at about 6:45 p.m. to catch the evening Shatabdi Express back to Delhi that departs at 7:02 p.m. It was here that some elderly people came up to me and said, 'Son, you have a voice in Delhi, please ensure that this does not escalate into a war with Pakistan.' Given that Punjab contributes substantially in terms of human material to the armed forces and shares a fairly long border with Pakistan that saw activity in 1965 and again in '71, war for people of this region is not an esoteric concept. It is a hard reality where your loved ones are in the firing line responding to the call of duty that often ends up in them coming home in caskets.

As I settled back into the Shatabdi Express, I was struck by the fact that there had been no communication of any sort from Delhi about the events in Mumbai. It seemed as if Mumbai could well be on another planet. As if on cue, my cell phone rang. It was Ambassador Singh. He informed me that a childhood friend, Deepak Bagla, who was the country head of a London-based private equity firm, 3i, was stuck in the Trident Hotel in Mumbai where the terrorists had laid siege and mowed down many innocent people. Ambassador Singh told me that he had spoken to Deepak a couple of times to keep his spirits up and keep him updated with what was going on outside.

Not again, I thought to myself as my trembling fingers dialled Deepak's mobile number. It rang and no one answered. I prayed and dialled again and again it went unanswered. Suddenly, I realized that since my number flashes as private or unknown he would not know who is calling. I texted him and called again. A small voice answered.

'Are you all right?' I asked Deepak.

He whispered yes. Fearing that his battery may run out, I told him that I would keep in touch via SMS and told him not to worry, that everything would be okay. He had an English colleague who was holed up with him in the same room.

The next four hours passed in a blur, praying for and texting Deepak a few times. The train rolled into New Delhi Railway station at 11:00 p.m. My driver whisked me home. Everybody was asleep. My wife was on an overseas flight.

I enquired about our daughter, Ineka, from her governess Leela ji, a wonderful lady who has now been with us for 24 years, from the time our daughter was born. Leela ji is the anchor of our home. She said Ineka was fine. I remembered how traumatized she had been when barely four years and four months old, she had seen on TV hijacked airplanes crashing into the World Trade Centre in New York on 11 September 2001. Her little mind had perhaps made a connection between the planes and her mother's profession as airline crew.

Reassured, I settled down with a stiff drink. It was 11:30 p.m. on 27 November. I switched on the television. One channel, perhaps Doordarshan, was replaying the Prime Minister's address to the nation from earlier in the day. His face was ashen, voice stilted as he sought to reassure the nation that the continuing assault on Mumbai would be dealt with resolutely.

As the Prime Minister faded from the screen, I flipped the channels to catch what others were reporting. The siege was continuing, with live television reportage giving a blow-by-blow account. India's great tragedy was being mercilessly milked for Television Rating Points (TRPs), replete with blazing by-lines—first on so and so channel. As I continued flipping channels, I suddenly stopped at India-TV[2] that was beaming a conversation with one of the terrorists, maybe taped earlier in the day.

The terrorist was explaining the rationale of the attack, and if I recall correctly after so many years as I write purely from memory, muttering something about being from the 'Deccan Mujahedeen'. I was quite struck by the fact that why would the terrorists pick India

---

[2]Randeep Ramesh, 'Indian TV agrees Code on Covering Terrorism after Mumbai Attacks', *The Guardian*, 18 December 2008, https://www.theguardian.com/world/2008/dec/18/mumbai-terror-attacks-india. Accessed on 15 March 2021.

TV of all the channels to give a phono. Not that India TV was not a popular Hindi TV channel, but it was known more for its religio-epigraphy at that time rather than hard news. It is another matter that its content put it in the top league as far as TRPs were concerned.

I thought either India TV had a tie-up with some Pakistani or Arabic channel, or the terrorists had picked out the name of India TV from the website of some TV channel in Pakistan or their host country. By then, it had become evident that operatives of LeT were carrying out the attack. If the Pakistani planners had indeed mapped out the TRPs of Indian television channels to get the widest possible coverage for their operations, it only convinced me of the operation's meticulous planning.

As channel surfing continued well into the night, other television anchors were screaming 'no politicians'. It seems that the late Gopinath Munde, a senior leader of the BJP from Maharashtra, had attempted to go near one of the sites under attack and the people, thanks to television-orchestrated hysteria, had booed him. It was made to appear as if politicians, and not terrorists, had attacked Mumbai. I tried calling Deepak. It was about 2 a.m. The phone was switched off. Maybe the battery had run out. I prayed for him and surrendered to fatigue. Sleep eluded me.

The next morning, 28 November, the attack had been on for 36 hours. I woke up to the visuals of NSG personnel trying to helicopter rappel down to the roof of Chabad House. The visuals were accompanied by a running commentary on exactly what the next steps would be. If the handlers of the terrorists were indeed in touch with them—as it became apparent later or maybe that morning itself, some newspaper was carrying transcripts of the conversation—there could not have been better intelligence inputs about the security forces' strategy than what even 10 precision positioned spotters could have provided. Here were 400-odd television channels swarming all over the place in a bid to outdo each other, if not directing then at least forecasting the next steps in the operation. They were ably assisted by packs of retired security personnel doubling up as experts, unconcerned about the implications of their mercenaryism on their colleagues who were waging a relentless struggle against the fedayeen.

This was the first full TV experience I had since the assault had commenced on the evening of 26 November. I wondered why the government was not trying to impose some order on the coverage, including, and not limited to, a delayed broadcast by at least one hour. I wondered whether there was no standard operating procedure (SoP), which was laid down to deal with such situations. I pondered why the government and, specifically, the Ministry of Information and Broadcasting, was not reading out the Riot Act to the media.

As I stepped into the park for my morning run, I was struck by the level of detachment of the people. Nobody came up to ask me why it was taking so long to bring the situation under control. What was the government doing? After all, Delhi was to vote in the Vidhan Sabha elections in a day's time on 29 November.

I recalled the same nonchalance when the bomb blasts in Sarojini Nagar market—in the heart of South Delhi—had killed and maimed a number of people on the eve of Diwali in 2005. A few days later, people were celebrating Diwali as if there was no tomorrow. Standing on the balcony of my modest apartment and seeing the fireworks pierce the sky, I was appalled at the sheer insensitivity of the people of Delhi. In some other country, Diwali would have not been celebrated or at worst it would have been muted.

Finally, as I was catching my breath after my run, a retired general, who is also a regular, came up to me. 'The government should launch a missile strike on the General Headquarters (GHQ) in Rawalpindi,' he said, with tears in his eyes. 'That is where the real rascals are.' The redness of his eyes showed that he had not slept much in the past few days.

I got dressed and left to attend a conference on the environment at the India Habitat Centre hosted by a dear friend Ligia Norona, who worked with The Energy and Resources Institute (TERI). She was quite surprised to see me, expecting me to be too preoccupied to find the time.

My phone vibrated while I was at that roundtable conference. There was a call from the late Ahmed Patel's residence. I stepped out and took the call. His office said that he wanted to speak to me. After an interminable round of music, he came on the line. He said, 'Manish, brief the media in the evening.'

I asked, 'Sir, about what?'

With an edge in his voice, he replied, 'About what is going on in Bombay.'

I said, 'Sir, it is Shakeel Ahmad's briefing today; he is the Minister of State for Home. He may be able to give more inputs and a perspective on the situation.'

He explained, 'That is why we do not want him to brief because in an evolving situation, we do not think it is appropriate for a government functionary to say anything that could be taken out of context.'

'What do you want me to say?'

'You know what to say. Nobody understands these issues better than you,' and with that he hung up.

Later, I was given to understand that Shakeel Ahmad took my replacing him as the spokesperson that fateful Friday rather amiss. It was conveyed to me that he had been possibly 'briefed' by some dodgy AICC beat reporters that I had snatched away his briefing by telling the 'powers that be' that it would be inappropriate for a Muslim to brief the media. This is totally untrue. I had been asked to brief for all the right reasons that day and had never requested for it. Such retrogressive and warped thinking is simply alien to my mental make-up.

In fact, when I think about it in retrospect, I was of the view that it would have been in national interest if a 'Muslim' had indeed briefed the media that day from the AICC podium. It would have reinforced the message that, cutting across caste, class and community, India stands as one when its national security is imperiled.

Be that as it may, at 4:15 p.m., as it was on every Monday, Wednesday and Friday, with only my discretion as the better part of valour to guide me, I mounted the podium and faced a larger-than-usual swarm of media persons. By my side, was the stoic Tom Vadakkan.

Anyway, after a matter-of-fact suo motu statement condemning the attack, the questions came in clusters—thick, fast and furious. Most of them, I was able to answer, deflect, sidestep and even evade till one asked by D.K. Singh of *The Indian Express* stumped me. 'Why has the Crisis Management Group not been convened?' he asked.

I replied, 'I will check and let you know,' as I did not want to falter on a factual query. The briefing ended and the debriefing began. The journalists were feisty and I was combative. I told them their actions were corrosive to national security, especially the TV coverage. Suddenly, there was a hush and then a senior gentleman from the Press Trust of India (PTI), Sunil Gatade agreed.

Even the TV journos gave a resigned sigh and confessed, 'What do we do? Otherwise, we would lose our jobs'.

After the ordeal, I sat in my car. The mobile phone buzzed; it was Ahmed Patel again wanting to know how it went. I replied that I made it out unscathed.

That same evening, I got conned into my first television appearance on the Mumbai tragedy on the CNN-IBN TV-18 network on Rajdeep Sardesai's show. He, along with others of his tribe, had camped outside the hotels where the terrorists were holed. Much against my better sense that a TV program at this juncture would be a blood fest, I took Rajdeep on face value that it would be a serious discussion devoid of histrionics.

What I got instead was a bunch of screeching Mumbai socialites and an 'ad Guru railing against the government.' One of them kept screaming why a 'nobody like me' was representing the government and why no minister was on the show. She was right; this was the time when people wanted to hear from the political executive directly.

I reminded her that while she had been living it up in Bombay in the '80s and '90s, it is people like me who had cut our teeth in the trench lines of the political struggle against terrorism in Punjab. That fortunately shut her up. Having done a lot of discussions on terrorist attacks and outrages over the years, what had always struck me was the absence of even manufactured anger among India's chattering classes if bombs went off on trains as they had done in Mumbai in 2006, or for that matter in areas that were peopled by the poor or the lower middle class. I had seen the terror incidents in Punjab, Kashmir or even the Northeast being reduced to a mere statistic in the minds of the Indian elite.

This time terror had invaded their living spaces, their watering holes, their haunts. The Pakistanis knew where to hit India in order to make the most noise. After being used as a punching bag from 9 to 10 p.m., and cursing Rajdeep a million times, I managed to keep a straight face, and the show ended.

Sick in my heart, I once again tried Deepak's number. It was still switched off. He had been in that hellhole for over 48 hours now. My text messages had also not elicited a response. I poured myself a stiff one and settled in front of the TV.

The next morning, 29 November, I woke up to the visuals of the penultimate terrorist crashing out of a hotel window apparently hit by a rocket-propelled grenade or something as lethal as that. Then, after a while, someone announced that all the terrorists had been neutralized and the security personal were in the process of making the final sweep.

Deepak and his colleague were among the last people to be escorted out of the hotel. When I got the news I called him, he seemed collected. The nightmares, I guess, came later, though he never once displayed any signs of the trauma.

Hundreds had died ruthlessly, wantonly slaughtered for no rhyme or reason but for being in the wrong place at the wrong time. A handful of terrorists had held India to ransom for close to 60 hours. It had taken the might of the Indian state that long to deal with them.

By then, the media was baying for blood. They wanted responsibility to be fixed for this negligence. The government was being roundly abused. The security forces were feted as heroes and rightly so. Many had died in reclaiming India's sovereignty.

On the evening of the 29th, at about 8 p.m., we were informed that Home Minister Shivraj Patil would brief us at his residence the next morning at 9. I reached there and was soon joined by my colleague spokesperson. Soft classical music was playing as Patil appeared and led us to the breakfast table. He looked flustered though outwardly he tried to radiate an air of serenity. He briefed us in detail about the attack as we listened patiently. My colleague was more direct than me. He asked a few pointed questions, each of which yielded a detailed response from the Home Minister. Finally, before leaving, I popped the question: Why had the Crisis Management Group not been convened? The Home Minister again provided a detailed timeline going back to when they got the first information about the attack. He further clarified, if I recall correctly, that given the sheer scale of the assault, the response was naturally being handled at the highest levels of government and that, effectively, was the Crisis Management Group insofar as 26/11 was concerned.

Among all this, even as the clear-up operations were in progress, on 30 November, the then CM of Maharashtra, Vilasrao Deshmukh, decided to take film director Ram Gopal Varma along to assess the damage. Maybe Deshmukh's intention was innocuous but coming as it did in that charged atmosphere, it lit a fuse. It was widely seen as an act of insensitivity. Varma is known for making action movies with plots revolving around terror situations. Since Deshmukh's son was a budding film star then, the media perceived the action through that lens.

I remember being on a live show with Barkha Dutt of NDTV. The moment she bounced it on me, I knew Deshmukh had made a cardinal error of judgement. I spontaneously condemned the action because I instinctively felt that the CM had stepped way over the line. Both he and his deputy were forced to resign subsequently.

However, the media was far from satisfied. They wanted the Home Minister's scalp. I recall the same afternoon I was sitting with Ahmed Patel at his Delhi residence, nervously trying to predict the outcome of the Assembly polls in New Delhi that was voting on 29 November.

He was simultaneously talking to P. Chidambaram, urging him to return to Delhi that very evening for an important meeting of the CWC. Chidambaram had gone to his constituency, Sivaganga, on a prescheduled visit. It was at the CWC meeting in the dying days of November 2008, that Shivraj Patil voluntarily offered to step down, and Chidambaram took over as the home minister a day later.

Later, in the month of December, I travelled to Muscat for a South Asia Security Summit hosted annually by a think tank. M.J. Akbar and Manvendra Singh, MP and son of BJP leader Jaswant Singh, were among the other Indian participants. However, what was particularly galling was the comment made to me over dinner by one of the generals from Bangladesh. He said, 'We had heard so much about the great Indian security forces, but it took them three days to deal with a motley group of terrorists.' In our hour of despair, an important functionary of a nation that we had created was mocking us.

I turned around and snapped, 'General, if we would not have created Bangladesh and intervened when your people were being butchered, we would not have been in the situation that we find ourselves today.' After all, for the Pakistani military establishment, their quintessential deep state, it all goes back to 1971. The creation of Bangladesh and the consequent defeat is a humiliation etched deep into the collective psyche of the Pakistani defence forces.

BACKCHANNEL TALKS: FIRST RAYS OF A NEW SUNRISE

The period from April 2003 to November 2008 had been relatively quieter in the proxy war unleashed by Pakistan against India. Unfortunately, there were a number of bomb blasts in various cities of India that claimed innocent lives. Notwithstanding these continuing depredations, the then UPA government still made an attempt to explore a modus vivendi with Pakistan. But 26/11 was that last straw that broke the proverbial camel's back. After that, the Indo-Pak relationship never really got back on track.

The Mumbai terror attacks came nine years and nine months after a backchannel dialogue was initiated by Nawaz Sharif with his Indian counterpart, Atal Bihari Vajpayee, in February 1999. 'It was basically on Kashmir,' Sharif opined. 'In the early days, we were not really having any consensus on anything. But the mere fact that the backchannel was established was itself a major milestone. It was doing some serious work.'[3] Islamabad designated Anwar Zahid and later Niaz Naik, and New Delhi named R.K. Mishra, founder chairperson of the Observer Research Foundation (ORF), as their respective representatives for these talks. While the backchannel was making good progress, the confabulations were disrupted by the reckless Kargil incursion authorized by General Musharraf. A few months after the Kargil incursions, Sharif tried to fire the General; but Musharraf captured power and threw Sharif in jail in 1999. Sharif was later exiled to Saudi Arabia in December 2000 through the intervention of 'friendly powers'.

It was a given, therefore, that India's leaders initially mistrusted Musharraf, but gradually, as Lalit Mansingh, then India's ambassador to the US, stated, 'We realized he was a man we could speak to.'[4] Eventually, the non-success of Operation Parakram, the assassination of Abdul Ghani Lone and the post-2002 economic boom, convinced Vajpayee to make one more attempt to arrive at a modus vivendi with Pakistan. The killing of Lone had made it fairly evident to him that a concurrent process with Pakistan was a sine qua non for an effective outreach to the separatists led by the Hurriyat Conference. The Vajpayee government had earlier taken the unusual step of talking to terror groups based in the Valley, through a dialogue

---

[3]Steve Coll, 'The Back Channel', The New Yorker, 22 February 2009, https://www.newyorker.com/magazine/2009/03/02/the-backchannel. Accessed on 19 July 2021.
[4]Ibid.

between the then Union Home Secretary Kamal Pande and Hizbul Mujahideen commanders in August 2000.

Musharraf's thinking about India was changing too. This was partly fuelled by the twin attempts by JeM to assassinate him, and partly by the US's diplomatic manoeuvres during Operation Parakram that led him to give the assurance that he would not permit Pakistani soil to be used to support terrorism in any manner. The two leaders, Vajpayee and Musharraf, began the journey of formal negotiations, known as the Indo-Pak Composite Dialogue, in February 2004. They also privately restarted the Kashmir backchannel talks. Vajpayee's man for the job was his principal secretary, Brajesh Mishra, and Musharraf chose his trusted aide, college mate and former income tax officer, Tariq Aziz.

When the UPA came to power in 2004, PM Dr Manmohan Singh picked up this baton and turned it into one of his foreign policy priorities. The thaw in the air made the climate conducive to try and initiate a sustained dialogue to resolve the conflict between the two countries. Both the leaders at least appeared to be on the same page. 'That you are a Pakistani Sikh ruling India and I am an Indian Muslim ruling Pakistan. A duty is divinely enjoined on us to buy peace for the people in the subcontinent. Let us summon courage and rid Indians and Pakistanis of sentimentalism that is bordering on insanity,'[5] Musharraf had prophesized.

To that end, once again, Tariq Aziz, secretary of Pakistan's NSC, and Satinder Lambah, who would later go on to be convener of India's NSAB, commenced another backchannel, the first one having died in the smouldering embers of the Kargil conflict and the second one was overtaken by a change of government in India. Altogether, there were about two dozen of these backchannel sessions between 2004-7.[6] Since the objective was to explore an

---

[5]Nadir Ali, 'General Musharraf's Four-Point Formula Can Provide an Effective Roadmap in Kashmir', *Institute of Peace and Conflict Studies Special Report 99*, 2011.
[6]Steve Coll, 'The Back Channel', *The New Yorker*, 22 February 2009, https://www.newyorker.com/magazine/2009/03/02/the-backchannel. Accessed on 19 July 2021.

end to the protracted fight over Kashmir, the meetings were aimed at essentially developing a 'non-paper'[7] on Kashmir.

By 2007, the backchannel talks seemed close to pulling off a solution not only on paper, but also on ground. The rate of terror strikes dropped, terrorist infiltrations had gone down, 'Pakistani artillery units stopped their salvos'[8] on Indian posts, and the Srinagar-Muzaffarabad bus service was inaugurated in 2005. The first rays of a new sunrise were quite obviously visible.

There were separate discussions between both General Musharraf and Dr Singh with the Hurriyat. Dr Singh had a long two-and-a-half-hour session with the Hurriyat on 5 September 2005 at his 7 Race Course Road residence. Such was the optimism that PM Singh had remarked, 'I dream of a day, while retaining our respective national identities, one can have breakfast in Amritsar, lunch in Lahore and dinner in Kabul.'[9]

The by-product of these talks was the pragmatic settlement formula known as the four-point formula, whereby the Kashmir problem was to be settled without either country having to cede the territory under its occupation. The formula set out an incremental four-step process for Kashmir resolution. The steps were: identifying conflict zones, demilitarization, self-governance and a consultative mechanism between India and Pakistan for the state of J&K.[10]

This was a drastic climb down from Islamabad's traditional stand on J&K. The corps commanders who ran Pakistan seemed to trust Musharraf's instinct. They knew that a peace settlement might be able to produce economic benefits for Pakistan through free movement of goods and services—resulting in potential enrichment for the people of Kashmir, in whose name Pakistan had initiated

---

[7]A non-paper is a text without any kind of names or signatures which can be denied but is detailed enough to act as a basis for a deal.

[8]Ibid.

[9]Editorial Board, 'Four Point Formula', *Kashmir Observer*, 24 October 2019, https://kashmirobserver.net/2019/10/24/four-point-formula/. Accessed on 15 March 2021.

[10]The broad contours of the four-point formula were defined in the speech delivered by Satinder Lambah at the Kashmir University.

the conflict. For the Indian side, as the PM had remarked, the four-point formula was a way out of the 'Kashmir impasse' making 'the whole idea of borders irrelevant, enable commerce, communication, contacts and development of the Kashmiri people on both sides that would end the cycle of violence.'[11]

However, Pakistan's domestic political cycle had begun operating against Musharraf. In the summer of 2007, Musharraf was beset by two major crises. First, was the siege of Lal Masjid involving a military assault on a mosque in Islamabad, thereby drastically reducing the president's credibility. Second, were the rock-tossing protests by lawyers, a consequence of Musharraf's dictatorial order to fire Chief Justice Iftikhar Chaudhry.[12] The General's popularity eroded daily. While he had enjoyed the popular support for many years, it became evident that it was starting to come down.

Delhi therefore dithered. It believed that 'it would be tougher for Musharraf to sell the peace formula in Pakistan than for it to get the majority opinion on its side.'[13] After all, India had been the recipient of Pakistan-sponsored terrorism for 27 years running by then. It needed peace on its periphery to focus more aggressively on its economic development and rising power aspirations. This is a fact that Indian people understand intuitively notwithstanding attempts by the then right-wing opposition party—the BJP, of accusing the UPA government of being soft on terror.

A once-in-a-lifetime opportunity to make a dramatic breakthrough in the frozen turbulence called the Indo-Pak dynamic, was therefore lost as Musharraf's political credibility plummeted and India continued to vacillate on taking the Manmohan-Musharraf formula to logical fruition. The UPA government calculated, perhaps erroneously then, that any Kashmir bargain forged by Musharraf

---

[11]Suhasini Haidar, 'Claiming the Four-Step Formula', *The Hindu*, 5 November 2016, https://www.thehindu.com/opinion/lead/Claiming-the-four-step-formula/article11634935.ece. Accessed on 15 March 2021.

[12]Steve Coll, 'The Back Channel', *The New Yorker*, 22 February 2009, https://www.newyorker.com/magazine/2009/03/02/the-backchannel. Accessed on 19 July 2021.

[13]Sanjay Baru, *The Accidental Prime Minister*, Penguin, 2014.

now, would be repudiated by the successor regime in Pakistan. The Indians were not confident that a provisional peace arrangement could be protected. There was also a hawkish view within the Indian establishment that Pakistan was negotiating the non-paper framework just to buy time and win favour with Washington DC while continuing to sponsor and support militant groups targeting India. It was the business-as-usual chicanery that Pakistan had perfected over the years. Ultimately, the hawks prevailed and India pulled back from the four-point formula.

In hindsight, the Indian decision to pull back was an error of judgement for that was the best shot India had had in years to bring quietus on its periphery. Whatever the formula may be called in future, in its kernel lies the key to both peace and the greater political and economic integration and development of South Asia. It is interesting that whenever I raised the Manmohan-Musharraf formula at Track I and a half, or Track II conferences, the Pakistani response was mixed. While 'official Pakistan' and the more hawkish retired elements of its security and foreign policy establishment would vehemently deny that such a formula ever existed, other cooler heads and sane voices opined to the contrary. Even the former foreign minister of Pakistan, Khurshid Mahmud Kasuri, has referred to it at length in his book, *Neither a Hawk Nor a Dove*.[14] Insofar as the Congress was concerned, since it was a part of the then UPA government it would invariably endorse the line taken by the government, especially on key foreign policy issues.

THE PARALLEL UNIVERSE OF TERROR

While all formal and backchannel attempts were being made to find an acceptable resolution to the outstanding issues bedevilling the India-Pakistan bilateral relationship particularly the 'Masla-e-Kashmir', it was not as if Pakistan-backed terror had completely abated. There was, however, definitely a bit of a lull in the proxy war

---

[14]Khurshid Mahmud Kasuri, *Neither a Hawk Nor a Dove*, Viking, 2015.

during the period between 2004 and 2008, primarily because both sides were exploring an acceptable modus vivendi. While there was certainly a thaw at the border and a seeming quiet in J&K, the rest of the country was as insecure as it had been since the Parliament attack of December 2001. There were several exogenous shocks every couple of months that repeatedly underscored the fragility of the entire peace process. Pakistan's strategy seemed to be: expand the horizon of terror but keep things on a slow burn on the border and J&K while incubating, operationalizing and sustaining a parallel universe of terror in the rest of the country.

The 29 October 2005 attack carried out by the LeT just three days before Diwali in Delhi's Sarojini Nagar market killing 67 innocent people and injuring more than 210 others, even while the composite dialogue process was going on, conclusively underscored the fact that the Pakistani deep state had indeed created a parallel universe of horror. This was followed by a series of blasts in other places like Hyderabad, Uttar Pradesh and Rajasthan over the next three years.

In early July 2006, a series of synchronized bomb attacks ripped through commuter trains and stations across Mumbai killing 160 people and injuring more than 400. Analysts attributed this attack to the LeT. This was followed by the bombing of the Samjhauta Express in 2007. Seventy people were killed. Most of the fatalities were Pakistani citizens. Four people were chargesheeted by the National Investigation Agency (NIA). However, the NIA special court in 2019 acquitted all four of them.

That period also saw the rise of the Indian Mujahideen (IM), a terrorist group led by Abdul Subhan Qureshi. This group received aid, training in sophisticated weaponry and support from the Pakistani deep state.[15] Its game plan was to establish itself as an Indian entity to take off the diplomatic pressure on Pakistan to act

---

[15] A backgrounder to the India Mujahideen and its links with the Pakistani state by the Manohar Parrikar Institute for Defence Studies and Analyses (MP-IDSA) is available at: can be found here: https://idsa.in/backgrounder/IndianMujahideen. Accessed on 15 March 2021.

against the LeT operating from its territory. The IM coordinated one of the deadliest attacks in the city of Jaipur. The attacks were a series of nine synchronized bomb blasts that took place on 13 May 2008, at different locations in the capital of Rajasthan. The alleged kingpin of the blasts, Atif Amin, was later killed in the Batla House encounter in Delhi in September 2008.

Not surprisingly, when New Delhi concluded that it had identified that the terrorists who had planned and executed these attacks were linked to Pakistan, it had the effect of further derailing what was left of the peace process that had continued to limp along despite the four-point peace formula being put on the back-burner.

Things took a turn for the worse when PM Manmohan Singh, the principal protagonist in the peace process had to, on the basis of available empirical evidence, point a finger directly at Pakistan for being complicit in these bombings across Indian cities. However, notwithstanding these grave provocations keeping the larger objective of peace in the subcontinent, the UPA government kept the negotiations in play. Select strategic commentators also canvassed and propagated an equally widely held view then that the Pakistan-based terrorist apparatus was acting semi-autonomously, that every act of terror did not have the sanction of the Pakistani deep state, as they were determined to derail the peace process at any cost.

One can say, with a reasonable degree of certainty, given Dr Manmohan Singh's sagacity and far-sightedness, that the only reason the peace process was allowed to chug along in fits and starts was because there was an abiding belief at the time, both inside and even outside government, that India would never be able to achieve its natural and true standing in the comity of nations if it did not resolve the vestiges of India's partition.

The central argument for continuing the dialogue then was that Musharraf was perhaps the only person, given his dual-hatted role at that point in time, who could perhaps even coerce the Pakistani military-terror complex, which remained primus inter pares, to shed its reluctance in negotiating an agreement with India. Such a rapprochement, if it would indeed have happened, would have dramatically proscribed their capacity to access considerable economic resources and retain their privileged role in the state's political order. With Musharraf stepping down as president on 18 August 2008 to avoid an impeachment, the unfettered Pakistani deep state fast tracked a stunning attack that could effectively abort the peace process once for all.

REACTIONARY RESPONSE TO INDIA'S 9/11

Why was Mumbai put in the cross hairs? For coordinated strikes on the financial capital of the country were aimed at undermining India's economic trajectory by perpetrating a spectre of dread. Hence, the choice of foreigners as targets also. Moreover, as India is home to the third largest Muslim population in the world, the expectation perhaps was that retaliatory attacks in India may set off communal conflagration and further inflame an already polarized polity.[16] However, all these calculations failed drastically notwithstanding the terrible human cost the carnage extracted.

Within hours, it felt like the city had come back to life. The Bombay Stock Exchange not only reopened the following day, but closed 0.7 per cent higher. The economy recovered very rapidly from the November 2008 tragedy. In the post-attack era, tourist arrivals from abroad declined by 10 per cent, but started to rebound by mid-2009. Above all, the economy grew at a better-than-expected 6.8 per cent rate during 2008–9, second only to China, despite the economic meltdown considered to be the worst economic crisis after the Great Depression of 1929.[17]

Within hours of this well-orchestrated attack, it became more than apparent that the police and security authorities of the city

---

[16]Shivshankar Menon, *Choices: Inside the Making of Indian Foreign Policy*. Penguin Random House, 2016.

[17]Rajesh Basrur, Timothy Hoyt, Rifaat Hussain and Sujoyini Mandal, 'The 2008 Mumbai Terrorist Attacks: Strategic Fallout'. S. Rajaratnam School of International Studies, 2009. 32-47.

were hopelessly ill-prepared for a terrorist outrage of this scale and dimension. Worse still, it also became clear that no substantive plans were in place to deal effectively with a major terrorist attack on a major metropolitan centre in the country.

That it took three days to neutralize the terrorists laid bare again the fact that an attack of this dimension had not been gamed by the counter terror response structure at various levels. It is a finding that the Maharashtra government's High-Level Enquiry Committee (HLEC) on 26/11, led by Ram Pradhan, also delineated while stressing the lack of cohesion in our counterterrorism approach.[18]

Like Kargil, can the attacks on Mumbai be also characterized as an intelligence failure, even though 26 warnings were issued by the intelligence agencies to the Mumbai police between 2006 and 2008 about a possible attack.[19] However, given the fact that most intelligence inputs are more in the nature of weather advisories, it is not surprising that they did not get the attention they deserved. Mechanisms like the Multi-Agency Centre (MAC) and subsidiary MACs, suggested by the Kargil review committee, continued to remain deficient in high-level coordination that essentially means breaking down the silos that segregate intelligence structures from their law-enforcement counterparts. It therefore would be no exaggeration to conclude that the Mumbai attacks, like various high-profile terror attacks in the past, did indeed constitute an intelligence failure once again.

The NSG, which was mobilized during the attacks, had its headquarters in Delhi and lacked bases anywhere else in the country and did not have access to a military aircraft for emergency mobilization.[20] A Russian IL-76 transport carrier, based in Chandigarh, was the only aircraft available to transport the 200

---

[18]Deepak Sinha, 'Targeting Mumbai: Future Imperfect', *ORF*, 24 November 2018, https://www.orfonline.org/expert-speak/targeting-mumbai-future-imperfect-45693/. Accessed on 15 March 2021.

[19]Ibid.

[20]Ibid.

commandos to Mumbai. After waking the pilot up, assembling a crew and fuelling the aircraft, it finally reached Delhi only at 2 a.m. (five hours after the attacks started and much of the killing was done). After that, it took another three and a half hours to reach Mumbai (compared to only two hours for a passenger jet).[21]

International standards require rapid reaction teams to enter a terrorist attack site no longer than 30–60 minutes after it has started. In Mumbai, however, nearly 10 hours elapsed before the elite counterterror force finally accessed the site. 'The lack of rudimentary devices, such as night-vision goggles, as well as inadequate intelligence and situational awareness, further hindered the NSG.'[22] It did not even have an operational command centre.

It is for these reasons that it took India's security forces the better part of 72 hours to neutralize the terrorists and restore order. Only one terrorist, Mohammad Ajmal Kasab, was captured alive. His testimony, other security inputs and intercepts made it amply clear that the attacks were carried out by the LeT. The Indians assembled a dossier, containing all the evidence that they had gathered and presented it to Islamabad and the rest of the world.

India demanded that Islamabad hand over 20 fugitives who were believed to enjoy sanctuary in Pakistan. Under sustained international pressure, Pakistani authorities finally had to arrest Zakiur Rehman Lakhvi, the individual accused of masterminding the attacks. It was only three months later that the Pakistani government formally banned the Jamaat-ud-Dawa (JuD), the parent organization of the LeT, froze their assets and sealed their offices across the country. However, it was yet again an exercise in tokenism.

The national security apparatus was also found inadequate in the maritime domain. The Indian Navy and Coast Guard failed

---

[21]Angel Rabasa, Robert D. Blackwill, et al, 'The Lessons of Mumbai', *RAND Corporation*, 2009.
[22]Deepak Sinha, 'Targeting Mumbai: Future Imperfect', *ORF*, 24 November 2018, https://www.orfonline.org/expert-speak/targeting-mumbai-future-imperfect-45693/. Accessed on 15 March 2021.

to detect and prevent the terrorists from sneaking into the city. According to a subsequent IB audit eight years later in 2016, out of 227 minor ports in India, 187 had little to no security.[23]

The real concern, analysts point out, was that the police apparatus has structural flaws. From the insufficient number of maritime police stations, to scarcity of personnel and unspent money, many systemic challenges plaguing the system are yet to be addressed by coastal administrators. Unfortunately, the plan for the creation of an apex maritime authority still remains frozen. The National Committee for Strengthening Maritime and Coastal Security, which currently oversees collaborative operations, is at best an ad hoc structure.[24]

Strategists underscored what has already been noted as India's reactionary response to defence reforms. What followed was a frenzied scramble of activity in our national security apparatus. NSG hubs were established at various places in the country. The idea of setting up a National Intelligence Grid (NATGRID) was germinated. While hubs for NSG have now been established in Mumbai, Kolkata, Bangalore, Hyderabad, Chennai and Ahmedabad, however, its expansion has also brought into question the quality of the elite force. In the Pathankot attacks in the wee hours of 2 January 2016, this deficiency manifested itself in a fairly forceful manner.[25] [26] [27]

[23]Ibid.

[24]Abhijit Singh, 'India's Coastal Security: An Assessment', *ORF*, 23 November 2018, https://www.orfonline.org/expert-speak/indias-coastal-security-an-assessment-45692/. Accessed on 15 March 2021.

[25]Deepak Sinha, 'Targeting Mumbai: Future Imperfect', *ORF*, 24 November 2018, https://www.orfonline.org/expert-speak/targeting-mumbai-future-imperfect-45693/. Accessed on 15 March 2021.

[26]Vijaita Singh, '20 NSG Commandos Were Injured in Pathankot', *The Hindu*, 22 December 2016, https://www.thehindu.com/news/national/20-NSG-commandos-were-injured-in-Pathankot-NIA/article16920713.ece. Accessed on 15 March 2021.

[27]'Why India's response to Pathankot attack was a debacle', *BBC*, 6 January 2016, https://www.bbc.com/news/world-asia-india-35232599. Accessed on 15 March 2021.

THE WORLD REACTS

The US started putting all its diplomatic efforts in preventing an armed conflict between the two nuclear states India and Pakistan rather than holding Pakistan to account. This is a tendency that has always underscored the double standards of the western nations when it comes to dealing with terrorist outrages on their soil vis-à-vis something that happened in the emerging powers or the developing world, as the West pejoratively likes to call it.

Post the 26/11 outrage, the Indo-Pak equation had become even more critical to the outcome of the war in Afghanistan and the war on terror in general. The newly elected Obama administration had delineated Afghanistan among its top foreign-policy priorities. The stability of Afghanistan depended on Pakistan's efforts to pacify the Taliban. Obama had remarked, 'We can't continue to look at Afghanistan in isolation. We have to see it as part of a regional problem that includes Pakistan, includes India, includes Kashmir, includes Iran.'[28] Veteran diplomat Richard Holbrooke was appointed as a special representative for both Afghanistan and Pakistan. Even India may well have been a part of Holbrooke's remit had it not been for serious objections by India at being lumped in the same basket as Pakistan and Afghanistan.

Given the sheer barbarousness of the assault, the international community could not ignore the atrocity. The United Nations Security Council (UNSC) put senior members of the LeT involved in the attack on sanctions list of terrorists. India was also successful in organizing unprecedented cooperation from countries like Saudi Arabia and even China to make the diplomatic pressure against the architecture of terror in Pakistan efficacious. The immediate Pakistani reaction to this coordinated international pressure was to place the alleged

---

[28]'Remarks by the President on a New Strategy for Afghanistan and Pakistan', Obama White House Archives, 27 March 2009, https://obamawhitehouse.archives. gov/the-press-office/remarks-president-a-new-strategy-afghanistan-and-pakistan. Accessed on 15 March 2021.

mastermind of the attack Hafiz Saeed under house arrest.

The fundamental problem however was that Pakistan's support to jihadi groups came indirectly from the US as its military and economic-assistance packages were the ones that were siphoned off and diverted to resource this monstrous machinery of mayhem and murder. The Bush administration did little after the 9/11 attack to question the duality of Pakistan's policies. They thought that there was no immediate threat to the US from Kashmir-focused jihadi groups. The administration supplied Pakistan with approximately $10 billion worth of military assistance, ostensibly for the war against the al-Qaeda, without any worthwhile oversight and without ensuring that the ISI does not fund international Islamist groups. 'The Pakistanis played the Americans,'[29] as much of this funding was not used for economic aid but to create home-grown militant groups and non-state actors with the sole purpose of carrying out attacks against India.

However, there have been serious suspicions in India that the US had much more information about the attack than it has admitted to. One of the prime conspirators of the 26/11 attack was David Coleman Headley, who was an agent of the US Drug Enforcement Agency (DEA) from at least 1997 onwards. He was also allowed to enter into a secret plea bargain with the access to his testimony restricted. It was only in 2013, five years after the attack, that he was sentenced to 35 years in prison.

India unrolled a diplomatic and media blitzkrieg to persuade the world to put greater pressure on Pakistan. The response to the cataclysmic developments in November 2008 was, however, fashioned by each nation based upon its perceived national interest. The world, including the US, was torn between its divergent interests qua India and Pakistan.

That is why the 26/11 attack failed to bring any systematic change in the way the international community deals with terrorism.

---

[29]Steve Coll, 'The Back Channel', *The New Yorker*, 22 February 2009, https://www.newyorker.com/magazine/2009/03/02/the-backchannel. Accessed on 19 July 2021.

The sanctions and limits placed on Pakistan after the attacks have withered away; the real perpetrators have not been brought to book. It is business as usual for the LeT. Given the past trajectory, this was almost a given.

UNDERSTANDING NEW DELHI'S POLICY OF RESTRAINT

It then begs an obvious question: why did India not retaliate with a massive conventional counter-attack that could have been both punitive and a future deterrent against state-sponsored terrorism? Why did we act with restraint and take only diplomatic measures and not undertake a kinetic response against Pakistan?

Why did India not go to war with Pakistan? Why, despite repeated provocations by Pakistan, did India restrain itself from an immediate and visible retaliation post 26/11? After all, that would have been the natural course of action to undertake under the given circumstances? This question has intrigued analysts. Many more have tried to discern and present reasons for the policy of restraint followed by Delhi after an assault that has become the scarred and perennial watershed in the Indo-Pak paradigm.

It was not that war was never an option. The armed forces had cranked up their readiness and surveillance levels all along the border, post the attack. There were several close calls and the IAF operational readiness platforms were also activated. One of these was the consequence of a hoax call made to the president of Pakistan posing himself to be India's external affairs minister.[30] Only when the US Secretary of State Condoleezza Rice intervened did it become evident that the call was a con, a deliberate provocation, to add fuel to the fire. It is also strange that the Pakistani president's office put the call through without even verifying the credentials of the caller. The caller's identity was never ascertained. Though a year later, it

---

[30]'A Hoax Call That Could Have Triggered War', *Dawn*, 6 December 2008, https://www. dawn.com/news/333312/a-hoax-call-that-could-have-triggered-war. Accessed on 15 March 2021.

was reported in some newspapers that the caller ostensibly was the British-born terrorist Omar Sheikh, then serving a life term in a high-security Karachi Jail for the murder of the *Wall Street Journal* correspondent, Daniel Pearl.[31] The Pakistani deep state however buried the investigation after the initial reports in November 2009.

Were the same actors who had perpetrated 26/11 now provoking both India and Pakistan to go to war? Was that the real objective of the Mumbai attack? In the absence of any sustained investigation by Pakistan and with every possible attempt by its intelligence agencies to bury this particular side show that may have actually unravelled a can of worms, the truth would never really come out.

There is, however, a school of thought that has been arguing from that time onwards that 'more was to be gained from not attacking Pakistan than from attacking it.'[32] What were these argued gains? Well for one, it states that if India would have indeed attacked Pakistan, it would have just become another India-Pakistan dispute. Any conventional attack would have meant taking the issue to the international corridors of justice. Considering all the previous Indo-Pak disputes, the world would have responded with the default, i.e., to call for peace and split the blame and credit equally between both the states in the name of fairness, yet again equating the victim with the aggressor. Additionally, such an attack would have united Pakistan behind the Pakistani Army and weakened the civilian government in Pakistan.

This school of thought further argues that Dr Manmohan Singh's approach appears to have been grounded in military realism. If India were to launch small, carefully chosen strikes, it would only further lessen Pakistan's apprehensions of a rigorous conventional attack in the future. Additionally, a limited strike would have not resulted in

---

[31]'How a Terrorist Called Zardari Posing as Pranab', *NDTV*, 27 November 2009, https://www.ndtv.com/world-news/how-a-terrorist-called-zardari-posing-as-pranab-405723. Accessed on 15 March 2021.

[32]Shivshankar Menon, *Choices: Inside the Making of Indian Foreign Policy*, Penguin Random House, 2016.

any substantial gain. If India were to attack the LeT HQ at Muridke, it would have hardly affected the terrorist organization. 'The LeT camps are tin sheds and huts which can be rebuilt easily.'[33] Moreover, these camps are deliberately set up near hospitals and schools so that any strike on these camps could result in heavy civilian casualties thereby handing over a propaganda tool to the Pakistanis.

Finally, a war, even one that India could have won, would have come at a heavy cost at a time when the world was in the throes of an unprecedented financial crisis, the economic meltdown of 2008 triggered by the sub-prime crisis. It would have set back the exceptional progress the Indian economy had made by at least a decade, if not more.

While in retrospect, it is always easier to find rational justifications for choices made, the problem is that this kind of restraint only produces results if both the parties to a negotiation are on the same page and have similar goals. Both parties should be stepping away from the ticking time bombs of history. However, if the other side (Pakistan in this case) continues to have mala fide intent and wants to run with the hare and hunt with the hounds, it becomes a self-defeating strategy for the side with kosher intent (India in this case).

It is evident that post 26/11, the Indian objectives had taken a drastic turn towards non-coercive diplomacy. Such an approach therefore lacks even the aspect of deterrence and is more difficult to execute. Moreover, it becomes difficult if not impossible to assuage inflamed public emotions that then rightly believe that no cost is being imposed on the belligerents for their murderous depredations. Such an approach naturally then lent itself to the 'soft on terror' cliché that stuck to the then UPA government like a noxious epithet for the remaining part of its first and second term.[34] It is these reasons and, above all, the imperatives of political messaging for the current

---

[33]Ibid.
[34]Ali Ahmed, 'India's Limited War Doctrine: The Structural Factor', *IDSA Monograph Series No. 10*. IDSA, 2012.

dispensation that since the September 2016 Uri attack, the policy of strategic restraint has given way to more tactical and forward leaning responses.

For the sake of argument, let us consider the outcomes of limited strike/Cold Start retaliation. Cold Start, as mentioned earlier, developed after it had taken the army more than a month to fully mobilize along the Pakistani border during Operation Parakram. However, even five years after Parakram, it was evident that the doctrine was not ready for operationalization and therefore virtually redundant in dealing with contingencies of this order. The land-based option thus was a non-starter from the word go.

However, air strikes against the LeT and JuD military camps in POK with a simultaneous presentation of dossiers indicating clear involvement of the Pakistani state (tapes of phone calls made by the terrorists from the high seas to their commanders in Pakistan, the micromanagement of the entire operation by Pakistan-based handlers and even Kasab's confessions later) would have prevented the Pakistani state from crying foul. It was an option that should have been actioned.

It would have then become extremely difficult for the international community to split the blame as it could have happened with the operationalization of a land-based option, as they had been historically programmed to do, for the attack had reverberated across the entire world. It had also targeted a number of foreign nationals as well.

If ever there was a moment to cash in all the IOUs that we had collected from the global community for the restraint that we had exercised over all these decades, by absorbing all the blows that Pakistan had hurled against us through their proxies and semi-state actors, 26/11 would have been the right occasion to do so.

While an attack certainly would have required robust intelligence inputs on the precise location of these terrorist camps, a limited strike on these camps that would have caused visible, tangible and undeniable damage would have sent out a salutary message.

It would have made it extremely difficult for Pakistan to retaliate with a nuclear threat. This is because it would have been too low a nuclear threshold even for Pakistan to escalate the conflict.

While it could be argued that the post-Uri surgical strikes in 2016 and air strikes on the Jaba hill-top in Balakot in 2019 did precisely this. However, the critical difference was that when these options were indeed operationalized, the punitive cost on Pakistan was negligible. Not only did they deny that a surgical strike had taken place, but more importantly, even the casualty figures put out in election rallies by the political dispensation in government was at a wide variance with assessments made by independent and non-partisan sources.

It is a fact that the perpetrators of the 26/11 attack have walked free. Except for some tokenism by Pakistan, and that too because of the Financial Action Task Force (FATF) sword hanging on its neck, precious little has really changed even after more than 14 years of that attack. The Pakistan Army is still at the helm of affairs. The international 'isolation' of Pakistan after the attacks has withered away and it is business as usual for everyone.

The attack definitely helped the LeT, as it assisted in healing the rift between a more active al-Qaeda and a passive LeT. The 26/11 attack helped in consolidating and profiling the LeT internationally after its al-Qaeda-style attack, thereby increasing its credibility and access to resources in the depraved subterranean world of international terror.

WANTED: A KINETIC RESPONSE

India should have reacted through the use of conventional force. The target should have been carefully chosen to impose significant punitive costs on Pakistan. Reliance on non-kinetic options can always be justified both in real time and retrospect, and could well have been very well-considered additional response prescriptions along with kinetic options.

However, the nation and the world saw that India had just absorbed a body blow to its solar plexus without as much as batting an eyelid in retaliation. For a state that has no compunctions in brutally slaughtering hundreds of innocent people, restraint is not a sign of strength; it is perceived as a symbol of weakness. There comes a time when actions must speak louder than words. 26/11 was one such time when it just should have been done. It, therefore, is my considered opinion that India should have actioned a kinetic response in the days following India's 9/11.

SIX

RISING TO THE CHINA CHALLENGE: THE UPA YEARS

The 10 years of the UPA government were characterized by a largely stable relationship with China. As both China and India's economies grew rapidly, the emphasis was more on looking ahead rather than peeking into the rear-view mirror. As someone who has closely followed China's transition over the decades—from its pauperized existence during the Mao years to the high growth paradigm commencing with Deng Xiaoping's rein—the latter efforts have undoubtedly borne fruit. They have made China both a prosperous and a powerful nation.

This stability in the relationship was also, in part, due to the assiduous work that both sides had carried out to bring the association back on track, going all the way back to 1988. Prime Minister Rajiv Gandhi broke the ice with his visit to China at the invitation of Premier Li Peng, between 19–23 December 1988. The last such visit by an Indian prime minister had taken place 34 years earlier in October 1954.

However, there is an episode that preceded that visit. It was perhaps the last major stand-off between India and China, before the current joust on the border that commenced with the Chinese transgression in eastern Ladakh in April 2020.

Despite the fact that 1962 had left a bitter aftertaste, an attempt was made by every successive government to try and manage a contentious relationship marked by an unsettled border. However, there was always a treacherous bed of live fuses that underpinned the relationship, waiting for the proverbial spark. Sumdorong Chu was one such spark.

SUMDORONG CHU AND A NEW MODUS VIVENDI

Sumdorong Chu is a rivulet north of the Tawang district of Arunachal Pradesh. The Wangdung pasture on this river is claimed by both India and China. India established an observation post at Sumdorong Chu in 1984. While officers were stationed there during the summer, they would evacuate the place in the winter. However, in June 1986, an Indian patrol found 40-odd People's Liberation Army (PLA) soldiers working to build permanent structures in this area.

This created a flashpoint as border tensions between India and China had started escalating in the early 1980s itself. The Chinese were neither willing nor able to bring things under control on the border, as they had done in the past, because of an increasingly assertive PLA in matters military after Mao Zedong's demise. The Chinese transgression in Sumdorong Chu led to military mobilization all along the LAC.

The Chinese had picked their ground carefully. Given the rudimentary nature of cartography back in 1913–14, sparsely populated regions were not delineated with needle-like precision. Sir Henry McMahon's original map showed Sumdorong Chu north of the McMahon Line, even though it was south of an elevated watershed. This was also due to a thick, red ink nib that had been used to draw the line. The consequence was that at some places, it obfuscated ownership of up to 5 km of land.[1]

What followed in Wangdung (Sumdorong Chu) is the stuff of legends. Indian forces marched in, occupied the dominant heights of Longrola and Hathungla, and set up posts a few metres away from the Chinese.[2] India also began Operation Falcon and deployed

---

[1]Shivshankar Menon, *Choices: Inside the Making of Indian Foreign Policy*. Penguin Random House, 2016.
[2]Ibid.

infantry combat vehicles and tanks.[3] However, it took several years to restore status quo in Sumdorong Chu and mutual withdrawal began only in 1995. The stand-off, however, served a political purpose. It became clear that a new modus vivendi was needed. Sumdorong Chu was a lesson for the India-China security apparatus for two reasons.

First, Operation Chequerboard, the name given to the Indian Army's response to the incident, was a highly effective deterrent. The speed at which the Indian Army had mobilized its troops made the Chinese realize that if a conflict ensued, it would be extremely difficult for them to counter-attack. The situation at the border had begun to change and it was no longer the India of 1962.

Additionally, no matter what the narrative was in New Delhi, the border forces were not living in the amnesia of the 1962 defeat as they were presented to be. The face-off also had dividends for India. It assimilated the erstwhile North-East Frontier Agency (NEFA), that was given Union Territory status in 1972 when it was named Arunachal Pradesh, as a full state of the Indian Union on 20 February 1987. This made the Chinese realize that a border conflict with India could not be solved through force anymore and would need political intervention.

Second, the intensity of the stand-off at Sumdorong Chu led to a bilateral effort to produce a substantial outcome. Joint working groups (JWGs) were set up and an atmosphere conducive for a settlement of the boundary issue was created. This is the reason why the Rajiv Gandhi visit to China, after the Sumdorong Chu incident, was a breakthrough. It was not a knee-jerk reaction to settle the immediate border dispute. Its aim was to create a foundation for a structured conversation to tackle the fundamental bottlenecks between India and China.

---

[3]Manoj Joshi, 'Making Sense of the Depsang Incursion', *The Hindu*, 8 June 2016, https://www.thehindu.com/opini/making-sense-of-the-depsang-incursion/article4689838.ece. Accessed on 15 March 2021.

RAJIV'S PRAGMATISM AND ITS IMPLICATIONS

The reason why a narration of events post 1988 is also germane is because it demonstrates continuity in handling, managing and finessing the China relationship across as much as two decades encompassing the tenure of nine Indian prime ministers. It demonstrates that experimentalism was not the favoured way forward, for there was an acute appreciation of the sensitivity of the relationship.

PM Rajiv Gandhi's visit to China was indeed an icebreaker. Although it did not bring about any resolution of the border dispute, it created the right kind of atmospherics for both countries to at least begin the dialogue process. For the first time, India did not demand resolving of the boundary question as a precondition for other matters to be taken up; in fact, the parties resolved to 'seek an equitable, rational and mutually acceptable solution to the issue of borders, and agreed to extend and establish bilateral relations in all other areas.'[4]

The move to not let the absence of a boundary settlement prevent India and China from developing relations in other domains became important from a strategic viewpoint. Beijing had refused to make any compromise on the border issue until there was a concession made in the Tawang region, something that any government of India would find difficult to accept.[5] Had it not been PM Gandhi's pragmatism, as global contexts had already begun changing, an obstinate position on the border question would have resulted in a stalemate.

It was this pragmatism that succeeded in laying the groundwork for a new modus vivendi. A JWG was formed at the foreign secretary-level, supported by an expert group to negotiate the border issue, and a joint economic group to promote cooperation in trade-related

---

[4]General J.J. Singh, *The McMahon Line: A Century of Discord*. HarperCollins India, 2019.
[5]Shivshankar Menon, *Choices: Inside the Making of Indian Foreign Policy*. Penguin Random House, 2016.

areas.[6] A truly multidimensional relationship was sought to be operationalized between the two nations.

However, nothing concrete came out between the period of 1989–91. As the beleaguered Chinese leadership was struggling in the aftermath of the 1989 Tiananmen Square massacre, India was going through the phase of short-lived coalitions. The transformation in the international arena—with the collapse of Soviet Union and the rise of the US as a hegemonic power—provided some momentum. China wanted to eschew any kind of provocation since it was paranoid that it might end up meeting the same fate as the erstwhile USSR and other eastern European countries.

If the US and its allies had applied sustained pressure on China in the wake of the Tiananmen Square massacre, the course of history may have been very different. However, in the first decade of the Deng Xiaoping years, many large American and European multinationals were reaping the benefits of record profits in the absence of any ethical human or labour standards in their production facilities in China. The stakes were too great to rock the boat. In any case, President George H.W. Bush, during whose presidency (1989–93) most of the epoch-making changes in the world took place, was already distracted by events that were unfolding in Europe and the Middle East.

The euphoria of those times was best summed up in Francis Fukuyama's seminal article, 'The End of History?' published in the summer of 1989 in *National Interest*. Fukuyama stated,

> What we may be witnessing is not just the end of the Cold War, or the passing of a particular period of post-war history, but the end of history as such: that is, the end point of mankind's ideological evolution and the universalization of Western liberal democracy as the final form of human government.[7]

---

[6]General J.J. Singh, *The McMahon Line: A Century of Discord*. HarperCollins India, 2019.

[7]Francis Fukuyama, 'The End of History?' *The National Interest*. https://www.embl.de/aboutus/science_society/discussion/discussion_2006/ref1-22june06.pdf. Accessed on 15 March 2021.

However, history never ended, Xiaoping was taking no chances at all. He articulated a way forward that held the field for a good two decades right up to the ascendency of Xi Jinping in November 2012. This approach is known as the Twenty-Four-Character strategy of 1990: 'Observe calmly; secure our position; cope with affairs calmly; hide our capacities and bide our time; be good at maintaining a low profile; and never claim leadership.' The Tiananmen Square incident had also revealed deep divisions within the Chinese leadership. It seemed logical that in these circumstances, it would serve the Chinese to try and maintain peace along its borders.[8]

ONE STEP FORWARD, TWO STEPS BACK

This provided an impetus to a border agreement between the two countries. During PM Narasimha Rao's visit to Beijing in 1993, India and China agreed to initiate discussions on the border dispute. The Agreement on the Maintenance of Peace and Tranquillity along the Line of Actual Control in the India-China Border Areas was signed by both parties, committing themselves to a policy of clarifying the disputed LAC wherever it was needed, and not some 'notional idea' of where it was in 1959 or 1962. Pending an ultimate resolution, both the countries agreed that 'neither side shall use or threaten to use force against the other by any means.'[9] Such an agreement was not to imply that both sides have resolved the difference on the alignment of the LAC. For this purpose, the JWG was to develop confidence-building steps and consult mutually to settle differences along the LAC.[10] Therefore, the use of force to address outstanding territorial claims was eschewed by both nations.

---

[8]Shivshankar Menon, *Choices: Inside the Making of Indian Foreign Policy*. Penguin Random House, 2016.
[9]'The Border Peace and Tranquility Agreement, 1993', *UN Peacemaker*, https://peacemaker.un.org/sites/peacemaker.un.org/files/CN%20IN_930907_ Agreement%20on%20India-China%20Border%20Areas.pdf. Accessed on 15 March 2021.
[10]Ibid.

The agreement of 7 September 1993 was the first of its kind to deal directly with the frontier between India and China. It was notable in various aspects and broke new ground. Both countries agreed to preserve the status quo and also agreed that there shall be no attempts to unilaterally alter it. Any dispute arising on the border would be resolved amicably at the negotiating table. It also essentially delinked the boundary settlement from the rest of the partnership.[11]

Three years after the 1993 Agreement, in November 1996, the two countries signed another crucial agreement, on CBMs in the military domain between the military forces of both countries. It went well beyond the Border Peace and Tranquility Agreement (BPTA), to actually prompt reduction of forces. This was to be based on the negotiations to resolve the border issue.[12]

The 1993 and '96 agreements were followed by a number of high-profile visits by national leaders to each other's countries (including 15 JWG meetings). However, they were not of much help in resolving contentious and convoluted claims not just limited to the LAC.

The 1996 agreement initiated a procedure to exchange maps, indicating their 'respective perceptions of the entire alignment of the LAC.'[13] However, the exchanging of maps was not without its quandaries. While the Indian side emphasized on discussing the alignment along the entire LAC, the Chinese side wanted to discuss only those border points where there was a dispute. Even then, the exercise on exchanging maps could only go as far as the Middle Sector of the LAC. By June 2002, when it was time to discuss the Western Sector, the situation reached a deadlock as both countries had taken 'maximalist positions'. The Eastern Sector being another kettle of fish.

According to an Occasional Paper written for the ORF titled

[11]Shivshankar Menon, *Choices: Inside the Making of Indian Foreign Policy*. Penguin Random House, 2016.

[12]'Confidence-Building Measures in the Military Field Along the LAC (1996)', *UN Peacemaker,* https://peacemaker.un.org/sites/peacemaker.un.org/files/CN%20 IN_961129_Agreement%20between%20China%20and%20India.pdf. Accessed on 15 March 2021.

[13]Ibid.

'Understanding Sino-Indian Border Issues: An Analysis of Incidents Reported in the Indian Media,'

> The India-China border is divided into three sectors, viz. Western, Middle and Eastern. The boundary dispute in the Western Sector pertains to the Johnson Line proposed by the British in the 1860s that extended up to the Kunlun Mountains and puts Aksai Chin in the then princely state of Jammu and Kashmir. Independent India used the Johnson Line and claimed Aksai Chin as its own. China initially did not demur when India said so in the early 1950s; however, in the years that followed, it reversed its position and stated that it had never acceded to the Johnson Line and therefore did not see why it should cede Aksai Chin to India. In the Middle Sector, the dispute is a minor one. It is the only one where India and China have exchanged maps on which they broadly agree. The disputed boundary in the Eastern Sector of the India-China border is over the McMahon Line. Representatives of China, India and Tibet in 1913–14 met in Shimla, where an agreement was proposed to settle the boundary between Tibet and India, and Tibet and China. Though the Chinese representatives at the meeting initialled the agreement, they subsequently refused to accept it. The Tawang tract claimed by China was taken over by India in 1951. Till the '60s, China controlled Aksai Chin in the West while India controlled the boundary up to the McMahon Line in the East.[14]

Why did the situation reach a deadlock? And why did map exchanges in the Western Sector not take place automatically, putting the territorial divergences beyond the pale of negotiations? While these revelations have not been made public, there have been some

---

[14]Mihir Bhonsale, 'Understanding Sino-Indian Border Issues: An Analysis of Incidents Reported in the Indian Media,' *ORF Online*, https://www.orfonline. org/research/understanding-sino-indian-border-issues-an-analysis-of-incidents-reported-in-the-indian-media/. Accessed on 15 March 2021.

conjectures about the same. The Chinese argue that the Indian side was adamant about first delineating the border between China and Pakistan and then settling the border between China and India. However, if this was the case, why did Beijing not agree to clarify the rest of the border?

For China, it has never been about contentious positions that need to be reconciled. Beijing has adopted a posture of strategic ambiguity about its territorial claims, an approach often seen in stances it has taken in other territorial and maritime disputes. Consistency is not a virtue that China adheres to when negotiating or even stating its boundary claims. It tailors its arguments to suit its concurrent strategic heft in terms of what concessions it can extract from the other side at a particular point in time. Not resolving its border disputes helps the Middle Kingdom in keeping its rivals off-balance while continuing to extend its claims.[15]

Whatever be the case, the LAC mechanism essentially stalled without any agreed-upon delineation of the LAC. The JWG and Expert groups had not yielded worthwhile results, despite a decade-and-a-half of negotiations.

It was fairly evident to India that without a political stimulus, resolution of the boundary problem would be impossible. Therefore, when PM Vajpayee visited China in 2003, both countries made a pledge at the highest political level to peacefully resolve the border issue. They also decided to nominate Special Representatives at the apex level, handpicked by the respective premiers, to explore the framework of a boundary settlement from the political perspective.[16]

The trajectory of the post Rajiv Gandhi Sino-Indo relationship has indeed been novel if not path-breaking in many respects. Not only did the 1988 visit mark the beginning of a thaw in the

[15]Ananth Krishnan, *India's China Challenge: A Journey through China's Rise and What It Means for India*, HarperCollins India, 2020.
[16]Manoj Joshi, 'Making Sense of the Depsang incursion', *The Hindu*, 7 May 2013, https://www.thehindu.com/opini/making-sense-of-the-depsang-incursion/article4689838.ece. Accessed on 15 March 2021.

relationship following the post-1962 freeze, it also set the framework for the relationship, which was essentially, as Deng suggested, to shelve differences and work on areas of common interest.[17]

While the 1993, 1996 and 2003 confidence-building agreements were critical and had far-reaching consequences, they have never been seriously implemented. For example, Article 3 of the 1996 agreement emphasizes on reducing military presence on both sides and that such 'ceilings shall be determined in conformity with the requirement of the principle of mutual and equal security, with due consideration being given to parameters such as the nature of terrain...'[18] Key clauses such as these have not been adhered to and remain in limbo. The Chinese strategy of salami slicing to create new facts on the ground, thereby giving it both an unequal and competitive advantage in the negotiations, has virtually rendered these agreements redundant, for the purposes of delineating the borders on the maps and demarcating it on the ground.

A question that needs to be addressed is: if the three agreements failed to create an architecture to resolve the disputed border, how come they were able to become instruments of maintaining relative peace and tranquillity on the borders, at least till the April 2020 conflagration?

This is because the patrolling habits of both sides are based on where they feel the LAC lies; each side has a pretty good idea of the other's ground positions, therefore provocation had largely been avoided till April 2020. Both sides had adopted operational procedures as enunciated in the CBMs required under the agreement/s. Both sides were not in direct contact along much of the sections of the LAC.

---

[17]Raviprasad Narayanan, 'India-China Relations: The United Progressive Alliance (UPA) Phase', http://dcac.du.ac.in/documents/E-Resource/2020/Metrial/25CihnnitaBaruah1.pdf. Accessed on 15 March 2021.
[18]'Confidence-Building Measures in the Military Field Along the LAC (1996)', *UN Peacemaker*, 29 November 1996, https://peacemaker.un.org/sites/peacemaker.un.org/files/CN%20IN_961129_Agreement%20between%20China%20and%20India.pdf. Accessed on 15 March 2021.

It should be borne in mind that even when the LAC is not accepted between the two countries, let alone delineated on a map or demarcated on the ground, the Sino-Indian border remained largely stable for over four decades, devoid of any cross-border infiltration or artillery exchanges. The last border deaths (except for the skirmishes in Galwan in 2020) occurred in October 1975, at Tulung La when four jawans of the Assam Rifles were shot by the Chinese soldiers.

CONTINUITY WITH CHANGE

The UPA government inherited a foreign policy that could be characterized as a broad continuum over the tenure of various past governments, going back to the origins of the Indian nation state. There had been stability of policy even with regard to China at least from 1988 onwards. They did not make any big policy reversals thereby underscoring a 'spirit of continuity.' This period saw Indian foreign policy mature with 'economic diplomacy' and multilateralism being South Block's preferred strategy in its interactions with the world.[19] In retrospect, however, one would have to admit that the UPA did manage rising China reasonably well. There was no unnecessary use of rhetoric to provoke the Chinese, and constant and structured dialogues were carried out at the highest levels. The UPA government cooperated with China on various global fora when necessary, and most important, the military was kept in readiness to meet any unforeseen eventuality that Beijing might try and inflict.

That period witnessed the signing of several bilateral agreements. The most important of them was the Agreement on the Political Parameters and Guiding Principles for the Settlement of the India-China Boundary Question (2005), which spelt out the contours of a settlement whilst taking into account the strategic interests of both

---

[19]Raviprasad Narayanan, 'India-China Relations: The United Progressive Alliance (UPA) Phase', http://dcac.du.ac.in/documents/E-Resource/2020/Metrial/25CihnnitaBaruah1.pdf. Accessed on 15 March 2021.

countries. Article VII, which lies at the heart of this agreement, states that 'in reaching a boundary settlement, the two sides shall safeguard due interests of their settled populations in the border areas.'[20]

Two other Articles—III and V—are also of seminal significance, as they have the potential to determine the basis for the proposed solution to the issue of frontiers in the future, notwithstanding the current stand-off. Article III calls for 'mutually appropriate changes to their respective positions on the border issue in order to arrive at a package settlement'; while Article V lays out the reasons that need to be kept in view, such as 'historical facts', 'national feelings' and 'sensitivities' of both sides while arriving at a settlement.[21]

Additionally, India reiterated its one-China policy and restated that Tibet was China's autonomous region.[22] The Chinese reciprocated, albeit rather belatedly, by allowing modest trade to commence between Sikkim and Chumbi Valley in the Tibetan Autonomous Region (TAR) through the historic Nathu La Pass in 2006.[23] This was agreed upon during PM Vajpayee's visit to Beijing in 2003.

Significantly, China accepted that India was a major developing country with a growing international footprint. China both recognized and endorsed the aspirations of India to play an active role in the UN and international affairs. During the same visit, the two sides also signed a protocol aimed at deepening the CBMs for

[20]'2005 Agreement on the Political Parameters and Guiding Principles for the Settlement of the India-China Boundary Question', MEA, https://www.mea.gov.in/bilateral-documents.htm?dtl/6534/Agreement+ between+the+Government+ of+the+Republic+of+India+and+the+Government+of+ the+Peoples+Republic+ of+China+on+the+Political+Parameters+and+Guiding+Principles+for+the+ Settlement+of+the+IndiaChina+Boundary+Question. Accessed on 15 March 2021.
[21]Ibid.
[22]'Joint Declaration by the Republic of India and the People's Republic of China', MEA, https://www.mea.gov.in/bilateral-documents.htm?dtl/6363/Joint+Declaratio n+by+the+Republic+of+India+an. Accessed on 15 March 2021.
[23]Atul Aneja, 'The Many Great Games in Chumbi Valley', The Hindu, 5 August 2017, https://www.thehindu.com/news/international/the-many-great-games-in-chumbi-valley/article19435857.ece. Accessed on 15 March 2021.

maintaining peace and tranquillity along the border. The modalities for implementation of the CBMs established an SoP. It envisaged that if there was a confrontation in the contested area, each side would display a banner with the following text emblazoned across it, 'This is Indian/Chinese territory' followed by a second banner, 'Turn around and go back to your side.' Such events of banners being displayed came to be known as face-offs.[24]

These modalities were followed by high-level meetings to improve upon the existing CBMs. President Hu Jintao, on a four-day visit to India in November 2006, negotiated a joint declaration with a 10-pronged stratagem to take the relations to a qualitatively new level. Besides the myriad initiatives launched under this agreement to reinforce the strategic and cooperative partnership, it was also agreed to establish new consulates in Guangzhou and Kolkata.[25]

ECONOMICS TRUMPS POLITICS

India and China were slowly seeing the fruits of their developmental reforms. While India opened its economy only in the 1990s, China however, had made a success of the reforms. It became the ticket to its legitimacy globally along with accelerated political institutionalization and systematic leadership at home. It was able to weather the 2008 global financial crisis reasonably well and its economy was not as battered as those of the developed countries. The India-China engagement began to look beyond the hard lines of security and border issues, and 'economics' became the new buzzword in the political corridors of both nations. The political leaders did not take much time to hop onto the train of economic incentives, trying to squeeze as much peace dividend as possible from this new dimension.

---

[24]Manoj Joshi, 'The Wuhan Summit and the India-China Border Dispute', *ORF Report June 2018*, 2018.
[25]General J.J. Singh, *The McMahon Line: A Century of Discord*, HarperCollins India, 2019.

As mentioned earlier, the Joint Economic Group set up after Rajiv Gandhi's visit to China, studied the feasibility of strengthening economic ties between the two nations. Consequently, China emerged as India's largest trading partner in the 2000s with bilateral trade increasing from $17 billion to $42 billion over the period of 2005/6–2009/10. Bilateral trade expanded 67 times between 1998 and 2012.[26] Joint military exercises were held in 2007, 2008 and 2013. Even now there are close to 25,000 Indian students in China, most of them studying medicine. Interestingly, China is today one of the rapidly growing overseas markets for Bollywood.[27]

The UPA government made efforts to deepen the economic relationship. Both countries assented to set up the India-China Strategic Economic Dialogue in 2010.[28] Its goal was to provide a platform to discuss macroeconomic cooperation. The India-China Financial dialogue was set up in 2005.[29] There was a growing recognition that trade was a new and important dimension of the bilateral relations between both the countries; this was also reflected in PM Manmohan Singh's visit to China in 2008. The resultant 'Vision Statement' underlined the value of both countries concentrating their respective capacities to leverage their economic potential in order to achieve comprehensive growth and social stability.

But there was a bitter pill to swallow; the biggest trade deficit that India was running with any country was with China. While on one hand, Indian markets were deluged with Chinese products, on the other, India's export basket had a very limited diversification to offer. The deficit had increased by a staggering 160 per cent by 2010–11. While both sides had consented to work on balancing the

[26]Raviprasad Narayanan, 'India-China Relations: The United Progressive Alliance (UPA) Phase', http://dcac.du.ac.in/documents/E-Resource/2020/Metrial/25CihnnitaBaruah1.pdf. Accessed on 15 March 2021.

[27]Ananth Krishnan, *India's China Challenge: A Journey through China's Rise and What It Means for India*, HarperCollins India, 2020.

[28]'India-China Bilateral Relations, MEA, https://mea.gov.in/Portal/ForeignRelation/China_2020.pdf. Accessed on 15 March 2021.

[29]Ibid.

trade dynamic better, this issue continues to trouble India even today. India's share in China's imports stood at a meagre 0.6 per cent during 2016.[30] It is not only the weak intensity of Indian products in the Chinese markets that is problematic but more worryingly, the majority of our exports are in the primary and intermediate category. Conversely, our imports from China are majorly in finished capital goods.

FLEXING MILITARY MUSCLE

The burgeoning trade and rapidly improving economic ties, however, did not mean that India was soft on China. The UPA government knew that the border issue lay at the heart of ultimately normalizing the relationship with Beijing, and that without any settlement on the LAC, peace would always remain tenuous and fragile. As a result, while the CBMs continued, India decided to bolster its border infrastructure. For a long time after the 1962 war, India had deliberately refrained from strengthening its military infrastructure, driven by the belief that this may end up creating lanes of invasion for the Chinese side, if hostilities were to ever break out again.[31] China, however, was uninhibited in this realm and had started its development and modernization projects along the LAC from the late 1990s itself. China's capacity to build was quicker than India's, given a relative terrain advantage, larger resources and even climatic advantage. India, on the other hand, has been trying to catch up ever since.

In 2006, on the recommendation of the China Study Group, the Indian government approved the completion of 73 China–India border

---

[30]'India-China Trade Relationship January 2018', *PHD Chamber of Commerce and Industry*, https://www.phdcci.in/wp-content/uploads/2018/11/India-China-Trade-Relationship_The-Trade-Giants-of-Past-Present-and-Future.pdf. Accessed on 15 March 2021.

[31]K. Bajpai, S. Ho and M.C. Miller, *Routledge Handbook of China–India Relations*, Routledge, 2020.

roads along with improving India's cross-border capabilities (this included building tunnels, as well as a trans-Arunachal highway).[32]

This was followed by the augmentation of the force structure along the LAC in an effort to strengthen the deterrence paradigm. The government decided to set up two new Mountain Divisions in 2009, and later in 2013, the CCS approved the creation of a new mountain Strike Corps—a 90,000-soldier force focused entirely on the Sino-Indo border.[33] The proposal envisaged an expenditure of ₹64,000 crore spread over seven years.[34] Unfortunately, in 2018, the current BJP-led NDA government pulled the plug on the complete raising of this Strike Corps citing a lack of resources for the same. Had the government diligently followed through this proposal, India would have had greater deterrence capacity against China by 2020.

Additional armoured units along the LAC were also approved by the UPA government. In Chushul, Fukche, Demchok and Daulat Beg Oldi (DBO), four advanced landing grounds were initialized, and top-of-the-line fighters such as SU-30MKI were also stationed.[35] The robust Indian economy helped to enhance military capabilities.

Owing to these improvements in the border infrastructure, the number of reported incursions by China began to increase significantly after 2010. In fact, they peaked at 500 in 2014.[36] India had to augment its border patrolling along the LAC, enhancing the frequency and size of the patrols and optimizing their efficiency.

---

[32]Manoj Joshi, 'Sino-Indian Border Deadlock: Time to Rewrite India Playbook', *ORF Occasional Paper 269*, 2020.

[33]K. Bajpai, S. Ho and M.C. Miller, *Routledge Handbook of China–India Relations*, Routledge, 2020.

[34]Josy Joseph, 'CCS Nod for Raising Mountain Strike Corps along China Border', *The Times of India*, 18 July 2013, https://timesofindia.indiatimes.com/india/CCS-nod-for-raising-mountain-strike-corps-along-China-border/articleshow_b2/21132826.cms?mobile=no. Accessed on 15 March 2021.

[35]Amitabh Dubey, 'How True Is the Claim that Modi Govt Is the Architect of the Border Roads Project?' *The Wire*, 3 July 2020, https://thewire.in/security/fact-check-india-china-border-roads. Accessed on 15 March 2021.

[36]K. Bajpai, S. Ho and M.C. Miller, *Routledge Handbook of China–India Relations*, Routledge, 2020.

The basic patrol limits were revised over time, especially after the 1993 BPTA and 1996 agreements, as per the differing perceptions on the alignment of the LAC. India was clear on where the LAC lay in its opinion, something that was delineated through a diligent survey using satellite imagery from 1976 onwards. This mapping was cleared by the China Study Group in 1976 itself.[37]

As suggested by various analysts and scholars, including Shivshankar Menon, former foreign secretary and NSA, India had done more in the past decade to strengthen military capabilities along our borders than in any decade since Independence, and given the state of India's security infrastructure, this move was indispensable. Even the Naresh Chandra Committee has ostensibly observed that 'China's development of military infrastructure in Tibet and the Indian Ocean region coupled with the PLA's modernization changes its military capabilities meaningfully.'[38]

XI RULES

While the economic, political and even the military dynamic between India and China appeared stable, the long shadow cast by the unresolved boundary dispute always imposed certain inherent limitations. Every now and then skirmishes on the border would remind both nations that they had outstanding issues to address. An episode of this nature that set off alarm bells coincided with the elevation of Xi Jinping in 2013.[39]

The rise of Xi Jinping and 'Xiplomacy' saw a marked break from the caution and circumspection that had characterized the approach of the Chinese leadership from Deng Xiaoping onwards

---

[37]Manoj Joshi, 'Sino-Indian Border Deadlock: Time to Rewrite India Playbook', *ORF Occasional Paper 269*, 2020.

[38]K. Bajpai, S. Ho and M.C. Miller, *Routledge Handbook of China–India Relations*, Routledge, 2020.

[39]Manoj Joshi, 'Depsang Incursion: Decoding the Chinese Signal', *ORF*, https://www.orfonline.org/research/depsang-incursion-decoding-the-chinese-signal/. Accessed on 15 March 2021.

to international relations and foreign policy:

> For the past four decades, China's diplomacy had followed Deng Xiaoping's cautious maxim of 'tao guang yang hui', or 'biding time, hiding brightness'. The new phrase of choice in Beijing however became the more confident 'fen fa you wei', 'strive for achievement', underlining its desire to 'proactively shape' its external environment. Xi is less shy about pushing China's goals and speaking up about its view of the world. It is a mix of strong nationalism and assertiveness on China's core interests and territorial disputes, coupled with a more proactive diplomacy in the neighbourhood. And all this is riding on, by Chinese standards, an extraordinarily personalized role for the country's leader.[40]

In March 2013, Xi Jinping made a statement at the 5th BRICS Summit in Durban that the border issue should be resolved 'as soon as possible'. He cautioned that a recessed military posture, while non-threatening, could still be construed as provocative. It was a portentous signal of what was going to become the behaviour template of a new and assertive China.[41] A confrontation looked imminent and it happened in the month of April.

On 15 April 2013, the PLA established an isolated camp 19 km inside what India considers its side of the LAC in the Depsang Plains, in Ladakh. It was completely unexpected, setting off a chain of events that led India to re-examine its position vis-à-vis China.

The incursion could be viewed at two levels. One, that it was a time-tested tactic of the Chinese to occupy an area, claim that it is part of their territory and then, through clever negotiation, agree on a smaller land grab. All this while expanding further than what was the status quo. This is the reason why the Chinese don't

---

[40]Ananth Krishnan, *India's China Challenge: A Journey through China's Rise and What It Means for India,* HarperCollins India, 2020.

[41]Manoj Joshi, 'Sino-Indian Border Deadlock: Time to Rewrite India Playbook', *ORF Occasional Paper 269, 2020.*

like to resolve a border dispute. Second, as mentioned above, the Chinese chariness over India's improving military capabilities across the border, even while China far outpaces India in border defence systems. (The Chinese had developed railway lines in Tibet and Xinjiang, had strengthened their border infrastructure and increased their military capabilities.)

India responded with countermeasures and mobilized its forces within days and quickly established their own encampment 300 metres (980 feet) away. It was made amply clear to the Chinese that the status quo must be restored. The insistence was to move back to the verified 'end point' of the withdrawal.[42] On the diplomatic front, India stopped all further negotiations until there was an assurance that the status quo would be restored.

The Manmohan Singh government was successful in getting the Chinese to vacate the region within three weeks, unlike the Sumdorong Chu incident, that took seven years to resolve. While, to a large extent, this was due to the enhanced capabilities of India's military, something that might have mortified even the Chinese, in part, it was also due to the institutions and CBMs both sides had put in place since the 1993 BPTA. Quiet, international persuasion also seems to have played a role although no Indian government ever acknowledges anything of this sort publicly.

On two counts, Indian strategic pundits who proposed a military counteraction to the Chinese incursion were incorrect. First, we were in the middle of our modernization period and still did not have essential elements of our security infrastructure like heavy lift helicopters and mountain artillery. Second, the situation would have been needlessly exacerbated by an over-the-top military response. What was needed was a calm and steady counter, both privately as well as in the public sphere. Finally, it was discerned that there were 'five tents, seven men and a dog' in the Chinese camp at the

---

[42]Suhasini Haidar and Dinakar Peri, 'Depsang Tensions Echo 2013 Stand-off', *The Hindu*, 3 June 2020, https://www.thehindu.com/news/national/depsang-tensions-echo-2013-stand-off/article31733947.ece. Accessed on 15 March 2021.

last count.[43] In retrospect, patient diplomacy, symmetrical non-threatening military reaction while displaying power coupled with giving the opponent a way out, paid off.

The Indian response leading to the rapid resolution of the incident at Depsang had a noticeable impact on Sino-Indo relations. Days after this stand-off on the border, Chinese Premier Li Keqiang visited India in May 2013. It was a trifle hard for the Indian side to even pretend that it was business as usual after what had happened, albeit without any provocation from the Indian side in Depsang just a month earlier. However, by visiting China later that year, Prime Minister Manmohan Singh ensured that the relationship stayed on an even keel.

During Li Keqiang's visit to Delhi, PM Singh hosted a dinner for the visiting Chinese Premier at his residence. It was a small affair. Among those invited were Sonia Gandhi, Rahul Gandhi, Arun Jaitley, Sushma Swaraj and I. Other officials from the PMO were also present, including the NSA Shivshankar Menon. The Chinese delegation, interestingly, were all busy scribbling notes when both prime ministers were talking. They did not want to miss a word of what transpired and considered any chit-chat with the person sitting next to them as a distraction. The Indians, on the other hand, were more relaxed, if not bemused by the Chinese behaviour. Nonetheless, they still went out of their way to make polite conversation with the Chinese guests seated adjacent to them.

There was a visible overture by the Chinese that Beijing wanted to preserve the relationship during Dr Singh's visit to the country in October 2013. Not only did President Xi host Dr Singh for dinner, but Li personally gave Dr Singh a walking tour of the Forbidden City. The Chinese practically brought Wen Jiabao out of retirement to meet Dr Singh. The visit was, ironically, helped by the fact that India took an assertive stand, impelled by the creation of formidable capabilities to tackle operational gaps along the LAC. This also

[43]Manoj Joshi, 'Making Sense of the Depsang Incursion', *The Hindu*, 8 June 2016, https://www.thehindu.com/opini/making-sense-of-the-depsang-incursion/article4689838.ece. Accessed on 15 March 2021.

included the ambitious proposal to raise a mountain strike corps by 2019–20, giving India the much-needed capability to launch a counteraction in Tibet against Beijing's assertiveness.

However, in July 2018, the defence and finance ministers of the subsequent Modi-led government shelved all the plans of raising a mountain strike corps against China citing financial constraints.[44] Mounting pressure on the LAC leading to the Doklam crisis in 2017 could have been averted, provided the mountain strike corps would have been raised, trained, resourced and efficaciously deployed. Scrapping the mountain strike corps is perhaps the greatest disservice that this government did to India's national security.

Since the early 1980s, China has dealt with the border dispute in an insidious manner, trying to create new facts on the ground. It has since then used this ambiguity to exploit its broader relationship with India. As Chinese analyst Zhang Jiadong put it, 'China's experience indicates that resolving border disputes is usually the result rather than the cause of improvement in relations.'[45] The two countries have a different understanding of the LAC and until such misgivings are resolved, their strategic divergence will linger on. The requirement is to find balance between competition and cooperation.

While the UPA government was successful in being able to maintain this peace with China while strengthening itself, the Modi government, by and large, has been caught off guard. Despite claiming to be a more assertive government with a larger electoral mandate, Modi seems to have failed the China test.

---

[44]Sujan Dutta, 'Indian Army Puts Mountain Strike Corps Aimed at China in Cold Storage', *The Print*, 12 July 2018, https://theprint.in/defence/indian-army-puts-mountain-strike-corps-aimed-at-china-in-cold-storage/82319/. Accessed on 15 March 2021.

[45]Zhang Jiadong, 'Challenges Linger in China–India Border Talks', *Global Times*, 26 November 2018, https://www.globaltimes.cn/content/1129040.shtml. Accessed on 15 March 2021.

SEVEN

THE CHALLENGE CONTINUES: CHUMAR-DOKLAM-GALWAN

In July 2010, I travelled to Kunming, the capital of the Yunnan Province in China, to participate in the International Conference of Asian Political Parties conclave on Poverty Alleviation hosted by the Communist Party of China (CPC). Later, we travelled to Beijing and called on Xi Jinping, then vice president of China and vice chairperson of the Central Military Commission. The interaction with the invited delegates from across Asia, who had come to attend the Poverty Alleviation Conference, took place at the Great Hall of the People in Beijing.

During the visit, our Chinese interlocutors told us that China had three main goals over the next three decades. The first was to turn China from a low-income into a middle-income country, to move manufacturing from the coastland to the hinterland, and to bring their conception of intra-party or party-less democracy to fruition.[1] The Chinese back then were experimenting with some form of 'one party, multiple candidates for one position' model of democracy at the grassroots level. For all this, they claimed that they needed peace on the periphery.

It would be instructive to recall that three decades earlier, on 18 December 1978, at the third plenary session of the 11th Central

---

[1]Cheng Li, 'Intra-Party Democracy in China: Should We Take It Seriously?' *Brookings*, https://www.brookings.edu/wp-content/uploads/2016/06/fall_china_democracy_li.pdf. Accessed on 15 March 2021.

Committee meeting of the CPC, the country had decided to turn the page on decades of suffering unleashed by Mao's maladministration and calamitous policies.

Under Deng Xiaoping's direction, China broke out of its self-imposed isolation. Deng realized that China needs to grow economically and for that it needs both a conducive environment for trade and investment and a break from the rigidities of the past. This paradigm held the field for three-and-a-half decades.

However, with Xi Jinping's accession as the President of China in March 2013, it soon became clear that this was not the playbook he had in mind. China became territorially aggressive towards its neighbours coupled with grandiose ambitions of global domination.

The question, therefore, that begs an answer is: how does India deal with an assertive China that refuses to play by the rules of international conduct and the various agreements signed between 1993 and 2005, especially those pertaining to the settlement of the vexed territorial imbroglio?

A TALE OF TWO LINES

At the core of the Sino-Indo border dispute is a tale of two lines, both disputed for over a century now. In the northern sector, it is called the MacDonald Line, whereas in the Eastern Sector, it is called the McMahon Line. While India recognized these lines as the successor state of the British Empire, the Chinese have always disavowed them.

On the history of these lines hangs an interesting tale of statecraft, intrigue, diplomatique and pure skulduggery.

The initial endeavour to delineate a boundary line between the erstwhile princely state of J&K and Tibet and Xinjiang was made in 1865. Its author was a surveyor named W.H. Johnson, who concluded that the border of J&K traversed right up to the Kunlun Mountains north of the Karakoram Range and included the entire Aksai Chin in its sweep. This trajectory was endorsed by the then London-headquartered director of British military intelligence, the versatile and multifaceted, Major General Sir John Ardagh. In 1897, it acquired the nomenclature of the Ardagh-Johnson Line. However, this initiative was stillborn for the grandiose nature of its geographical expansiveness.

Back in the early 1890s, the Indo-Russian frontier till the Little Pamir was delineated to the satisfaction of both the British and the Tsarist empires. However, the Russian, Chinese and British domains also converged in the Great Pamir, where there was considerable fuzziness, if not an overlap of claims. As the great game was in full swing, the British were always circumspect of Russian intent.

The clashing claims of the British-protected state of Hunza and the Chinese Empire to the Taghdumbash and the Raskam Valley created the possibility of a Russian intervention. To surmount this uncertainty, the British government proposed to the Chinese a solution to this imbroglio through a demarcation of the whole Sino-Kashmir border. This pitch was penned in 1899 by C.M. MacDonald and addressed to His Highness Prince Ch'ing and the ministers of the Tsungli Yamen. It has a substantial bearing on the stand-off with the Chinese on the Northern borders even today. The operative part of the proposal was as follows:

> In the year 1891 the Indian Government had occasion to repress by force of arms certain rebellious conduct on the part of the ruler of the state of Kanjut [Hunza], a tributary of Cashmere. The Chinese Government then laid claim to the allegiance of Kanjut by virtue of a tribute of one and a half ounces of gold dust paid by its ruler each year to the Governor of the New Dominion (Chinese Turkestan) who gave in return some pieces of silk. It appears that the boundaries of the state of Kanjut with China have never been clearly defined. The Kanjutis claim an extensive tract of land in the Tagdumbash Pamir extending as far North as Tashkurgan and they also claim the district known as Raskam to the South of Sarikol. The rights of Kanjut over part of the Tagdumbash Pamir were admitted by the Taotai of Kashgar in a letter to the Mir of Hunza dated February 1896,

and last year the question of the Raskam district was the subject of negotiations between Kanjut and the officials of the New Dominion in which the latter admitted that some of the Raskam land should be given to the Kanjutis.

It is now proposed by the Indian Government, that for the sake of avoiding any dispute or uncertainty in the future, a clear understanding should come to the Chinese Government as to the frontier between the two States.[2]

The line proposed by the Indian government is briefly as follows.

It may be seen by reference to the map of the Russo-Chinese frontier brought by the late Minister Hung Chiin from St. Petersburg and in possession of the Yamen. Commencing on the Little Pamir from the Peak at which the Anglo-Russian Boundary Commission of 1895 ended their work, it runs South-East crossing the Karachikar Stream at Mintaka Aghazi; thence proceeding in the same direction it joins at the Karchenai Pass the crest of the main ridge of the Mustagh Range. It follows this to the South passing by the Kunjerab Pass and continuing Southwards to the peak just north of the Shimshal Pass. At this point the boundary leaves the crest and follows a spur running east approximately parallel to the road from the Shimshal to the Hunza post at Darwaza. The line turning South through the Darwaza post, crosses the road from the Shimshal Pass at that point and then ascends the nearest high spur and regains the main crests which the boundary will again follow, passing the Mustagh Gusherbrun and Saltoro Passes by the Karakoram. From the Karakoram Pass the crests of the range run east for about half a degree (100 li) and then turns South to a little below the thirty-fifth parallel of North Latitude. Rounding then

---

[2]Manish Tewari, 'A Tale of Two Lines at the Core of India-China Border Dispute', *Outlook India*, 29 June 2020, https://www.outlookindia.com/website/story/opinion-a-tale-of-two-lines-at-the-core-of-india-china-border-dispute/355644. Accessed on 15 March 2021.

what in our maps is shown as the source of the Karakash, the line of hills to be followed runs northeast to a point east of Kizil Jilga and from there in a South-easterly direction follows the Lak Tsung Range until that meets the spur running South from the Kunlun Range, which has hitherto been shown on our maps as the Eastern boundary of Ladakh. This is a little east of 800 East-longitude.[3]

The Chinese never ever replied to the letter. Their lack of response was deemed by the British as acceptance of their proposal by implication—a concept recognized by international customary law. Thus, the MacDonald Line squarely puts not only the Galwan valley and other current flashpoints, but also large tracts of Aksai Chin, squarely in the Indian Territory.

In the Eastern Sector, the tale unfolded as follows: in 1913, the British convened a tripartite conference in Shimla with the Tibetans and Chinese. The objective of this conclave was to formalize the de facto independence that Tibet acquired in 1912, consequent to the overthrowing of the Manchu dynasty and the resultant chaos in China.

Tibet was to be maintained as a buffer state between India and China. The Simla Conference collapsed. China would not agree to a draft proposal drawn up by the British that proposed the partition of Tibet in inner and outer regions. It was identical to what the Russians had extracted from China with regard to Mongolia. After initialling the draft, the Chinese representative baulked and refused to sign it.

However, the British were successful at Shimla in getting from the newly independent state of Tibet a settlement on a new boundary alignment, that advanced the contours of British territory in eastern India from a line along the foot of the hills to the crest line of the Assam Himalayas, some 60-odd miles to the north. This new configuration not only put a wide swathe of tribal no-man's land within India, but also incorporated a salient of Tibetan territory adjacent to Bhutan that ran right down to the plains, called the Tawang Tract.

---

[3]Ibid.

The Anglo-Tibetan negotiations were led on the British side by Charles Bell, a political officer in Sikkim. It resulted in an exchange of letters, dated 24 and 25 March 1914, in which both sides agreed to this new boundary that ran along the crest-line of the Assam Himalayas, and thus incorporated the Tawang Tract into British India. The boundary was not described in the letters, but was referred to on a map, on two sheets that were sealed and exchanged with the letters. This came to be known as the McMahon Line.

The British attempted to obtain Chinese approval of this new, yet undisclosed, agreement with the Tibetans. On the map, on which the proposed zonal division of Tibet had been drawn, the boundary of 'Inner' Tibet and China was shown in red; that line curved round to its southern extension to show what would have been the boundary between Tibet and India. In that sector, it followed the alignment which McMahon had agreed with the Tibetans.

However, Sir Henry McMahon's diplomacy could only achieve a Chinese initial on the map, not a full-fledged ratification. However, between 1913 and 1962, before the Chinese tried to change the status quo by force after the illegal annexation of Tibet in 1950–1, the McMahon Line, all through World War I (WWI) and WWII and even after that, was recognized as the border between India and China. Recognition through usage and convention are valid concepts in customary international law.[4]

The Chinese however have deliberately dithered on settling the boundary question with India. Ever since 1962, they have resorted to creeping aggression to try and get India to acquiesce to its perception of where its borders with India lie. More often than not, over the years, they have been checkmated as described in the previous chapters but that does not stop the Chinese from trying again and yet again. The same sordid story of Chinese bellicosity played itself out once again in Chumar in 2014.

---

[4]Ibid.

CHUMAR INCURSION AND A FAILED GAMBLE

Barely a year after Xi Jinping's anointment, Narendra Modi's election victory in 2014 sparked of an unusual amount of optimism in China, leading to renewed focus on Sino-Indian relations. Part of this was because of Modi's own tenure as the chief minister of Gujarat. Modi, then persona non grata in the West because of the 2002 Gujarat riots, had made four visits to China. His state, at that point in time, had become a favourite among Chinese companies as an investment destination.

Barely four months after taking office as prime minister, Modi decided to take a political gamble by going out of his way to host Xi in his home state of Gujarat.

The first leg of Xi's trip, to the capital Ahmedabad, did make for some quixotic optics—the Chinese supremo and his Indian counterpart sitting on a jhula (swing) on the banks of river Sabarmati ('jhula diplomacy' as it was disparagingly called). However, despite the heady optimism brought by the bewildering optics, the first Modi-Xi meeting in India was nothing short of a gamble that failed miserably.

By the time the two leaders were in Delhi the next day, news had broken on India's boisterous television channels that a stand-off at the border in Chumar had escalated.

Chumar is situated in southern Ladakh. It lies to the west of the prominent frontier outpost of Demchok. The disputed area to its south-west has a vehicular track that links it to both the Indian and Chinese sides.[5] This is one of those places on the LAC where patrols frequently run into each other as each side has a different perception of where the LAC runs. This time, the trigger was the PLA extending a road from Chepzi towards Chumar (which India considers as territory on its side of the LAC).

The Chumar incident was an exercise in coercive signalling.

---

[5]Arjun Subramaniam, *Full Spectrum: India's Wars, 1972-2020*, HarperCollins Publishers, 2020.

The Chinese objective was to establish themselves on the plateau south-west of Chumar and send out a message that they did not agree with the contours of the LAC in that area.

A post near the disputed area of the LAC on a point called 30R was established by Indian patrols. When the PLA decided to expand their track beyond 30R, matters began to heat up. There was a rapid troop induction by both sides. Human chains of several hundred infantry soldiers and personnel from the Indo-Tibetan Border Police (ITBP) blocked the site where the PLA wanted to build a road.[6] Soon enough, 1,500 Indian soldiers stood face to face with 750 PLA troops.

The stand-off lasted for 16 days and was resolved after intense diplomatic and military negotiations. A quid pro quo was arrived at. While the Chinese decided not to follow the Chepzi-Chumar road development, India agreed to demolish its observation hut at Tible and refrain from building any further there.[7]

For the Chinese PLA, simultaneously violating the LAC in Ladakh's Chumar sector while Xi was being wooed by the Indian leadership was characteristic of their behaviour pattern. However, the assumption made by the Indian establishment then, perhaps erroneously, was that it was probably the handiwork of some PLA generals acting without Xi's approval.

It was a bad act at concealing an error of judgement, or even worse, ill preparedness with even the reasoning predicated upon, if not conditioned, by India's experience of dealing with Pakistan where a distinction has always been made between the civilian dispensation and their military counterparts to let a part of the Pakistani state off the hook. But this was not the case, as the generals involved in the Chumar adventure, instead of being reprimanded,

---

[6]Ibid.

[7]Srijan Shukla, 'How India and China Resolved Three Major Stand-Offs in the Modi Era', *The Print*, 27 May 2020, https://theprint.in/defence/how-india-and-china-resolved-three-major-stand-offs-in-the-modi-era/430594/. Accessed on 15 March 2021.

were all promoted.[8] Modi's political gamble hadn't worked. He was left facing criticism at home for indulging in 'jhula diplomacy' while the PLA was sending in more troops. Even though the stand-off was resolved within 16 days, the illusion of 'heady optimism' was shattered.

When Xi invited Modi to Xi'an in 2015 to mark the second leg of what was called the 'hometown diplomacy' after Xi's Gujarat visit, the Chinese side went to somewhat extreme lengths to demonstrate its hospitality. As Ananth Krishnan writes in his book *India's China Challenge,*

> One of the more peculiar sights of Modi's first day in Xi'an was a clearly prearranged cheering squad (by the Chinese government), which greeted the Indian prime minister as he got down from his car at the Daxingshan temple, chanting 'Modi! Modi!'[9]

Disappointments from Depsang to Chumar were put on the back-burner. Hometown diplomacy soon became targeted at tempering expectations with the focus becoming more on managing—rather than resolving—thorny issues, such as the boundary question. The Modi and Xi declaration was short-sighted. Rather than marking a new beginning, it turned out to be yet another false dawn—this time at the 100-square-kilometre-area called the Doklam plateau.

DOKLAM AND AN UNEASY TRUCE

In 2017, India and China faced a crisis that was not a typical stand-off. The flashpoint was unrelated to the main India-China territorial

---

[8]Shekhar Gupta, 'How Modi Has Made a "Nehruvian" Half-Blunder on China & Ignored Investing in the Military', *The Print*, 14 November 2020, https://theprint. in/national-interest/how-modi-has-made-a-nehruvian-half-blunder-on-china-ignored-investing-in-the-military/543859/. Accessed on 15 March 2021.

[9]Ananth Krishnan, *India's China Challenge: A Journey through China's Rise and What It Means for India*, HarperCollins India, 2020.

dispute. The Doklam plateau stands at the tri-junction between India, Bhutan and China, surrounded by the Chumbi Valley to the North, Bhutan's Ha Valley on the east and Sikkim on the west. This plateau was contested, with China claiming it as a part of Yadong County in Tibet, but India and Bhutan see it as Bhutanese land. China's claim is south of where India and Bhutan see it.

On 16 June 2017, PLA border forces brought construction equipment to the region to expand a previously constructed road southward to a Bhutanese Army camp near the Jampheri Ridge. Both India and China have been aware of their differences on the tri-junction, even agreeing in 2012 to mutually negotiate the matter. The PLA's road building towards the tri-junction was, therefore, given the Chinese tactics, like a fait accompli. As a matter of fact, much across the rest of Doklam plateau, the PLA had already made inroads, building roads deep into what Bhutanese government saw as its territory. Resistance from the Bhutanese Army was little.[10] However, the Chinese intention to unilaterally change the status quo prompted India to intervene.

For China, it was about 'territorial sovereignty'; India had crossed an international boundary to enter into Bhutan, which was seen by China as an intervention in the bilateral issue between Bhutan and China. For India, however, the PLA road, just a short distance from an Indian border post, was a tactical red flag as it brought the Chinese presence uncomfortably close to comfort. Moreover, it was heading straight into the Chicken's Neck—the 27-kilometre-wide Siliguri corridor linking the rest of India with the Northeast. A long-held tactical concern of India has been that in a future war, the PLA would send its troops pouring down this valley, severing India's connection with its Northeast. Therefore, when news of the incident first broke, it was instantly seen in India as the latest in an unending series of surreptitious 'salami slicing' military moves by China.

---

[10]Zorawar D. Singh, *Powershift: India-China Relations in a Multipolar World*, Pan Macmillan India, 2020.

A distinguished school of strategic punditry has sought to interpret the 2017 crisis. While some argued, to a limited extent rightly, that the unresolved Himalayan conflict was the key cause of recurring tensions; others suggested that broader threat perceptions have turned the area into a zone of geopolitical rivalry. Despite this, there were some specifics that did not make sense about the Doklam flare-up. The fact that PLA had communicated to the Indian border post, not once but thrice, that construction work would be carried out was surprising. For a stealth salami-slicing mission, the PLA was overtly communicative.[11] The Indian officials, however, had made their concerns clear on the road development. China nevertheless went ahead. The Doklam episode illustrated a new threat that India faced from an assertive China. It was the beginning of what many call China's 'wolf warrior diplomacy.'

This aggressive approach marked a new Chinese posture that would be repeated in future boundary disputes where perceptions of where the LAC lay diverged widely. The *PLA Daily*, the army's official newspaper, termed the posture, during the Doklam crisis as an 'information warfare' strategy, aimed 'to fully integrate the publicity forces of public opinion, radio, TV, newspapers and social media, and carry out a multi-wave and high-density centralized publicity in a fixed period of time to form favourable public opinion situation to allow for a final victory.'[12]

It would have been difficult for the NDA government if skirmishes had escalated. Reports of various Parliamentary Committees and recent disclosures have suggested that our tank and howitzer ammunition were sufficient for just 10 days in the event of active combat against the prescribed 40 days. Coupled with it were reports that the Navy was also underfunded and facing a short supply of both submarines and anti-submarine warfare helicopters. All this

---

[11]Ananth Krishnan, *India's China Challenge: A Journey through China's Rise and What It Means for India*, HarperCollins India, 2020.
[12]Ibid.

was disquieting to say the least.[13] As discussed earlier, the Indian security apparatus seems hobbled by both stalled military reforms and non-upgradation of vital defence infrastructure.

Fortuitously, the crisis did not intensify. Both sides were fortunate enough to surmount the situation. What helped in Doklam was the BRICS Summit that China hosted at the beginning of September in Xiamen. For the Chinese, this was a big dilemma. While on one hand, they had used their information warfare tactics to create a wave of nationalism in their country, pegging it on fanning an anti-India sentiment, on the other hand, Xi Jinping had to play a good host to PM Modi. Although nearly all normal bilateral interaction had ceased during the Doklam crisis, the preparations for BRICS continued, allowing top Indian ministers to go to Beijing for meetings in the midst of the crisis.

Ultimately, if there would have been an armed clash unleashing a new Cold War in the region, both countries had everything to lose. India and China agreed at the end of August 2017, after a 72-day stand-off to pull back their troops from the Doklam face-off site.

As far as the Chinese road construction is concerned, Delhi took the risk and did succeed in stopping the road from reaching a strategically vital ridge. Yet, China responded by fortifying its position pretty much everywhere else on the plateau, to an extent that it is today far better positioned in Doklam than it was before the crisis.

While in the past, the response to Chinese incursions were strong counterattacks or a call for status quo, this time around, the NDA government, albeit taking direct action in Doklam in 2017 and commendably so, unfortunately then chose to withdraw without adequate guarantees. The Modi government's stop-start intervention in Doklam set a bad precedent. China 'learned a vital lesson that as long as the NDA government could be allowed to walk away with what they thought was a propaganda victory, they could actually

---

[13]Ibid.

make gains and change the outcomes on the ground.'[14]

What are the takeaways from Doklam? The key takeaway was that the Chinese disengage to reconsolidate. With them, one has to be eternally vigilant as tactical withdrawals are just a part of their larger strategic land grab. Their occupation of the Doklam plateau is proof of this. Even the withdrawal was sequential and not simultaneous, with India withdrawing first. It would come back to bite India in the years ahead. India needs to be ever more cautious of these tactics now that only that part of the disengagement in eastern Ladakh that suits China more than India has been operationalized so far.

WUHAN AND MAMALLAPURAM: THE LOVE THAT WASN'T

Despite the agreements reached after the Doklam crisis, tensions did not subside. The air was filled with mutual suspicion on both sides. It was in this situation that India and China agreed to hold an 'informal summit' in Wuhan in 2018. However, there are also reports that the summit did not come out of the blue, despite the surprise announcement. It was ostensibly first suggested in June 2017 by Modi at a bilateral meeting with Xi in Astana, Kazakhstan, according to China's ambassador to India. Therefore, an informal summit was in the works well before the Doklam military confrontation in June 2017.[15]

In April 2018, Modi travelled to Wuhan for the first summit. Xi and Modi agreed that they would provide 'strategic guidance' to their respective militaries to enhance coordination, introduce various confidence-building steps and reinforce existing institutional structures to avoid and handle situations in border areas.[16]

---

[14]Amitabh Dubey, 'A Few Questions on China that Narendra Modi Cannot Evade', *The Wire*, 22 August 2020, https://thewire.in/security/china-ladakh-narendra-modi-lac-disengagement. Accessed on 15 March 2021.

[15]Dhruva Jaishankar, 'The India–China summit in Wuhan Was No Reset', *The Interpreter*, https://www.lowyinstitute.org/the-interpreter/india-china-summit-wuhan-was-no-reset. Accessed on 15 March 2021.

[16]Sudha Ramachandran, 'India-China Relations: From the Wuhan Spirit to the

The informal summit was organized with the expectation of creating a framework for dealing with instability and handling the outbreak of any unforeseen fissures in inter-state ties. However, the effect of the summit was both shallow and transitory. China may have taken measures to resolve India's concerns about its large trade deficit, but this has had negligible impact. It went up from $51.7 billion in 2017 to $57.86 billion in 2018.

As an aside, in 2020, the trade deficit was down to $45.8 billion as a consequence of various import restrictions imposed by India,[17] the lowest since 2105.

China remains on edge, if not frustrated, with India's ambitions in the subcontinent. India's apprehensions at Doklam or along the disputed border over another face-off with China, did not decrease in the months following the Wuhan summit—one must not forget that Chinese expansionism in Doklam continued well after the 'Wuhan Spirit' was established. Even the larger areas of concern between India and China, such as the NSG membership and China's funding of the China-Pakistan Economic Corridor (CPEC) still persist.

Among the decisions taken at the Wuhan Summit was to hold more such summits, aimed at ensuring higher levels of strategic communication. Therefore, despite the dissipating outcome from the Wuhan summit, a second summit would be held in Chennai in October 2019, in the old town of Mamallapuram on the city's outskirts. The seaside town was chosen for its ancient civilizational links between the rulers of the Pallava dynasty and the Chinese. Attempts in the more recent past to capitalize on this ancient linkage have not had a happy history. A guided tour of Mamallapuram was also offered to Chinese Premier Zhou Enlai in 1956. The historical convergences did not seem to have impressed

---

Chennai Connect', *Jamestown*, https://jamestown.org/program/india-china-relations-from-the-wuhan-spirit-to-the-chennai-connect/. Accessed on 15 March 2021.

[17]Ibid.

him. India and China were at war six years later.[18]

The Mamallapuram summit, however, in the weeks preceding the gathering, would remain under a cloud of uncertainty. This was because the summit was arranged despite tensions rising again. The Indian government's legislative moves on 5 August to revoke J&K's autonomy and statehood, and to divide it into two centrally administered union territories, Jammu and Kashmir, and Ladakh, was the key cause for the bilateral tension. The NDA government asserted that Aksai Chin, a disputed plateau, was part of Indian territory. If one were to go as far back as 1890 or even earlier, it is not an incorrect assertion. However, this affirmation did not go down well with the Chinese.[19] [20] Subsequently, many bilateral visits were cancelled or postponed. Even for the Mamallapuram summit, Xi Jinping's confirmation came less than two days before the summit.[21]

As was the case with the Wuhan Summit, the Mamallapuram Summit was no different—they were both, at best, designed as a palliative, with each side exploring how they could stop rubbing each other the wrong way. It is therefore not surprising that despite the fact that these informal summits emerged from the aftermath of the Doklam crisis, they did not address the border issue in any substantive manner, if one goes by the official press release.

[18]Ipsita Chakravarty, 'Beyond Modi-Xi Summits: To Avoid Military Escalation, What Are India's Options?' *Scroll*, 5 September 2020, https://scroll.in/article/972235/beyond-modi-xi-summits-to-avoid-military-escalation-what-are-indias-options. Accessed on 15 March 2021.

[19]Sujan R. Chinoy, 'The Forgotten Fact of China-Occupied Kashmir', *IDSA*, 13 November 2020, https://idsa.in/specialfeature/forgotten-fact-of-china-occupied-kashmir-srchinoy-131120. Accessed on 15 March 2021.

[20]Nyanima Basu, 'Creating Ladakh UT, Amit Shah's Aksai Chin Remarks Got China's Attention', *The Print*, 18 July 2020, https://theprint.in/india/creating-ladakh-ut-amit-shahs-aksai-chin-remarks-got-chinas-attention-says-mit-professor/463669/. Accessed on 15 March 2021.

[21]Sudha Ramachandran, 'India-China Relations: From the Wuhan Spirit to the Chennai Connect', *Jamestown*, https://jamestown.org/program/india-china-relations-from-the-wuhan-spirit-to-the-chennai-connect/. Accessed on 15 March 2021.

The press release of the Mamallapuram summit devoted only a paragraph to the subject, speaking on the need to strengthen the CBMs. Para 16 of the joint statement stated as follows:

> The two leaders have exchanged views on outstanding issues, including on the boundary question. They have welcomed the work of the Special Representatives and urged them to continue their efforts to arrive at a mutually-agreed framework for a fair, reasonable and mutually acceptable settlement based on Political Parameters and Guiding Principles that were agreed by the two sides in 2005. They reiterated their understanding that efforts will continue to be made to ensure peace and tranquillity in the border areas, and that both sides will continue to work on additional Confidence Building Measures in pursuit of this objective.[22]

The writing on the wall was clear. Wuhan and Mamallapuram provided us with the limits of informal summitry. Based on the personality of the two men, the summits relied on symbolism, optics and woolly assertions of civilizational relations. Happily isolated from the bureaucratic or military talks, the Modi-Xi meetings were mere distractions from the prickly deadlock on border conflicts. But it worked well for both leaders. For Modi, because he could not have been seen as making no attempts to resolve the border issue. For Xi, because bonhomie offered an appropriate cover for aggression along the LAC. Additionally, the informal summitry took away from the relationship both established foreign office institutionalism and, more importantly, public accountability of the government that is the sine qua non of every democratic dispensation's interaction on questions that have a profound bearing on both national security and stability.

The clashes in Galwan that would follow the Mamallapuram summit would be a testimony to the fact that these informal summits

---

[22]Manoj Joshi, 'Sino-Indian Border Deadlock: Time to Rewrite India Playbook', *ORF Occasional Paper 269*, 2020.

created a false sense of security, the foundations of which were grounded in quicksand. They only depended on a veneer of mere optics.

GALWAN: BEGINNING OF THE NEW NORMAL

On 24 March 2020, at a four-hour notice, India was thrust into a draconian lockdown to contain the spread of COVID-19, a Chinese export to the world. A day prior to that, India had only 433 confirmed cases and seven deaths.[23] Barely three weeks later, the news broke that China, under the cover of a military exercise, had moved across a broad front and illegally occupied territory that India claims as its own in eastern Ladakh. This led to the most medieval kind of jousting between the two armies with the worst clash taking place in the Galwan Valley.

The Galwan River, from China's side of the LAC flows west into the Ladakh region, where it converges with the Shyok River on India's side of the LAC. The Shyok River and the Darbuk-Shyok-Daulat Beg Oldi (DSDBO) road, a crucial motorway from the tactical perspective, made operational in 2019 connecting India's northernmost areas, lies to its west.

The preponderance of maps issued by China erroneously depict significant portions of the Galwan River abut its border line. China asserts that the LAC cuts right across the Galwan curve, where it then pivots to converge with the 'Y-Nallah' called Shyok.

Nonetheless, the PLA commenced transgressing across the LAC from the early part of May 2020.

It started opposing any Indian maneuvers east of the Y-Nallah. The Indian stance was unequivocal. Beijing was obtusely and suo-

---

[23]Deepak Nagpal, 'Coronavirus New Cases in India: 433 Confirmed COVID-19 Cases, 7 Deaths, 402 Active Cases as on March 23, 6 pm', *Times Now*, 23 March 2020, https://www.timesnownews.com/india/article/coronavirus-new-cases-in-india-confirmed-covid-19-cases-death-active-cases-as-on-march-23-6-pm/568388. Accessed on 15 March 2021.

moto attempting to alter the LAC in a bid to synchronize it with the position that they had wrongly delineated on their maps. Doing so was in complete violation of the key and cardinal principles of all preceding covenants. To add insult to injury, the Chinese simply declared that 'China's traditional customary boundary is in line with the LAC' on the northern bank of the Pangong Tso lake.[24] This is again not true. Indian and Chinese patrolling patterns have existed for the past 50 years. But it is this very ambiguity—the fact that the LAC has not been clarified yet—that the Chinese leveraged to cross the LAC.

Since 5 May 2020, violent melees, face-offs and skirmishes started taking place between Chinese and Indian troops at myriad spots, including and not limited to the Pangong-Tso Lake Finger areas and other locations even along Sikkim's border with the TAR. There were additional clashes at other locations in eastern Ladakh along the LAC. However, it was the events of 15–16 June 2020 which transformed what was limited to jostling and jousting into a dead serious conflagration.

In the Galwan Valley, alarming reports began flowing in from Indian Army sources that a violent conflict had unfolded. It started with an Indian patrol discovering a Chinese tent still standing on India's side of the LAC. A conflict over the tent escalated into a brawl and according to Indian officials, the Chinese dispatched a large number of troops in a premeditated assault to attack a vastly outnumbered Indian patrol. Most of the Chinese soldiers were armed with iron rods and nail-studded batons, a somewhat cynical workaround the firearms rule observed since the 1975 Tulung La ambush.[25] Twenty Indian soldiers lost their lives along with five Chinese soldiers. (This is according to Chinese official reports. There is absolutely no way of confirming if four or five casualties is indeed what the PLA suffered in Galwan.) It was the worst violence on the border since 1967. All

---

[24]Ananth Krishnan, *India's China Challenge: A Journey through China's Rise and What It Means for India*, HarperCollins India, 2020.
[25]Ibid.

at once, it shattered decades of hard-won peace.

This would mark what would be the beginning of the longest India-China stand-off in the post-Cold War era. At the peak of the crisis, nearly 100,000 troops from the Indian Army and PLA stood mobilized and forward deployed along the disputed border of the Western Sector. With China unilaterally trying to alter the status quo, this was the fait accompli that many had feared.

Foreign ministers of both the countries met in September 2020 on the sidelines of the SCO meeting in Moscow and reached a five-point agreement. The Indian media was quick in declaring this a victory and finally a restoration of peace—a premature declaration of triumph—as any kind of tangible settlement was still at least five months away.

With Indian troops occupying the heights overlooking the south bank of Pangong Tso by September 2020, it provided a bargaining chip to New Delhi. A counter-intrusion immediately after multiple encroachments by the Chinese over the years—be it Chumar in 2014, Depsang a year earlier in 2013 or even ones before that—sent a salutary message to the Chinese that the shoe would not always remain on the same foot. However, the restoration of status quo ante was even more challenging this time around as the stand-off continued, with clashes taking place even in Naku La in north Sikkim on 20 January 2021.

Military purchases were fast tracked. They included emergency procurement of 12 Sukhoi Su-30MKI and 21 Mikoyan MiG-29 fighter aircrafts from Russia, and emergency purchases of winter clothing from the US. Every source, however diverse, was tapped.[26]

The Chinese had once again demonstrated marked deftness in land-grab enabled by sharp military action, assisted by information war, psychological warfare and AI-enabled military platforms.

---

[26]Shekhar Gupta, 'Modi's Bid to Sway China's Xi with Personal Outreach Was a Big Error. India's Paying for It', *The Print*, 18 July 2020, https://theprint.in/national-interest/old-obsessions-electoral-politics-why-modi-govts-strategic-policy-is-a-glass-only-half-full/463310/. Accessed on 15 March 2021.

THE DISENGAMENT AGREEMENT

On 11 February 2021, more than 10 months after the clashes in eastern Ladakh had commenced, Defence Minister Rajnath Singh told Parliament that sustained military-to-military talks had led to an agreement to disengage on the north and south banks of the Pangong Lake. He clearly underscored that 'we have not conceded anything.'[27]

The crux of the agreement was as follows: first, disengagement would be limited to the North and South Bank of Pangong Tso Lake in eastern Ladakh. It would not encompass other flashpoints. The statement made by the defence minister implicitly implied that disengagement at all other points would continue to remain the focus of discussions with the Chinese. The exact formulation in his statement being: 'The House should also know that there are still some outstanding issues with regard to deployment and patrolling at some other points along the LAC in eastern Ladakh. These will be the focus of further discussions with the Chinese side.'[28]

Second, the Chinese would keep their troops to the east of Finger 8 and the Indians would remain at their permanent base at the Dhan Singh Thapa Post near Finger 3. It meant that India would have to give up its sovereign rights to patrol over its claimed territory up till Finger 8. Hopefully, this will be a transitory situation with patrolling rights being restored over a period of time.

Third, 'any structures that had been built by both sides since April 2020 on both the north and south banks would be removed and landforms will be restored.'[29]

---

[27]The Print Team, 'Full Text of Rajnath Singh's Statement in Rajya Sabha on India, China Disengagement', The Print, 11 February 2021, https://theprint.in/defence/full-text-of-rajnath-singhs-statement-in-rajya-sabha-on-india-china-disengagement/603056/. Accessed on 15 March 2021.

[28]Ibid.

[29]'Defence Minister of India Rajnath Singh's Statement in Rajya Sabha on "Present Situation in eastern Ladakh", https://www.rajnathsingh.in/speeches-in-english/raksha-mantri-shri-rajnath-singhs-statement-in-rajya-sabha-on-present-situation-

The disagreement in essence meant that India would have to surrender its sole bargaining chip by vacating the heights on the south bank of Pangong Lake or the Kailash range.

This agreement could hardly be termed as a negotiating triumph. By agreeing to restrict itself to Finger 3 and not patrol up to Finger 8, the farthermost point of its LAC claim, at least temporarily, India seems to have acquiesced to the classic Chinese shuffle—two steps forward, one step back. It should not end up leaving China with a net gain in terms of territory over time.

Additionally, this disengagement agreement, as of 17 March 2021, has yet to agree on withdrawal from the other flashpoints, including the Depsang plains. The Chinese have a strategic interest in the Depsang plains given both its location and terrain. Even the sole bargaining chip that India had in terms of the heights it was occupying on the Kailash range, vital even for the defence of Chushul Valley, had to be traded in. Thus, there is no real leverage available to India now were the push come to a shove again. With China and India now agreeing to disengage in Gogra, the focus would now move to Hot Springs but the real litmus test is Depsang plains. The Chinese stubbornly and trenchantly refuse to discuss this inflection point that is of immense strategic and tactical value for India for myriad reasons.[30]

Any Chinese withdrawal must be taken with a pinch of salt always. Lt Gen. Rana Pratap Kalita, former general officer commanding (GOC) of the Dimapur-based 3 Corps, opined in an interview, 'We are already seeing massive infrastructure development in Tibet opposite the Eastern Sector, which is an indication of things to come in the future.'[31] It is therefore hard to say how long the Chinese

in-eastern-ladakh/. Accessed on 15 March 2021.

[30]Sudha Ramachandran, 'Indian and Chinese Troops Disengage from Gogra', *The Diplomat*, 8 August 2021, https://thediplomat.com/2021/08/indian-and-chinese-troops-disengage-from-gogra/. Accessed on 15 September 2021.

[31]Prabin Kalita Interviews Lt Gen. Rana Pratap Kalita, *The Times of India,* 16 February 2021, https://timesofindia.indiatimes.com/blogs/the-interviews-blog/we-are-already-seeing-massive-infrastructure-development-in-tibet-opposite-the-eastern-

side will abide by the current terms, after having seen the utility of transgressions in pushing the envelope.

While all of this continues, Indian strategic circles have started considering a two-front situation as a very real possibility. It would be nothing short of extraordinary, if given the decades of Sino-Pakistan bonhomie, India is still unprepared to surmount such a possibility.

UNDERSTANDING THE CHINESE MOTIVE

'Objective not to occupy territory, but to paralyse the adversary.'[32]

Why did China do what it did? While the true motivation and intent is yet unknown, there are several factors that might have influenced Chinese behaviour along the LAC. From the point of view of China, the reactivation of the landing grounds and the completion last year of the DSDBO road that runs in this area, more or less parallel to the LAC, significantly enhances India's leverage in the local balance of power and enhances its capabilities to operate across the LAC. Although this construction activity lies on the Indian side of the LAC, China probably considers it to be a threat to its position on the LAC and perhaps its stability.

The coronavirus pandemic and the deteriorating US-China relationship have led to growing insecurity within the CCP leadership. China feels that it must take a hard line anywhere it sees its sovereignty being challenged, given Xi Jinping's uncompromising commentary to protect Chinese sovereignty, especially if Beijing feels that others may perceive it as weak or distracted by the coronavirus pandemic and its economic aftershocks. This is true not only regarding the border with India today, but also its assertiveness qua Taiwan, Hong Kong and in the South China Sea.

It is possible that similar crises are bound to recur with the LAC

sector-indicators-of-things-to-come/. Accessed on 15 March 2021.
[32]Ananth Krishnan, *India's China Challenge: A Journey through China's Rise and What It Means for India*, HarperCollins India, 2020.

continuing to remain un-demarcated and disputed. Moreover, the Aksai Chin region remains a coveted piece of real estate for China when juxtaposed against the historical backdrop and the PLA's resolve to preserve its security in the Western Sector of the border between India and China. This is because the only direct road link (National Highway G219) between the Xinjiang Uyghur Autonomous Region of China and the TAR is provided by Aksai Chin. China will have to rely on G219 for access, in case of major unrest in either of these areas which is home to millions of ethnic minorities—in other words, losing Aksai Chin will jeopardize the security of the entire western frontier of China.[33]

China has already started solidifying its presence along its border, as evidenced by the integration of its armed forces into five theatre commands. It is globally expansionist, as demonstrated by its multimillion-dollar Belt and Road Initiative (BRI)—the Silk Road of the twenty-first century and debt diplomacy.

Strategically, India would be strangulated if its neighbours begin using Beijing as leverage against New Delhi. In fact, the second Belt and Road Forum in 2019 was attended by 40 member countries including delegates from Moscow and Islamabad. 'With the possibility of connecting 65 countries, representing 55 per cent of world's Gross National Product, 70 per cent of population and 75 per cent of energy resources, Yidai Yilu, in Chinese, or BRI in English, is one of the top priorities of Xi Jinping's leadership.'[34]

While the move to stay out of the BRI is a strategic compulsion for India, it remains to be seen how the US, the Blue Dot Network and the Quad counter the BRI. There is a need for sturdy policies that transcend domestic political implications, looking not just at

[33]Zorawar D. Singh, *Powershift: India-China Relations in a Multipolar World*, Pan Macmillan India, 2020.

[34]Captain T. Sugreev, 'The Belt and Road Initiative of China: Security Implications for India and the Indo Pacific Region and Response Strategies', *The United Service Institution of India*, https://usiofindia.org/publication/usi-journal/the-belt-and-road-initiative-of-china-security-implications-for-india-and-the-indo-pacific-region-and-response-strategies/. Accessed on 15 March 2021.

the aftermath of the Galwan clashes but also the tail risks that we are missing out. China's intelligence gathering through complex internet models, combined with its multipoint information gathering approach, termed by many as the 'thousand grains of sand' approach, are challenges that India seems just not ready for. It should not take another Kargil for India to understand the security implications of fourth generational warfare. India needs to understand that it can no longer afford to go soft on China—the Wuhan spirit is long dead.

WAY FORWARD: NEED FOR A NEW MODUS VIVENDI

Despite the disengagement agreement at eastern Ladakh, one thing is clear: there is no going back to the situations that subsisted post the CBM agreements. The 1993, 1996, 2005 and 2013 agreements have been rendered virtually redundant. The LAC remains un-clarified, and the final settlement remains in limbo. It would be instructive to note that even when China was at its weakest, historically speaking, it had rejected both the McCartney-MacDonald Line and the McMahon Line.

If the fundamental postulates of Chinese policy qua India have changed, New Delhi too must recalibrate its own thinking. It cannot allow Beijing's policy of stabilizing and destabilizing the border at will to perpetuate its own ends. Global historical experience suggests that more sensitive border control systems have evolved after major border crises.

The 2020 Ladakh crisis should give rise to a similar sensitivity from both Delhi and Beijing. Both sides should speed up work to conclude new CBMs to preserve and strengthen stability and tranquillity in border areas. Until then, India needs to increase its spending on defence after six years of waffling. The NDA government could learn from its own predecessors—the Vajpayee-Brajesh Mishra doctrine, that stated, 'for coercive diplomacy to work, the threat of war had to be so real, even we would believe it was for real.'

UNCANNY PARALLELS: 1962 AND 2020

As I have argued elsewhere,[35] a difference of 58 years divides the 1962 Sino-India border war and the current developments playing out between India and China in the high Himalayas. However, the parallels are spooky.

Spectre of Betrayal

India became independent in 1947 and the Chinese Communist state was established in 1949. The two Asian subcontinents, emerging from a devastating World War and rapacious imperialism, began charting their own respective destinies in a world where colonialism was in full retreat across Asia, Africa, Latin and South America. The respective helmsman of India and China—Nehru and Mao Tse-tung—were both fierce patriots and men of global stature.

The '50s saw a great bonhomie between India and China—the Panchsheel Agreement was signed on 29 April 1954. While the historical record on whether India gave up its UN Security Council seat for China is fuzzy, Nehru's biographer Sarvepalli Gopal in 1979 wrote: 'He (Jawaharlal Nehru) rejected the Soviet offer to propose India as the sixth permanent member of the Security Council and insisted that priority be given to China's admission to the UN.'[36] Whether the offer of the US followed by the USSR was serious or a dud to create a divide between India and China, the jury is still out. The fact, however, remains that India was not ready to break with China even if a seat on the UN Security Council was the bait.

There was that niggling issue about unsettled boundaries

---

[35]Manish Tewari, 'India-China in 1962 and 2020: Uncanny Parallels but Difference in Leadership Is a Telling', *Outlook* India, 27 July 2020, https://www.outlookindia.com/website/story/opinion-india-china-in-1962-and-2020-uncanny-parallels-but-disparity-in-leadership-is-a-telling/357484. Accessed on 15 March 2021.

[36]Anton Harder, 'When Nehru Refused American Bait on a Permanent Seat for India at the UN', *The Wire,* 14 March 2019, https://thewire.in/diplomacy/when-nehru-refused-american-bait-on-a-permanent-seat-for-india-at-the-un. Accessed on 15 March 2021.

between the inheritors of British India and Imperial China on which negotiations were underway between Chou En-lai and Nehru personally right up till 1961. However, this bonhomie did not stop the Chinese from invading India in October 1962.

Mirror this to what happened between Xi and Modi. After becoming the prime minister, Modi met Xi no less than 18 times in six years, including two record informal summits in Wuhan and Mamallapuram. Modi also visited China four times as Gujarat chief minister and perhaps a couple of times as a BJP functionary before that. But what did the PM get in return is Doklam in 2017 and the theatre-level incursions playing out currently in quick succession. Given that Bhutan's security is guaranteed by India, Doklam was the payback for the boycott of the BRI conference by Bhutan and India in May 2017.

While Nehru, in the years of innocence of the Indian republic, should be excused of being waylaid by the Chinese guile, nations are supposed to have an institutional memory. Why was Prime Minister Modi led up the garden path by the Chinese 58 years later?

Ghost of Intelligence Failure

During 1955–7, Indian sleuths completely missed the construction of the Xinjiang-Tibet Highway. It was only on 31 August 1959 that Nehru informed the Rajya Sabha,

> According to an announcement made in China, the Yehcheng-Gartok Road, which is also called the Sinkiang-Tibet Highway, was completed in September 1957... Two reconnaissance parties were accordingly sent last year. One of these parties was taken into custody by a superior Chinese detachment. The other returned and gave us some rough indication of this newly constructed road in the Aksai Chin area.[37]

---

[37]Rakesh Sinha, 'History Headline: Aksai Chin, from Nehru to Shah', *The Indian Express*, 18 August 2019, https://indianexpress.com/article/opinion/columns/aksai-chin-from-nehru-to-amit-shah-china-karakoram-great-game-5913508/. Accessed on 15 March 2021.

Similarly, the Forward Policy was a product of bad advice by B.N. Malik, then director, Intelligence Bureau, supported by Lt General B.M. Kaul, then chief of the general staff, contrary to the counsel given by the military intelligence.

Compare this with 2020. Eminent strategic commentator Saikat Datta wrote in a piece in the *Deccan Chronicle*,

> In October last year a senior Indian security official on a visit to Ladakh met the General Officer Commanding (GOC) of the Indian Army's 14 Corps. The Corps was raised in the aftermath of the Kargil war between India and Pakistan in 1999 and has its headquarters in Leh...The Indian security official gave a detailed briefing to the Lieutenant General Harinder Singh, a former Director General of Military Intelligence, who took over as the GOC of 14 Corps late last year. The Indian security official explained that the change of the status of Jammu & Kashmir had irked the Chinese. In the coming months they would up the ante and try to capture more land and shift the LAC deeper into Indian-held territory...[38]

While in 1957-9, the instruments of intelligence collection were rudimentary and limited to human intelligence, as Nehru pointed out in his intervention to the Rajya Sabha; six decades later, with all the sophisticated technical assets at our disposal, how did we miss the Chinese military build-up in the western Himalayas? Who bears responsibility for this massive failure?

Apparition of Military Failure

On 23 May 2001, Neville Maxwell, author of *India's China War*, placed the tactical responsibility for the debacle as follows. In an article on rediff.com, Maxwell wrote,

---

[38]Saikat Datta, 'Chinese Intrusions and India's Limited Options', *The Deccan Chronicle*, 18 June 2020, https://www.deccanchronicle.com/opinion/columnists/180620/chinese-intrusions-and-indias-limited-options.html. Accessed on 15 March 2021.

HB/B [Henderson Brooks-Bhagat report that went into the causes of the 1962 defeat] place the immediate cause of the collapse of resistance in NEFA in the panicky, fumbling and contradictory orders issued from Corps HQ in Tezpur by a 'triumvirate' of officers they judge to be grossly culpable: General Sen, General Kaul, and Brigadier Palit.[39]

At the higher defence management level, COAS General P.N. Thapar and Defence Minister Krishna Menon had to resign taking responsibility for the debacle. Even Nehru came in for withering criticism for his idealistic foreign policy predilections.

Compare this with the situation today. At least 144 veterans of the armed forces in a signed letter to the PM wrote: 'The incident at Galwan could only have happened because of failure at one or more levels in the political, civil and military establishments, especially in continuous intelligence acquisition and dissemination.'[40] They demanded that a fact-finding commission be constituted and its report be tabled in the Lok Sabha.

The fundamental question remains: can and should the service brass and the political leadership escape from responsibility for these theatre-level incursions? Don't these questions still demand cogent answers?

The Solace of Redemption

In both 1962 and 2020, our deliverance lay in the grit and bravery of the Indian Army. At Rezang La, on 18 November 1962, 13 Kumaon Regiment, under the command of Major Shaitan Singh Bhati, made their last stand. Each man fought to the last bullet before embracing

---

[39]Manish Tewari, 'India-China In 1962 And 2020: Uncanny Parallels But Difference In Leadership Is A Telling' *Outlook India*, 27 July 2020, https://www.outlookindia.com/website/story/opinion-india-china-in-1962-and-2020-uncanny-parallels-but-disparity-in-leadership-is-a-telling/357484. Accessed on 15 March 2021.
[40]The Wire Staff, 'The Wire, India-China Standoff: 144 Armed Forces Veterans Appeal for Accountability, Reforms', 9 July 2020, thttps://thewire.in/security/veterans-statement-ladakh-galwan-valley. Accessed on 15 March 2021.

martyrdom. Similarly, on 15–16 June 2020, 16 Bihar Regiment, led by Colonel Santosh Babu, though ambushed by an overwhelmingly superior force, bravely fought the Chinese aggressors with their bare hands, killing an unspecified number of PLA soldiers and losing 20 of their compatriots in turn. The unmatched valour of the Indian Army in 1962 is on display again as Indian and Chinese troops try and stare each other down.

Even the Headlines Are the Same

On 6 July 2020, India's former Foreign Secretary, Nirupama Menon Rao, shared a newspaper clipping from 15 July 1962 on Twitter, that stated: 'Chinese troops withdraw from Galwan post.'[41] (Three months and 14 days later, the Chinese invaded India on 20 October 1962.) The same day, a piece by another erudite strategic commentator, Pranab Dhal Samanta, appeared in *The Economic Times* titled 'First Signs of Chinese Withdrawal in Galwan; India and China to Issue Statements.'

This is where the similarities end. In 1962, Nehru did not try to cover up the Chinese betrayal. On 26 October 1962, Nehru accepted a young Vajpayee's demand and called a Parliament session on 8 November. He brusquely brushed aside L.M. Singhvi's suggestion that the House meet in a secret session. He said: 'The issues before the House are of high interest to the whole country. Right at the beginning to ask for a secret session would have a bad effect on the country.' Unfortunately, PM Modi did the exact opposite when at an all-party meeting on 19 June 2020 he declared 'not an inch of land has been occupied by anyone,' thereby squarely playing into the Chinese narrative of events. More than a year has passed since the commencement of the Chinese incursions and illegal occupation of our lands. Parliament till date has not had one single substantive discussion on the Chinese situation.

---

[41]Nirupama Menon Rao, Twitter, https://twitter.com/NMenonRao/status/1280148354681339904. Accessed on 15 March 2021.

History repeats itself, first as tragedy, second as farce: Karl Marx had warned in *The Eighteenth Brumaire of Louis Bonaparte* (though in a different context).

EIGHT

CDS: INTEGRATING CIVIL
AND MILITARY ECOSYSTEMS

On the last day of December 2019, the NDA government announced the appointment of a chief of defence staff (CDS), a numero uno position in the military hierarchy. In line with many western countries that have a unified command, India has decided to follow a similar path to ostensibly improve coordination among its forces. However, questions, concerns and issues remain.

Would India move towards a more autonomous military with lesser degree of civilian oversight? Should the civilian establishment be wary that its supremacy could be challenged in the future? Would the institution of CDS as a single-point military advisor to the government take away from the diversity of views currently available to the government? Can the CDS really catalyse greater jointness and more operational integration of the services?

Most of these questions can perhaps only be fully addressed after at least a decade or so has elapsed. The impact of this newly created position coupled with the rearrangement of relationships of authority within the military establishment would take that amount of time to fully manifest themselves. However, an interim and periodic assessment is equally vital given the nature of the position. Its daily impact on the armed forces and the dynamic vis-à-vis the civilian establishment are ever-evolving paradigms that may require concurrent course corrections, should the need ever arise.

India inherited both its armed forces and the Westminster

system of government from Imperial Britain. The Westminster system ordains both civilian oversight and control over the armed forces. However, many former colonies that attained independence from their colonial rulers around the same time as India did either fall under the jackboot of military rule, or even ended up as one-party totalitarian states. India has so far managed its civil-military relationship with a degree of sangfroid. To fully appreciate these dynamics, a historical perspective spanning over a century and a half is imperative.

ARMIES OF THE RAJ

The East India Company had set up its legions namely the Bengal Army, Madras Army and the Bombay Army to protect its commercial interests. In no time however, they also became the principal tool for attaining the overlordship of India.

The armed forces of the East India Company were then consolidated as the British Indian Army in 1858 after the Crown assumed charge of India from the East India Company. However, it was only in 1895 that the three armies could be fully amalgamated to create the Indian Army headed by a commander-in-chief.[1]

The war of independence in 1857 had changed British perspectives with regard to recruitment and management of the armed forces. Before 1857, it is noteworthy that the British Indian Army was primarily composed of upper-caste Hindus. The company was sensitive to both the rituals and dietary requirements of their troops. Even the community celebration of religious festivals was encouraged. The army therefore became more or less a homogenous entity. In 1830, the Adjutant General (AG) of the British Army, Colonel C. Fagan, had suggested that while Brahmin recruitment

---

[1]Syed Hussain Shaheed Soherwordi, "'Punjabisation" in the British Indian Army 1857-1947 and the Advent of Military Rule in Pakistan, *Edinburgh Papers in South Asian Studies,* http://www.csas.ed.ac.uk/__data/assets/pdf_file/0011/48674/WP24_ Shaheed_Hussain.pdf. Accessed on 15 March 2021.

may be continued, more soldiers should be enlisted from Rajput and Muslim communities to balance the increasing Brahminical dominance in the ranks of the armies.[2]

The real object of this structural shift in recruitment paradigms was that the 1857 uprising was led by the Sepoys of the Bengal Army. This had made the British government chary of recruiting from the usual stomping grounds from where the Bengal Army had been drafted.

The Jonathan Peel Commission (1859) was therefore given the responsibility of identifying social groups and communities from which loyal soldiers could be recruited. Thereafter, by the 1880s, the British began recruitment along caste lines by classifying certain communities as 'martial races', thereby implying that the rest were 'non-martial races'. The rationale used to justify this arbitrary pattern for recruitment was that certain communities are more 'battlefield friendly' than the rest.

The races categorized as martial were the Dogras, Pathans, Rajputs, Sikhs, Janjuas, Mahars, Garhwalis, Gujjars, Gorkhas, Gakhars, Ghumman, Khokhar, Jats, Kumaonis, Kodavas and Yadavs. As a consequence, very heavy recruitment into the British Indian Army started taking place from undivided Punjab and the North-West Frontier Province (NWFP), now in Pakistan, from around 1870.

This massive recruitment from Punjab has often been called 'Punjabisation of the Army'.[3] The great game between Britain and Russia had pushed the British government to secure the NWFP and Afghanistan. Recruiting soldiers from these areas also served this objective well. Courage was thus converted into a convenient racial quality rather than a personal trait.[4]

---

[2]G. Rand and K. Wagner, 'Recruiting the "Martial Races": Identities and Military Service in Colonial India', Patterns of Prejudice, 46 (3-4): 232-254, 2012.
[3]Santanu Das, 'Why Half a Million People from Punjab Enlisted to Fight for Britain in World War I', Quartz India, 19 October 2018, https://qz.com/india/1425486/british-indian-army-recruited-half-a-million-from-punjab-in-ww1/. Accessed on 15 March 2021.
[4]Aravind Ganachari, 'The British Used "Low-Caste" Indian Soldiers Only When WWI

All throughout WWI, Britain recruited heavily from the erstwhile undivided Punjab that stretched from Delhi to Rawalpindi and even beyond, right up to the Khyber Pass before 1901. As many as half a million men were recruited from the province. As per some historians, 50 per cent of these recruits were Punjabi Muslims, 36 per cent were Hindus, 12 per cent Sikhs and 1 or 2 per cent Christians. However, Sikhs had a larger proportion than Punjabi Muslims when it came to people being recruited upon the cusp of military age. Moreover, during WWI, 75,000 acres of land around the Lower Bari Doab Canal (in Punjab, Pakistan) alone was awarded on peasant conditions to the men who had distinguished themselves in various battles of WWI.[5]

There was a spike in recruitment during WWII with the numbers from Punjab crossing a million. 'Incentives for soldiers during the war had included the gifting of traditional swords, weapons that featured, along with all manner of homemade and ancient weapons, in the horror of communal violence.'[6] When the war ended in 1945, most of the recruits were demobilized and sent back to their respective villages. They were permitted to retain their weapons in most instances.[7] A British policeman remembered 'continually finding dumps of live grenades' in the countryside left by soldiers who had brought back 'souvenirs' from WWII.[8] The Partition of India followed in 1947. The worst-affected provinces were Punjab and Bengal. More than a million

Intensified, Rejected Them After', *The Print*, 21 February 2020, https://theprint.in/pageturner/excerpt/the-british-used-low-caste-indian-soldiers-only-when-wwi-intensified-rejected-them-after/369092/. Accessed on 15 March 2021.

[5]Manish Tewari, 'How Farm Laws Might Hurt National Security', *The Asian Age*, 12 October 2020, https://www.asianage.com/amp/opinion/columnists/121020/manish-tewari-how-farm-laws-might-hurt-national-security.html?cv=1. Accessed on 15 March 2021.

[6]Robin James Fitch-McCullough, 'Imperial Influence on the Postcolonial Indian Army, 1945–1973', *University of Vermont*, 2017.

[7]Sarah Ansari, 'How the Partition of India Happened—and Why Its Effects Are Still Felt Today', *The Conversation*, 10 August 2017, https://theconversation.com/how-the-partition-of-india-happened-and-why-its-effects-are-still-felt-today-81766. Accessed on 15 March 2021.

[8]Yasmin Khan, *The Great Partition: The Making of India and Pakistan*, Yale University Press, 2007.

innocents were slaughtered between July and September of 1947 in Punjab alone. This was the direct consequence of dismembering a heavily militarized region with no thought of its implications.

PAK ARMY'S STRATEGIC IMPORTANCE

In India, the military was brought under the control of an elected civilian government at the very commencement of nationhood. Unfortunately, in Pakistan, the military was impelled to owe its allegiance to an unelected governor general and not the elected prime minister or the civilian government.

Lawyer Aditya Sondhi explains this succinctly in an interview to a London School of Economics (LSE) blog in June 2014. He states,

> I think this is the strongest reason for the nature of civil-military relations in the two countries. Pakistan had her constitution after a lapse of close to six years, by which time her tallest leader, Jinnah, had passed away and power was vested in bureaucrats. The people had no direct say in governance and the future of their young country. This is a delicate phase in the making of the DNA of any country, and the absence of strong, democratic leaders led to the military being seen as the only institution that was sincere and nationalistic. The fatal error came from Prime Minister Khwaja Nazimuddin who invited the army under General Ayub Khan to quell sectarian riots in the Punjab province, permitting the army to dominate the political high table of its nation. India not only had strong civilian leaders at her birth with a leaning toward democratic practices, but also leaders who distrusted the army and saw it as a remnant of the Raj that had not involved itself in the freedom movement. The army has therefore been not 'politically relevant' since India's inception.[9]

---

[9]Aditya Sondhi, 'The Civilian-Military Balance: Why Institutional Relations in India and Pakistan Are Different', *LSE South Asia*, https://blogs.lse.ac.uk/southasia/2014/06/18/the-civilian-military-balance-why-institutional-relations-in-

In an opinion piece titled 'What India Owes to Nehru' for the *Dawn*, Pervez Hoodbhoy, a well-known Pakistani academic, opined as follows:

> Nehru must also be credited with keeping a lid on his generals. In a democracy, the army should be subordinate and answerable to civilian authority, not the other way around. And so, immediately after Partition, Nehru ordered the grand residence of the army chief to be vacated and instead assigned to the prime minister. This move carried huge symbolism—it said clearly who was boss. When Ayub Khan's coup across the border happened in 1958, it led to rules that further diminished the role of the Indian Army in national affairs. Gen Cariappa, who had retired but praised the coup, was told to refrain from making such observations. Officers, serving or retired, were strongly discouraged from commenting on matters related to public affairs and economics—and particularly their pensions and retirement benefits. There was no concept of army owned enterprises and businesses.[10]

In 1958, the military had staged its first coup in Pakistan. Since then, the country has witnessed a number of coups that have constantly challenged democracy and the civilian government. To this day, a very powerful military establishment and a deep state in Pakistan exercise vast control over both its governance structures and foreign policy. The ethnic base of recruitment was also responsible for alienation of Bengalis of East Pakistan as the Pakistani military was largely composed of Punjabis from West Pakistan. The resultant genocide that was perpetrated on the people of East Pakistan by the West Pakistani military can be catalogued as one of the worst military excesses, a war crime of gargantuan proportions in the post-WWII era.

---

india-and-pakistan-are-different/. Accessed on 15 March 2021.
[10]Pervez Hoodbhoy, 'What India Owes to Nehru', *Dawn*, 21 April 2018, https://www.dawn.com/news/1402940. Accessed on 15 March 2021.

EVOLVING CIVIL-MILITARY DYNAMIC

Strategic scholars ascribe many reasons for the civil-military dynamic institutionalized in India over the past seven decades whereby the civilian government has, till now, exercised supreme authority in the administration of the country, its foreign relations and the defence of the realm. One of them is the professional conduct of the British armed forces, of which the Indian troops were a part until 1947. As Aditya Sondhi again opines in the above-mentioned interview,

> A great deal of credit for the healthy civilian-military relations in India must go to the early generals, who were trained in the highest traditions of the British army to be professional soldiers. No more and no less. King George IV exempted his officers from drinking to his health or standing for the national anthem, as their loyalty could never be in doubt. This ethos has carried the Indian army forth, making it remain loyal to the civilian leadership of the day.[11]

The British government had a clear demarcation of authority when it came to the function of the military. Many erstwhile colonies like India had inherited these trained armies, however that did not translate into a harmonious civil-military equation everywhere. Many former colonies, such as Sierra Leone and Nigeria, were rocked by rather unpleasant situations.

That begs the question as to what was different in the Indian case, in addition to, of course, the ethos that was intrinsic to the British armed forces and became ingrained in the gene pool and the DNA of the Indian armed forces too.

A part of the answer lies in the initial composition of the then Government of India. It was mostly composed of leaders from the

---

[11]"The Civilian-Military Balance: Why Institutional Relations in India and Pakistan Are Different", LSE South Asia, https://blogs.lse.ac.uk/southasia/2014/06/18/the-civilian-military-balance-why-institutional-relations-in-india-and-pakistan-are-different/. Accessed on 15 March 2021.

INC that was more a diverse platform rather than just a political party in the conventional sense of the word. It was, therefore, better equipped to manage internal dissent in the country, as opposed to the Muslim League in Pakistan. The Muslim League, from the late 1930s right up to 1947, was an instrument of reaction patronized by the British to both split India and undermine the freedom struggle by injecting the vitriol of communalism into its very vitals. Moreover, the internal contradictions of India never ever reached a flashpoint that it could have impelled military generals to attempt a coup d'état.

Another part of the answer stems from the sterling discipline of the Indian armed forces right from the day of Independence in August 1947. A tradition flowed from the ethos of the British model of armed forces management. Senior officers have always set examples of conduct for succeeding generations to emulate. Notwithstanding his candour on certain issues, it was Field Marshal K.M. Cariappa who memorably had termed politics in the Army as poison and advised both officers and men alike to keep away from it.

This is not to say that civil-military relations have been entirely satisfactory over the decades. Back in the day, many military leaders were overt admirers of authoritarian administrations led by the army. General J.N. Chaudhuri had called General Ayub Khan's coup an effort to 'put things right'.[12] Hence, the effort to maintain civilian supremacy is an exercise in constant vigil.

A HISTORY OF CLASHES

Even though the armed forces have been proscribed from getting involved in politics in India, there still have been cases where military leaders have been fairly liberal with their opinions about matters political. A rough and ready barometer of deducing the tautness between the civilian government and the military leadership would

---

[12]Sushant Singh, 'Lessons From Nehru, Cariappa', *The Indian Express*, 10 May 2018, https://indianexpress.com/article/opinion/columns/lessons-from-jawaharlal-nehru-km-cariappa-pm-modi-speech-5170511/. Accessed on 15 March 2021.

be an assessment of the ups and downs in the relationship between the prime minister and the COAS. Both these positions are vested with the highest level of authority and functionality in each vertical, and therefore, it is the working equation between them that largely sets the tone of the civil-military relationship.

Prime Minister Nehru had to write to the then army chief, General (and later Field Marshal) K.M. Cariappa, to avoid articulating his opinions in the public domain. Cariappa had led the Indian Army with distinction during the war with Pakistan over J&K in 1947–8. He was a widely respected General.[13] However, after his retirement in 1953, he spoke several times about 'disbanding political parties and suspension of Parliament' to restore law and order in the country, reflecting his belief that the armed forces are better equipped to run the civilian administration.[14]

This trend continued well into the 1960s when he again suggested that Universal Adult Franchise should be replaced by allowing only literates to vote. Considering the state of education and literacy in India of those times, such a step would have meant grant of suffrage to a very limited population. That would not have been a representative democracy by any stretch of imagination.

One of the key inflection points in civil-military relations was the 1962 Sino-Indo border war. Much before the conflict turned kinetic, the then army chief, General K.S. Thimayya, had repeatedly flagged deficiencies in the battle preparedness of the Indian armed forces, especially qua China.[15] The defeat exposed the cracks in

[13]K.C. Mehta, 'Trust Our Generals, They Are Patriots', *The Hindu*, 12 July 2016, https://www.thehindu.com/opinion/open-page/trust-our-generals-they-are-patriots/article3436815.ece. Accessed on 15 March 2021.

[14]Sushant Singh, 'Lessons from Nehru, Cariappa', *The Indian Express*, 10 May 2018, https://indianexpress.com/article/opinion/columns/lessons-from-jawaharlal-nehru-km-cariappa-pm-modi-speech-5170511/. Accessed on 15 March 2021.

[15]Shekhar Gupta, 'The Saga of Krishna Menon and the Indian Army', *Hindustan Times*, 10 January 2020, https://www.hindustantimes.com/columns/the-saga-of-krishna-menon-and-the-indian-army/story-KKfqngk8ZukvoS1Zqn1QQL.html. Accessed on 15 March 2021.

civil-military relations like never before. The rather irascible style of Defence Minister V.K. Krishna Menon was greatly responsible for the disruption of this delicate relationship. The high commissioner of the UK to India from 1955–60, Malcolm MacDonald, had a close relationship with Thimayya, and the account of events that he sent to London outlines the more than prickly equation between the then defence minister and his army chief.

MacDonald's account reveals that Thimayya found Menon to be a grave impediment in executing his remit. Menon insistently painted Pakistan as the main enemy and largely ignored the Chinese threat. Menon's imperious attitude towards army officers made it difficult to work with him. He would continuously interfere in postings, promotions and transfers, motivated by his whims and fancies, totally ignoring the impact of such randomness on a highly hierarchical organization.[16] [17]

Apparently, Thimayya made substantial efforts to accommodate Menon's quirks, but when it became impossible to continue any further, he offered his resignation to the prime minister. PM Nehru talked Thimayya out of it and persuaded him to withdraw his resignation. The news of his resignation was, however, leaked to the media, and when Nehru spoke in Parliament, he acknowledged that he had persuaded Thimayya to withdraw his resignation. However, he 'spun' it off, and perhaps rightly so, given the rather delicate nature of the matter at hand, as more of a case of temperamental differences of the army chief with his immediate civilian superior rather than a disagreement on substantial issues.

Menon's penchant for playing favourites in the armed forces even extended to encouraging a few of his favoured generals to

[16]Karan Thapar, 'This Book Spills Secrets of a General & His Boss', *The Tribune*, 12 December 2019, https://www.tribuneindia.com/news/comment/this-book-spills-secrets-of-a-general-his-boss-8197. Accessed on 15 March 2021.

[17]Jairam Ramesh, 'Was Krishna Menon Thinking of a Coup Against Nehru? COAS Gen Thimayya Had Privately Said This', *The Print*, 13 January 2020, https://theprint.in/pageturner/excerpt/krishna-menon-thinking-of-coup-against-nehru-coas-thimayya-privately-said-this/348690/. Accessed on 15 March 2021.

malign the image of their peers and superiors. It, therefore, would not be incorrect to conclude that there was clearly a power struggle between the civilian and military dispensations whose crowning discord was the continuing spat between Thimayya and Menon.

It is believed that Thimayya had strong views on defence policy and wanted to accept Pakistani President Ayub Khan's offer of a joint defence arrangement. Nehru and, very likely, Menon were against the idea.[18] Menon also pushed for change of norms to ensure greater civilian control over the army. Thimayya naturally resented Menon's involvement in the day-to-day running of military affairs. Menon remained categorically opposed to creating the post of CDS that was floated and pushed by Lord Louis Mountbatten at that point in time.

The publicly available version of the *Henderson Brooks-Bhagat Report* that explored the causes of the debacle during the Sino-Indo border war in 1962, held the chief of general staff and later commander of the 4 Corps, Lt Gen. B.M. Kaul, director military operations, Brigadier D.K. Palit, director of the Intelligence Bureau, B.M. Mullick, Foreign Secretary M.J. Desai and Defence Minister Krishna Menon, responsible for the military defeat though the problems, as pointed out above, had commenced much earlier.[19]

The *Report* did not comment on the role played by PM Nehru and his army chief, General P.N. Thapar. The remit of the Henderson Brooks exercise was to examine the military aspects of the operation. This however did not mitigate the factum of the immediate resignation of General Thapar from the post of army chief on 22 November 1962, the day after China announced a ceasefire.

How much was PM Nehru responsible for the 1962 debacle?

[18]Shoaib Daniyal, 'Fact Check: Did Nehru Insult General Thimayya in 1948 after the Indo-Pak War, as Modi Claimed?' *Scroll.in*, 3 May 2018, https://scroll.in/article/877830/fact-check-did-nehru-insult-general-thimayya-in-1948-after-the-indo-pak-war-as-modi-claimed. Accessed on 15 March 2021.

[19]Manish Tewari, 'India-China in 1962 and 2020: Uncanny Parallels but Difference in Leadership Is a Telling', *Outlook*, 27 July 2020, https://www.outlookindia.com/website/story/opinion-india-china-in-1962-and-2020-uncanny-parallels-but-disparity-in-leadership-is-a-telling/357484. Accessed on 15 March 2021.

Nehru was a colossus, a world statesman, who rightly believed that Asia's time had finally arrived and therefore was loath to break with the Chinese while simultaneously believing that firmness on the border was essential to safeguard India's interests. However, there is near concord among defence policy experts that Nehru's Forward Policy was undoubtedly a strategic misstep. Nehru's fault, if any, lay in his implicit faith in Menon. He did not read the smoke signals that were rising repeatedly from the defence establishment that things in the higher defence management were going horribly wrong.

A prime minister must trust his cabinet colleagues, but where the behaviour of one of them undermines the basic tenets of both organizational synchronicity and personnel management, especially in highly hierarchal and tightly structured establishments, the PM must not hesitate to wade in. Nehru was perhaps culpable only to that extent and not anymore.

For some strange reason, the *Henderson Brooks-Bhagat Report* remains classified 59 years later. Its declassification, including pages 112–57 that are not in the public domain, would help in understanding the contours of civil-military relations and its impact on higher defence management better during a critical period when the Republic was still consolidating.

PREPARING FOR 1971

The defeat of 1962 has had a debilitating impact on the psyche of the Indian state. It cast a doubt on the capability of India to defend its sovereignty. However, by the time India fought the 1971 war, the state of the civil-military relationship had improved substantially. Prime Minister Indira Gandhi and the army chief General S.H.F.J (Sam) Manekshaw had mutual respect for each other. Moreover, PM Gandhi was not averse to deferring to the judgement of her army chief on matters military.

When PM Gandhi asked Sam Manekshaw whether India was ready to go to war with Pakistan to stop the genocide in East Pakistan, he demurred and asked for a couple of months more to get the army into a state of battle readiness. She accepted his professional judgement.[20] With the creation of Bangladesh, 1971 became the year after 1947 when the political map of South Asia stood redrawn again.

However, Manekshaw too had a penchant for talking out of turn that became a source of embarrassment for both himself and the government at times. Once he jocularly told a reporter that if he had taken up Pakistan's offer to join its army in 1947, the results of the 1971 war would have been different.[21] It obviously did not go down well with the government of the day.

Even though Manekshaw always accepted and deferred to the supremacy of the civilian political leadership, C. Uday Bhaskar, a distinguished strategic commentator, wrote on Manekshaw's demise that he acquired for himself the reputation of being a totally apolitical professional solider who could not be pushed around by the civilian establishment.[22]

One can observe a sea change in the relationship between the Indian civilian and military leadership between the two wars. On one hand, Menon had an increasingly difficult working relationship with Thimayya and did not receive or was not receptive to candid military advice from General Thimayya's successor or other generals whose advise he should have actively solicited in the lead up to the 1962 conflict. This majorly contributed to the lack of battle readiness and the subsequent reverses.

On the other hand, the sound understanding between PM Gandhi

[20]Rahul Bhonsle, 'When Jagjivan Ram Played Moderator between Indira Gandhi and Sam Manekshaw in 1971', News18, 5 April 2019, https://www.news18.com/news/india/when-jagjivan-ram-played-moderator-between-indira-gandhi-and-sam-manekshaw-in-1971-2091061.html. Accessed on 15 March 2021.

[21]Achyut Mishra, 'Sam Manekshaw, the General Who Told Indira When Indian Army Wasn't Ready for a War', The Print, 27 June 2019, https://theprint.in/theprint-profile/sam-manekshaw-the-general-who-told-indira-when-indian-army-wasnt-ready-for-a-war/254796/. Accessed on 15 March 2021.

[22]C. Uday Bhaskar, 'A Legend in Uniform', Frontline, 1 August 2008, https://frontline.thehindu.com/other/obituary/article30196947.ece. Accessed on 15 March 2021.

and General Manekshaw, and for that matter Defence Minister Jagjivan Ram in 1971, was a consequence of the lessons learnt during the 1962 debacle. Harmonious civil-military relationship became the sine qua non for the success of 1971.

UNSETTLING TIMES?

However, there were several events that affected this relationship. These episodes should not ever be taken for granted. For more than just personality differences, they perhaps are a reflection of the institutional supremacy of the civilian establishment over the military not having yet fully ripened in India.

Lt Gen. S.K. Sinha was one of the most senior military officers in service during the 1971–7 tenure of the Congress government. He had served in the British Indian Army during WWII. He had worked closely with Manekshaw and former Pakistan President Yahya Khan in the Indian Army before Independence. He was also close to leaders like Nehru and Patel. Even though Sinha was supposed to be the army chief in 1983 when Gen. K.V. Krishna Rao retired, the government chose Gen. A.S. Vaidya to succeed Gen. Krishna Rao. Gen. Vaidya was junior to Gen. Sinha. The government claimed that the reason for supersession was Sinha's lack of active service during the war years. However, it was widely speculated that the supersession was because of the government's disapproval of his activism within the forces, particularly his advocacy of soldiers' rights, perks, status, etc. Sinha did the honourable thing. He resigned from service.[23]

The strain in civil-military relations was never as bad as it got during the Vajpayee administration in 1998, which resulted in the controversial and, as considered by many, unnecessary dismissal of

---

[23]Sushant Singh, 'Lt Gen S K Sinha (1926-2016): The Lieutenant General Who Could Not Be Army Chief', *The Indian Express*, 18 November 2016, https://indianexpress.com/article/india/india-news-india/lieutenant-general-s-k-sinha-dead-governor-jk-assam-army-chief-indira-gandhi-4381197/. Accessed on 15 March 2021.

the Chief of Naval Staff (CNS), Admiral Vishnu Bhagwat—a first in the history of independent India when the government resorted to such an extreme step. Hopefully, it would be the last.

A lot of dramatic prose has been woven around Bhagwat's dismissal from office. Comparisons were drawn with the Dreyfus affair in France during the nineteenth century and even General Douglas MacArthur's dismissal by the Harry Truman administration in 1951.

The public record states that the government's dissatisfaction with Bhagwat largely stemmed from two things—his comments on the Sagarika anti-ship missile project and divulgence of details on the undercover Operation Leech in the Andaman and Nicobar Islands.[24] He had also ostensibly violated protocol in communicating directly with the Pakistan High Commission after an incident relating to naval air space violation. Very often, he would also take internal military disputes to the court[25] and that had added to the displeasure of the MoD.

On 1 December 1998, he had told reporters, 'We have no project called Sagarika,' adding that the truth was that the navy was developing a short-range anti-ship weapon system. 'At the moment all other speculations are wrong,' he stated.[26]

Operation Leech was an ignominious if not murky chapter that did not cover those involved with any glory. The story collated from various publicly available reports suggests that on the night of 8 February 1998, activists of an organization called Arakan Army, led by one Khaing Raza, commenced their journey from the Thai-Myanmar border in vessels carrying arms. The boats laden

---

[24]Manoj Joshi and Prabhu Chawla, 'Naval chief Admiral Vishnu Bhagwat sacked for "defiance of civilian authority"', *India Today*, 11 January 1999, https://www.indiatoday.in/magazine/cover-story/story/19990111-naval-chief-admiral-vishnu-bhagwat-sacked-for-defiance-of-civilian-authority-779870-1999-01-11.   Accessed on 28 July 2021.

[25]Ibid.

[26]'Prithvi to Find Naval Platforms on Republic Day', *Rediff*, 1 December 1998, https://www.rediff.com/news/1998/dec/01navy.htm. Accessed on 15 March 2021.

with weapons were to first break journey at the Landfall Island situated in the archipelago of Andaman and Nicobar. The plan was to then move to Cox's Bazar in Bangladesh. The final recipient of the arms was their Myanmar-based militia. On 9 February, the insurrectionists paused at the Narcondam Island and continued their journey towards Landfall Island. On 10 February, the rebels were informed that Saw Tun, an activist of the Arakan militia, was in touch with certain Indian officials. On reaching Landfall Island, the militants were arrested, their boats sequestered and arms commandeered.

Of the 73 persons detained, 35 asserted that they were mere fisher folk. They were released after a year in detention. Two of the detainees maintained that they were nationals of Thailand and were engaged in the business of seafaring. They were released, while two more ostensibly tried to get away. These two were categorized, to use a rather military expression, as Absent Without Leave (AWOL). The remaining 34 were interned in Indian prisons for nearly 13 long years until they were finally released in 2011.

While they were in custody, the prisoners kept affirming that they were cadres of the Karen National Union (KNU) and the National Unity Party of Arakan (NUPA). They presented themselves as dissenters who were waging a struggle for democracy against the military Junta of Myanmar. The militiamen vociferously and unequivocally kept alleging that they were entrapped in a game of smoke and mirrors. They had claimed to have been guaranteed protection and sanctuary by certain unidentified Indian spooks but were allegedly duped by an officer who seemingly held himself out as an Intelligence officer with the Armed Forces.

Quixotically, the 34 men incarcerated and charged walked free on 20 May 2011 as the CBI was unable to substantiate the charges against them. Granted refugee status by the United Nations High Commissioner for Refugees (UNHCR), they were later relocated to the Netherlands.

Much has been written about the smoke and mirrors nature of

this episode, but at that point in time, it became a bone of contention between Defence Minister George Fernandes and Admiral Vishnu Bhagwat.[27]

Other points of contention between the government and the Naval Chief included staffing issues. The Appointments Committee of the cabinet had rejected the CNS's recommendations for Deputy Chief of Naval Staff (DCNS), compelling Bhagwat to argue that it was incorrect to do so. Bhagwat asserted that politicians with no direct experience of the staffing patterns unique to the armed forces were remiss to disregard recommendations from the forces. The Naval Chief was also reluctant to accept the supremacy of the defence secretary. Bhagwat apparently refused to implement the order which had cleared Vice Admiral Harinder Singh's name for the post of DCNS.

The dismissal of the CNS was a cataclysmic event. Admiral Bhagwat's wife, Niloufer Bhagwat, an eminent lawyer, characterized the government's action as a 'communal' design. It was condemned by the Opposition and strategic thinkers who argued that it had set a bad precedent.[28] The defence secretary was also concurrently transferred to the Department of Industrial Policy and Promotion.

Two decades later, questions remain. Were Admiral Bhagwat's alleged indiscretions so grave in nature that they warranted his dismissal from service? Was it a case of extreme heavy handedness by a government that otherwise had seasoned politicians in its ranks? The latter seems definitely to be the case.

There are always ways of handling delicate situations in an elegant manner. Presuming that the government in its wisdom was convinced that Admiral Bhagwat was overreaching his remit and therefore

[27]Ritu Sarin, 'Operation Leech - George vs Bhagwat', *The Indian Express*, 10 May 1999, https://indianexpress.com/article/news-archive/operation-leech-george-vs-bhagwat-the-inside-story/. Accessed on 15 March 2021.

[28]D.P. Satish, 'Admiral Bhagwat to Admiral Joshi, Bad 15 years for Indian Navy', *News18*, 26 February 2014, https://www.news18.com/news/india/admiral-bhagwat-to-admiral-joshi-bad-15-years-for-indian-navy-670879.html. Accessed on 15 March 2021.

needed to be chastened, they could have given him the option of either resigning or could have given him some gubernatorial or diplomatic assignment with the explicit understanding that bygones would be bygones as long as there are no public recriminations.

Something as draconian and humiliating as what was handed over to him on 30 December 1998 as he prepared to leave his office for the day could certainly have been eschewed. Admiral Bhagwat's termination order read:

> The President, in exercise of powers conferred by Section 15(1) of the Navy Act 1957 ... is pleased to withdraw his pleasure for continuance of Admiral Vishnu Bhagwat in the Naval Service on account of loss of confidence in his fitness to continue as CNS and he is relieved of his services with immediate effect.[29]

To the credit of the armed forces, they took this lightning bolt hurled by the government stoically in their stride. However, the reverberations of 'governmental arrogance' lingered long after.

TENUOUS STATE OF RELATIONS

The civil-military relationship boat was rocked once again in 2011 and 2012. This time over an issue that otherwise would have been considered laughable had it not involved the COAS. The dispute pertained to the COAS's date of birth.

The public record concerning this specific question states that the AG's branch is charged with the responsibility of maintaining the personal information of the officers of the Indian Army. Conversely, the Military Secretary's (MS) branch preserves the proceedings and minutes in respect of ranks of officers and their career progression.

---

[29]Manoj Joshi and Prabhu Chawla, 'Naval chief Admiral Vishnu Bhagwat sacked for "defiance of civilian authority"', *India Today*, 11 January 1999, https://www. indiatoday.in/magazine/cover-story/story/19990111-naval-chief-admiral-vishnu-bhagwat-sacked-for-defiance-of-civilian-authority-779870-1999-01-11.   Accessed on 28 July 2021.

Unfortunately, the AG's office and the MS, in their records, had noted two different dates of birth qua Gen. V.K. Singh. This anomaly ostensibly arose right after his formal induction into the army, post completion of the mandatory training in 1970.

The AG's branch had logged the General's date of birth as 10 May 1951. This was in accordance with what was declared in the Secondary School Certificate (SSC) supplied by the Rajasthan Board of Secondary Education. On the other hand, the MS had recorded it as 10 May 1950. This particular date was contained in the application filed by him with the Union Public Service Commission (UPSC) to appear for the entrance examination of the National Defence Academy (NDA). This apparent contradiction should have been ideally reconciled eons back.

Either Gen. Singh never noticed this discrepancy or did not really attach any importance to this contradistinction. It seems until 2006, his date of birth apparently had no impact on any of his promotions or official assignments and thus it never became a subject of contention.

The first time this discrepancy surfaced was ostensibly in 2006 when the then MS, Lt Gen. Richard Khare, wrote to V.K. Singh, then a major general. That letter, dated 3 May 2006, pointed to the variance in his date of birth and advised him to either reflect the correct date of birth as 10 May 1950 in future or otherwise explain the inconsistency to delineate the correct date of birth.

In his rejoinder datelined 10 May 2006, V.K. Singh attempted to explain that the discrepancy was on account of his birth date being erroneously noted into his NDA form. He further submitted that in the year 1971 when he gained possession of his SSC credentials, he had presented the original certificate itself to the office of the AG. Consequently, that office had amended his birth date and reflected it as 10 May 1951.

He also averred that twice in the past, once in 1985 and again in 2002, he had notified the MS branch to make the necessary corrections in the Army List. Gen. V.K. Singh was apparently informed by the MS office that since matters pertaining to personal information of officers was preserved rather meticulously by their office, the requisite amendments would be carried out. He ostensibly wrote, 'I have always retained the impression that the necessary corrections would have been done by the MS branch at the behest of the AG's branch.' 'It appears this impression has been wrong as a doubt has come up almost 35 years after submission of correct certificates,' the General penned in another missive to the Military Secretary's establishment in the year 2008.[30]

The age hullabaloo continued to manifest itself sporadically. The AG's office kept restating that his birthdate according to their records was 10 May 1951. On the other hand, the MS branch was insistent that in their official record, the date of birth stood reflected as 10 May 1950. They strongly averred that notwithstanding the textual substantiation proffered, his year of birth would be held to be 1950 and not 1951 as the General had been arguing.

The MS branch on 25 January 2008 informed the MoD that the general had acquiesced to the fact that his date of birth may be treated as 10 May 1950. The variance, the communication elaborated, was on account of lack of coordination between the two branches at that point of time. Whether this was voluntary or presented as a fait accompli to the General, given the strict hierarchal nature of the armed forces, is a matter of conjecture now. However, since the General was a rising star in the army who anyway would have been in the top echelons of the armed forces notwithstanding the one-year variance in his age, he may have just erred on the side of caution. It would not have made much sense to get into a running battle with his superiors.

Matters should have rested there. However, after becoming the COAS, Gen. Singh filed a statutory complaint to get his birthdate rectified to 10 May 1951 from 10 May 1950. The government, after

---

[30]Purnima S. Tripathi, 'Age of Controversy', *Frontline*, 24 February 2012, https://frontline.thehindu.com/the-nation/article30164500.ece. Accessed on 15 March 2021.

consulting the Attorney General, rejected the COAS's complaint and said that his date of birth would remain 10 May 1950. The General decided to take the government to the Supreme Court. The Supreme Court's unwillingness to side with the General's contention left him with no other option but to withdraw his petition. Had he pressed his petition, he may have invited a speaking order perhaps even upholding, or at worst, dismissing his plea on merits. The matter would have conclusively ended there once the apex court would have spoken.

Like the proverbial bolt from the blue, on 4 April 2012, *The Indian Express* carried a story that was splashed three-fourth across its front page. Captioned 'The January Night Raisina Hill Was Spooked: Two Key Army Units Moved towards Delhi Without Notifying Govt'.[31] It would perhaps be instructive to produce the report in full for its contents are both either too grave or too sensational to attempt any paraphrasing:

This is a story you would tell with extreme care and caution. But it so starkly characterizes the current state of top-level politico military relations that it is a folly to keep it under wraps, as the entire establishment has tried to do for a full 11 weeks now.

It has also taken this team of *The Indian Express* reporters that long to establish the story and the dramatic developments during, say, about 18 very difficult hours on January 16-17 earlier this year.

While many, including the spokesmen for the defence establishment, say it was much ado about nothing, it is a story of a most unusual night when Raisina Hill was spooked as never before in peace time.

Essentially, late on the night of January 16 (the day Army

Chief General V.K. Singh approached the Supreme Court on his date of birth issue), central intelligence agencies reported an unexpected (and non-notified) movement by a key military unit, from the mechanised infantry based in Hisar (Haryana) as a part of the 33rd Armoured Division (which is a part of 1 Corps, a strike formation based in Mathura and commanded by Lt Gen. A.K. Singh) in the direction of the capital, 150 km away.

Any suspicion was still considered much too implausible, but lookouts were alerted as a routine step. This was part of a protocol put in place in June 1984 when some mutineers from Sikh units had moved towards the capital in the wake of Operation Bluestar.

The lookouts confirmed the movement of what looked like a sizeable unit. It was soon identified as an entire unit of Mechanised Infantry, with its Russian-made Armoured Fighting Vehicles (AFVs), carried on 48 tank transporters. The movement was towards the capital, which was odd.

No such thing had been notified. The Army Day celebrations had ended just the previous day (January 15).

It was still a cause for curiosity and some confusion—more than much concern—because, over the decades, New Delhi has come to be totally relaxed and trustful of the apolitical and professionally correct nature of its military leadership.

The situation changed rapidly, though. Reports came in of yet another military movement 'towards' Delhi. This unit was identified as a large element of the airborne 50 Para Brigade based at Agra.

The lookouts were activated south of Delhi as well and the column was identified.

By this time, both columns were being tracked and 'watched'. A bemused establishment raised an alert of sorts. The Defence Minister was informed. Immediately, the Centre put in motion an old contingency plan to delay just such a move.

It issued a terror alert with instructions to police to

carefully check all vehicles on the highways leading to Delhi. The objective was to slow down traffic. The Prime Minister was informed at the crack of dawn on January 17. Quiet checks carried out on the location and status of key formations and their commanders, particularly in the northwestern region, revealed nothing abnormal at all. Defence Secretary Shashi Kant Sharma was asked to cut short his visit to Malaysia. He returned.

After the briefing, he opened his office late at night and asked Lt Gen. A.K. Choudhary, Director General Military Operations, to see him and explain what was going on. Gen. Choudhary, it seems, knew about the move of the Paras (the Para Brigade is controlled directly by the DGMO) and said it was a routine exercise.

He was asked to return with full facts about the mechanised unit. This he did soon enough. The explanation was still the same: the Army was carrying out exercises to check its ability to make quick deployments of key units during fog. He was told to send the units back immediately. Both formations were halted, and sent back within hours.

The mechanised unit, sources said, had parked itself at an industrial park near Bahadurgarh abutting West Delhi's Najafgarh. The Paras were staying put in the barracks of an artillery regiment—79 Medium—not far from Palam.

The Army's explanation that it was all a simple fog-time exercise was then viewed with scepticism at the highest level. The question: Why was the well-set protocol, that any military movement, at any time, in the NCR (National Capital Region) has to be pre-notified to MoD (Ministry of Defence) not followed?

The Army's justification for the specific movements did sound plausible though. The mechanised units, they said, were checking out their ability to move and deploy rapidly in fog, should a contingency arrive. It could not have driven westwards (towards Ferozepur or Fazilka) as that would have alarmed Pakistan since the move had not been notified to them.

There was a more elaborate explanation for the paratroopers' movement. The mandated time for the Agra-based Paras to get airborne in an emergency is just two hours. It was simpler when they were transported by aircraft based 'in situ', at the same military complex in Agra.

The new designated transport for them is the faster, bigger and brand new C-130J Hercules. The IAF has based the C-130s at Hindon, across the Yamuna, east of Delhi. Since fog lifts in Agra much later (11.30 am) than at Hindon (8.30 am) in January, the Army was checking out the possibility of transporting the paratroopers to Hindon by road to 'marry' them with the C-130s, rather than wait for the planes to land at Agra, and thereby save time.

In the process, the Army said, they discovered many glitches. These are now being ironed out. For example, it was found that the shoulder-fired missiles, standard equipment with Para units, were stored not in Agra, as decided several years earlier, but at Bharatpur as was the case originally.

So the columns were delayed by that detour and the stop at Bharatpur to pick up their missiles, and thereby also forced to take a longer route to Delhi. The good lesson learnt: all of the Paras' equipment must now be based where their home is, at Agra.

But this was questioned too. Did the mechanised units have to come as far as the outskirts of Delhi to check out their readiness? And Hindon is a long distance from Palam/Gurgaon. Even on a reasonable day, an Army convoy might take longer moving from here to Hindon given the snarls on Outer Ring Road and NH-24, than if only it had crossed the Yamuna at Agra itself and driven through Uttar Pradesh, parallel to GT Road. Why was the IAF not informed of this exercise? Again, the Army's explanation is they did not want to hold an elaborate exercise involving the IAF etc, or cause alarm.

The government also noted the fact that the C-130s were not even in Hindon then. They were in Jaisalmer, rehearsing at their staging base for the Republic Day flypast. Yet another reason some in the government were curious was that between Army Day (January 15), and Republic Day (January 26), when so many Army units are involved in parades, such exercises are rare, particularly around the capital.

The Indian Express has had detailed conversations with key people and sources at the very top of the political, civil and military leadership. There is unanimity over General V.K. Singh's impeccable reputation as a sound, professional soldier, earned over nearly 42 years of distinguished service to the Army. Nobody is using the 'C' word to imply anything other than 'curious'. All else is considered an impossibility.

But so strained has the political-military relationship been these weeks, that nothing is easily dismissed as a routine misdemeanour. The timing—the Chief's petition on his date of birth was filed on the morning of January 16—did not help.

Sources speak of confusion and unease in the government. To be fair, the MoD's considered view now seems to be that it was a false alarm, caused by some non-adherence to Standard Operating Procedures (SoPs) by the Army and an alarmist civil/political reaction on a particularly distrustful day.

We learn, however, as a consequence, that certain 'important correctives' have been put in place. Incidentally, the Home Ministry has turned down the Army Headquarters' recommendation (subsequent to the events of January 16/17) to appoint Lt Gen. Choudhary as D-G Assam Rifles, the paramilitary force it controls.

These are the bare facts of an unusual set of events. It is too early to answer all the 'hows, whys and the what-nexts' of this. Or to say whether it was an avoidable case of neurosis the

Indian establishment is—mercifully—not familiar with.

These facts may indeed be officially denied for now. But these will be debated for a long time, forcing the UPA to introspect on its mismanagement of the delicate civil-military relationship, bruised as it is now by charges of corruption, bribes and bribe offers and indiscipline. These will also have a bearing on the future course of higher defence organisation and control in India.

The government at the highest level debunked *The Indian Express* report, with both the prime minister and the defence minister calling it alarmist and absolutely baseless, respectively. However, whether the report was baseless or it did have a substratum to it would be clear if some of the dramatis personae involved or those who were in the know of the matter do decide to speak or write candidly at some point.

However, certain things are self-evident from this news report and developments preceding its publication. There was tension between Gen. V.K. Singh and the political leadership. Troops had indeed moved. There was an advertent or inadvertent communication gap between Army Headquarters and the MoD with regard to the movement of these formations. The fact is that it caused a degree of consternation in the highest echelons of the Indian state. The then defence secretary had to open his office late at night and ordered the troops back. A fact not specifically denied by the government while debunking the report.

The defence secretary 'formally' told the Standing Committee of Defence (of which I was a member) on 9 April 2012 that the troop movements were routine and no permission was required.[32] However, the fact remains that when such meetings take place, there are a number of other MoD officers and military brass who attend the

---

[32]ET Bureau, 'Troop Movement Was Routine: Ministry of Defence', *The Economic Times*, 10 April 2012, https://economictimes.indiatimes.com/news/politics-and-nation/troop-movement-was-routine-ministry-of-defence/articleshow/12603128.cms?from=mdr. Accessed on 15 March 2021.

hearings as the demands for grants of the Defence Ministry have to be considered/approved by the Parliamentary Standing Committee and a report presented to Parliament. Conversations with officials of the MoD and the service headquarters on the sidelines or pull asides during these hearings, that go on for 2–3 days at a stretch, can at times be far more illuminating than formal pro forma positions taken during actual meetings. There has been, and will remain, a gap between institutional positions and the inputs provided informally. It enables one to arrive at a more rounded and a holistic perspective on a given situation or issue.[33] [34]

How did things come to such an unfortunate pass? Why did the COAS take his own government to court? Why did sensational stories appear where the 'C' word was all but a thinly disguised veneer in the manner it was used, notwithstanding the spin put into the story to the contrary. Why were things not handled in a more skilful and discreet manner? Should the government or the CCS not have collectively ensured that matters did not get out of hand? Ultimately, Gen. V.K. Singh retired a month after this story went public but questions still remain especially about the rather tenuous state of civil-military relations at that point.

To be fair to Gen. Singh, perhaps he had a point. It is quite possible that he was compelled, albeit reluctantly, to accept a date of birth much to his discomfiture as perhaps he did not have a choice then. However, after becoming COAS, was it correct and proper to raise a 'personal' issue or should he have let bygones be bygones? The jury remains out on that.

A legion of distinguished commanders has led the Indian Armed Forces with quiet dignity and exemplary military rectitude, both

---

[33]Standing Committee on Defence, 'Fifteenth Report', 30 April 2012, https://eparlib.nic.in/bitstream/123456789/63938/1/15_Defence_15.pdf. Accessed on 15 March 2021.

[34]Express News Service, 'Manish Tewari: Indian Express Story on Troop Movement Unfortunate but True', *The Indian Express*, 10 January 2016, https://indianexpress.com/article/india/india-news-india/indian-express-story-on-troop-movements-unfortunate-but-true-manish-tewari/. Accessed on 15 March 2021.

before and after Independence. Over the course of time, structures and institutions within the defence establishment also evolved. It would perhaps be instructive to look at this bygone era with the benefit of hindsight.

REVOLUTION IN MILITARY COMMAND PARADIGMS

During 1861–1947, there were 20 commanders-in-chief in the British Indian Army. The Headquarters of the Army in India (AHQ India) was shifted to Delhi in 1911 when the capital moved from Calcutta to Delhi. During summer, some components of the headquarters would be moved up to Shimla, as the imperialists could not stomach the Delhi heat.[35]

As WWII began, AHQ India was re-designated as the General Headquarters (GHQ India) Command. GHQ India remained in actuality up till 15 August 1947. It was disbanded upon the partition of undivided India. Pakistan Army's new headquarters were formed out of the Northern Command of the British Indian Army, while the Indian Army took over the HQs in Delhi. Field Marshal Sir Claude Auchinleck, the last commander-in-chief of the British Army in India, was appointed as the supreme commander of the Army in India and Pakistan. His role was to transfer responsibilities to the new armies, and to organize the withdrawal of British Army units, former officers and men of the British Indian Army.

On 15 August 1947, both India and Pakistan assumed operational control over their respective armed forces. From 15 August, Auchinleck was re-designated as the supreme commander in order to avoid abstruseness with the new commanders-in-chief of the two Dominion states.

---

[35]Manish Tewari, 'BJP Govt Created Chief of Defence Staff Post without Addressing Several Fundamental Questions', *Outlook*, 31 December 2019, https://www. outlookindia.com/website/story/opinion-bjp-govt-created-chief-of-defence-staff-post-without-caring-for-these-fundamental-questions/344930/?cv=1&next=. Accessed on 15 March 2021.

Auchinleck had limited authority vide the Joint Defence Council Order of 11 August 1947. He had no responsibility for law and order or operational control over any units except those in transit from one Dominion to another. Even in the exercise of his limited authority, he would be dependent on the cooperation of the two Dominions. Even though he represented a legally constituted authority, his position was tenuous, at best.

Whether Field Marshal Auchinleck formally retired on 1 December 1947[36] or was asked to leave due to his frequent run-ins with Lord Mountbatten,[37] remains ambiguous. Nonetheless, what is fairly clear is that the office of the Supreme Commander attained quietus. Major General L.G. Whistler was appointed the General Officer Commanding British Troops in India in 1947 and remained in the saddle until the last British unit, the 1st Battalion of the Somerset Light Infantry (Prince Albert's), left on 28 February 1948. The 2nd Battalion, the Black Watch (Royal Highland) Regiment, was the last British Army unit to leave Pakistan earlier on 26 February 1948.

On 24 September 1947, Lord Ismay, the chief of staff to Lord Mountbatten, Governor General of India, recommended a three-tier Higher Defence Management Structure to PM Nehru. Three committees were constituted: the Defence Committee of Cabinet presided over by the prime minister, Defence Minister's Committee chaired by the defence minister and Chiefs of Staff Committee integrated into the Military Wing of the Cabinet Secretariat. The chair of the Committee would be rotational and the service chief

---

[36]Margaret M. Wright, *The Military Papers, 1940–48, of Field-Marshal Sir Claude Auchinleck: A Calendar and Index,* Available at https://www.escholar.manchester.ac.uk/api/datastream?publicationPid=uk-ac-man-scw:1m2193&datastreamId=POST-PEER-REVIEW-PUBLISHERS-DOCUMENT.PDF. Accessed on 15 March 2021.

[37]Claude Auchinleck, *The Open University,* https://www.open.ac.uk/researchprojects/makingbritain/content/claude-auchinleck#:~:text=Auchinleck per cent20stayed per cent20on per cent20as per cent20Supreme,where per cent20he per cent20died per cent20in per cent201981. Accessed on 15 March 2021.

longest in the Committee would become the chairperson.[38]

This paradigm held the field well into the mid-1950s, despite the commander-in-chief being only an invitee to the Defence Committee of Cabinet and not a member. The position of the chief of the Indian Army was also known as commander-in-chief from 1947–55. There were four officers who had served in this position. However, in 1955, the government consciously took a decision to re-nomenclature this designation as the chief of the army staff. Gen. Maharaj Shri Rajendrasinhji Jadeja was the last commander-in-chief and the first chief of the army staff of the Indian Army. It may be pertinent to note that while the army chief was called the commander-in-chief till 1955, the designation was limited to the Indian Army only; and the Air Force and the Navy were headed by their respective Commanders.

Post the Sino-Indo War of 1962, the Defence Committee of Cabinet first morphed into the Emergency Committee of Cabinet and then later into the Cabinet Committee of Political Affairs. It is now known as the Cabinet Committee on Security (CCS). This system has served India well over all these years.

Sixty-four years later, on 24 December 2019, the PIB put out a press release about the Cabinet clearing the appointment of a CDS. The communiqué inter alia stated:

> The following areas will be dealt by the Department of Military Affairs headed by CDS: The Armed Forces of the Union, namely, the Army, the Navy and the Air Force; Integrated Headquarters of the Ministry of Defence comprising Army Headquarters, Naval Headquarters, Air Headquarters and Defence Staff Headquarters; The Territorial Army; Works relating to the Army, the Navy and the Air Force and Procurement exclusive to the

---

[38]Manish Tewari, 'There Is a Design Flaw with This Military Post', first appeared in *The Hindu*, on 8 January 2020 https://www.thehindu.com/opinion/op-ed/there-is-a-design-flaw-with-this-military-post/article30506758.ece. Accessed on 15 March 2021.

Services except capital acquisitions, as per prevalent rules and procedures.

It further read that,

> The Chief of Defence Staff, apart from being the head of the Department of Military Affairs, will also be the Permanent Chairman of the Chiefs of Staff Committee. He will act as the Principal Military Adviser to Raksha Mantri on all tri-Services matters. The three Chiefs will continue to advise RM on matters exclusively concerning their respective Services. CDS will not exercise any military command, including over the three Service Chiefs, so as to be able to provide impartial advice to the political leadership.[39]

Herein lay the contradiction. As Secretary to the Government of India, in charge of the DMA and having superintendence over the Army, Navy and Air Force, there would be an implied subordination of the three service chiefs to the CDS, notwithstanding any declaration to the contrary. Moreover, the President of India is the Supreme Commander of the Armed Forces.

Moreover Article 53 (2) of the Indian Constitution declares: 'Without prejudice to the generality of the foregoing provision, the supreme command of the Defence Forces of the Union shall be vested in the President and the exercise thereof shall be regulated by law.'[40] What then would the position of the CDS be qua the Supreme Commander—the President of India? There are also other questions that need to be looked at.

What implication does the nomenclature, Principal Military Advisor to the Defence Minister qua the three service chiefs, have in relation to military advice tendered to the government? Will the

---

[39]'Cabinet Approves Creation of the Post of Chief of Defence Staff in the Rank of Four Star General', *PIB*, 24 December 2019, https://pib.gov.in/PressReleaseDetail.aspx?PRID=1597425. Accessed on 15 March 2021.
[40]'Article 53 in the Constitution of India 1949', https://indiankanoon.org/doc/1597349/. Accessed on 15 March 2021.

advice of the CDS override the advice of the respective service chiefs as he heads the newly created DMA? Will the CDS as Permanent Chairperson of Joint Chiefs of Staff Committee outrank the three service chiefs even though theoretically all are four-star officers? Would the three chiefs now report to the defence minister through defence secretary or CDS? In theory, the service chiefs report directly to the defence minister, while in practice all files and decisions are routed through the defence secretary.

What will be the position of CDS qua the defence secretary? Would the defence secretary, in terms of Rule Eleven of Transaction of Business Rules, continue to be the administrative head of the MoD? What is the remit/mandate of the proposed DMA? Would the CDS override the service chiefs with regard to operational command and control of tri-service agencies and organizations? And finally, what are the implications of the appointment of a CDS for civil-military relations? The last part is profoundly serious, for the singular success of India going back to 1947 has been the supremacy of the civilian leadership over the military even in military matters.

Given that the new DMA will govern all the activities of the three services,[41] the CDS, who will now control the DMA, would be a very important interface between the service chiefs, the defence minister and by extension, the CCS and the Cabinet. It will perhaps take a decade before the structural impact of the CDS on the armed forces becomes evident in the fullness of time.

India's civil-military relations were fortunately handled well during the transition from colonial rule to Independence and especially during Partition. For any erstwhile institution to be divided into two and made into opponents of each other overnight would have been nothing short of severely traumatic.

However, notwithstanding this un-elective surgery, the armed forces of independent India have faithfully risen to the occasion

---

[41]Ibid.

whenever required. The relationship between the armed forces and the governments has endured many ups and downs over the years, reiterating its strong foundations. It could be a variety of factors difficult to quantify, such as proper training of the armed forces, strict discipline within the institution and India's institutional design that is an antidote to the concentration of power. However, shifts in the existing institutions can bring change in the scheme of things. It can be both positive and negative.

To be cognizant of the fact that India may perhaps move towards a more autonomous military is a preemptive hypothesis. Institutional inertia will prevent the Indian armed forces from moving down that road. Such a possibility in the given national and global context seems very remote. Notwithstanding that, it might constitute a leap of faith to countenance such a situation. It would be both prudent if not sagacious to observe the evolving revolution in military command and control paradigms carefully.

It must also be noted that the interests of India as imagined by its political leadership and the military leadership cannot be at cross purposes. Both sides therefore must also make efforts to have a continuous dialogue and try and mitigate all such differences of opinion that do arise as a consequence of daily interaction.

For India to consolidate a permanently resilient template of civil-military relations in the coming decades, any changes to institutional structures must be carried out with absolute care and caution after a thorough assessment of its implications. Transformations, if any, must always be both incremental and reversible, such that they cause minimum disruption in the ethos of the forces. This should hold true for the proposed theatre commands under consideration. A consensus must be arrived at and the process of transformation should be implemented through legislation. It must be supervised by a Standing Committee of Parliament especially created for this purpose, assisted by military and strategic advisors specifically tasked for this purpose.

What the above overview tells us is that notwithstanding the successes that India has attained in maintaining civilian supremacy over its armed forces and the professionalism that the armed forces have displayed specially to remain apolitical, even a slight misstep can raise the spectre of suspicion very quickly. A fracture in the civil-military relationship is hazardous in more ways than one, and therefore, both the civil and military leadership must walk the extra mile to ensure that there is no space for any misunderstanding or second-guessing of each other's intent or actions.

NINE

SURGICAL STRIKES: TESTING PAKISTAN'S REDLINES

I t was 29 September 2016; I was supposed to address a press conference at the AICC headquarters at noon on the unfortunate suicide of B.K. Bansal, director general in the Ministry of Corporate Affairs, and his son, earlier on 27 September. His wife and daughter had also taken the same unfortunate path in July of that year. In their alleged suicide notes that were published in public domain, the family had blamed the CBI for torturing them and driving them to this tragic end.[1] Just then the news came in of a government-scheduled press conference. We decided to postpone our presser till after the government's announcement.

The Director General of Military Operations (DGMO) and spokesperson of the MEA jointly announced in their media briefing, resplendent with Indian flags in the background, that surgical strikes had been carried out against certain Pakistani terrorist launch pads.[2] This changed the public script for the days to come; Bansal and his family's tribulations were swept under the carpet. As I write this

---

[1]IANS, 'Bansal's Suicide Note Names DIG Who Bragged About Being "Amit Shah's Man"', *Business Standard*, 28 September 2016, https://www.business-standard.com/article/news-ians/bansal-s-suicide-note-names-dig-who-bragged-about-being-amit-shah-s-man-116092801280_1.html. Accessed on 15 March 2021.

[2]'Full Text of DGMO Lt Gen. Ranbir Singh's Press Conference', *Live Mint*, 29 September 2016, https://www.livemint.com/Politics/02IQNHAgeQ3sqUEuZwQTON/Full-text-of-DGMO-Lt-Gen-Ranbir-Singhs-press-conference.html. Accessed on 15 March 2021.

chapter, a petition by retired bureaucrat E.A.S. Sarma in the Supreme Court demanding a probe into the tragic demise of an entire family because of alleged police excesses continues to hang fire.[3]

However, to return to post-Uri surgical strikes and Balakot air raids, there are certain questions that should be asked. Did the abandonment of strategic restraint practised by India between 1980 and 2016 help in mitigating the problem of Pakistan-sponsored terror? Is kinetic action using conventional forces across the LoC and International Border the correct and proportionate response to cross-border terrorism, given that we live under a nuclear overhang? Do India and Pakistan have a playbook or off-ramps to contain the escalatory spiral of actions and reactions that such a move can initiate? Will India be able to deal with the joint threat of Pakistan and China on its northern borders—the classical two-front situation that such actions by the use of conventional forces may just initialize? In the future, how should India deal with the Pakistani deep state that has consistently endeavoured to destabilize India? More importantly, perhaps, have these two strikes made India more secure than it was before?

MODI'S PAK POLICY: A CHEQUERED HISTORY

PM Modi came to power in 2014 and invited all South Asian Association for Regional Cooperation (SAARC) leaders to his swearing-in ceremony. The prime minister of Pakistan, Nawaz Sharif, was also invited and the gesture was seen by analysts as a bold step towards increasing regional engagement and improving bilateral relations between India and Pakistan.[4] It would not be amiss to

---

[3]Anthony S. Rozario, 'Three Years On, Centre Ignores SC Notice on Bansal Family Suicide', *The Quint*, 2 August 2019, https://www.thequint.com/news/india/three-years-on-centre-remains-quiet-on-bk-bansal-family-suicide-in-supreme-court. Accessed on 15 March 2021.

[4]Jason Burke and Jon Boone, 'Narendra Modi Invites Pakistani Prime Minister Nawaz Sharif to Inauguration', *The Guardian*, 21 May 2014, https://www.theguardian.com/world/2014/may/21/narendra-modi-invites-pakistan-nawaz-sharif-inauguration.

mention that Sharif has always been perceived as a votary of a deeper engagement between India and Pakistan, notwithstanding the fact that Kargil happened on his watch soon after the path-breaking Lahore Declaration in 1999. Sharif accepted Modi's invitation and attended the swearing-in ceremony.

This outreach by PM Modi could have set the tone for renewed engagement in the bilateral relationship with a fresh effort to bury the ghosts of the past. Barely three months later, this new-found bonhomie was blown away in the cold wind of mutual antagonism as foreign secretary-level talks were cancelled due to disagreements over the Pakistani outreach to the Hurriyat Conference.

This was totally unnecessary and the outreach should have been ignored for even the former president of Pakistan, Pervez Musharraf, had met Hurriyat leaders at the Pakistan High Commissioner's residence in New Delhi on the eve of the Agra summit in July 2001 with PM Vajpayee. There had been, and continued to be, many such interactions with the Hurriyat whenever a senior official or politician from Pakistan had visited India. This should be viewed as a domestic political necessity of the visiting Pakistanis, given all the imprudent lip and other service they have paid over the years to the cause of Kashmir's liberation. In any case, the Pakistani High Commissioner, Abdul Basit, merrily went ahead with his consultations with the separatist leaders of the Hurriyat Conference of Jammu & Kashmir despite the Indian government's explicit displeasure over the meeting.

Although the move was seen as a stronger riposte against Pakistan's support to Kashmiri separatists, many analysts believe the cancellation of the talks could have been avoided. As pointed out above, Pakistani officials and politicians have met Kashmiri separatists ad nauseam and it had always been perceived as something which was being done to appease the hard-line elements in domestic Pakistani politics. Kashmir is a sensitive political issue in both countries and therefore allowing it to sabotage resumption

Accessed on 15 March 2021.

of a bilateral dialogue was, at best, churlish. The talks would have laid the ground for resumption of a formal dialogue between the two countries.

The cancellation of the talks once again set the ball rolling downhill in the tortured bilateral relationship. It played right into the hands of the hardliners on both sides of the border who yet again rediscovered how easy was it to derail the bilateral dynamic.

However, notwithstanding this overt posturing, New Delhi and Islamabad continued to engage with each other quietly. The NSAs of both countries ostensibly led this interaction. Another effort to get the relationship back on track came a year later on 10 July 2015, when prime ministers Modi and Sharif met on the sidelines of the Shanghai Cooperation Summit (SCO) in the Russian city of Ufa. A joint statement emanated from the meeting that stressed on combating terrorism. Both sides agreed that terrorism is a grave threat to peace and stability in the region and efforts must be made to prevent it.[5] It was decided that the NSAs of both countries and personnel from the security establishment will meet and interact to devise a strategy for attaining counterterrorism objectives.

The statement was met with withering criticism in Pakistan and the popular opinion there was that it was skewed in favour of the established Indian position. Nasim Zehra, Pakistani security analyst, summed up the sentiment by stating, 'A dialogue that fails to factor in Pakistan's concerns will obviously be short-lived. Sharif's task was now to convince the opposition and Pakistan's other stakeholders that more was discussed and agreed upon than was reflected in the Ufa statement.'[6] Considering the dissatisfaction with the statement

---

[5]'Full Text of India-Pakistan Joint Statement on PM Narendra Modi-Nawaz Sharif Talks in Russia', *The Hindu*, 10 July 2015, https://www.thehindu.com/news/resources/full-text-of-the-joint-statement-by-the-foreign-secretaries-of-india-and-pakistan-in-russia/article10566559.ece. Accessed on 15 March 2021.
[6]Nasim Zehra, 'Ufa Statement Has Put Nawaz Sharif on the Mat in Pakistan', *Hindustan Times*, 16 July 2015, https://www.hindustantimes.com/analysis/ufa-statement-has-put-nawaz-sharif-on-the-mat-in-pakistan/story-2gKqO90ZipHGPF9AtxsaDI.html. Accessed on 15 March 2021.

back in Pakistan, it quickly became fairly evident that the Ufa joint statement would turn out to be another red herring, if not a dead letter.

Only three weeks after the Ufa statement came out on 27 July 2015, there was a terrorist attack in the Gurdaspur district of Punjab.[7] The region shares its borders with J&K and Pakistan, and the attackers are believed to have come either from Kashmir or infiltrated into the Gurdaspur district at Bamiyal or in the areas near Tash in Punjab.[8] The perpetrators holed themselves up in a residential quarter inside a police station and fired continuously. A later analysis of the GPS devices of the perpetrators revealed that they were in Pakistan about a week prior to the attack. The exact location had been erased from the devices.[9] It is quite possible that fringe terrorist groups, not entirely in the control of the Pakistani deep state or even affiliated to the more hard-line elements in the ISI, could have carried out the attack less than a month after talks between the two leaders in Ufa. This problem has been perennial in the trajectory of the relationship between the two countries, now going back a couple of decades.

Any diplomatic overture or even minor progress towards starting a modicum of dialogue between India and Pakistan has always been undermined by state and semi-state actors, especially in Pakistan and maybe indigenous elements in J&K who want the relationship— for various reasons ranging from ideological to revenge—to remain

[7]'Gurdaspur Attack: Ten Killed in Indian Police Station Siege', *BBC*, 27 July 2015, https://www.bbc.com/news/world-asia-india-33671593. Accessed on 15 March 2021.

[8]RSTV Bureau, 'Gurdaspur Attackers Came from Pakistan: Home Min', *Rajya Sabha*, 30 July 2015, https://rstv.nic.in/gurdaspur-attackers-came-pakistan-rajnath-singh.html. Accessed on 15 March 2021.

[9]Rahul Tripathi and Aman Sharma, 'Gurdaspur Attack: GPS of Terrorists Shows Pakistan Location on July 21', *The Economic Times*, 13 July 2018, https://economictimes.indiatimes.com/news/defence/gurdaspur-attack-gps-of-terrorists-shows-pakistan-location-on-july-21/articleshow/48259397.cms. Accessed on 15 March 2021.

in a state of a perennial freeze.

Five months later, on 25 December 2015, PM Modi made another of his 'grand gestures' when he flew from Kabul to Lahore and from there to Raiwind to greet PM Sharif and his family on the occasion of his granddaughter's wedding. That the initiative was novel needs to be acknowledged. At another level, it was deeply personal and should be the norm in any civilized part of the world. However, given the very contentious, contested state of Indo-Pak relations, such diplomacy on the hop does not become an icebreaker, as subsequent events demonstrated.

Moreover, the decision to fly from Kabul to Lahore should have been carefully planned. Given the fact that Afghanistan, like India, has been at the receiving end of the Pakistani deep state's terrorist depredations including, and not limited to, support of the Taliban and sheltering not only of the Quetta Shura, Osama bin Laden and a host of other such notorious characters, but even terror syndicates like the Haqqani network that constantly seek to undermine the territorial integrity and sovereignty of Afghanistan, the impact of this journey on the Afghans should have been carefully assessed and factored in. Especially given that they have always looked to India for support against the continuing Pakistan-sponsored territorial and other pillages into their country. A fact today unequivocally demonstrated by the Pakistan-backed Taliban taking over Afghanistan. India will have to carefully calibrate its approach in Afghanistan for the great game version 3.0 has only now begun in Afghanistan. The original version had played out between the British, Russian and to a lesser extent by the Chinese imperialists in the closing decades of the nineteenth century. Version 1.0 was the partition of India and creation of Pakistan to give the US-led allies a foothold so that they could keep a neo-imperial eye on both Central and West Asia. Version 2.0 commenced in December 1979 with the Soviet invasion of Afghanistan and ended with ignominious withdrawal of the US in August 2021.

Considering the historical antagonism between Afghanistan and

Pakistan, Modi's visit reminded me of the dash that Defence Minister Pranab Mukherjee made from Tokyo to Beijing in May 2006. Though both China and Japan have normalized their relationship for many decades now, the memories of the brutal Japanese conduct during WWII linger not only in China, but across the North and South East Asian region.

As far as Modi's Kabul to Raiwind odyssey was concerned, though the Afghans never made an issue out of it (for that would have further complicated their already contentious relationship with Pakistan), I am sure some quiet eyebrows must have been raised in Kabul.

As had become the established pattern, only eight days after Modi's attempt to make a personal overture to Sharif, a deadly terror attack targeted the Pathankot airbase in Punjab in the early hours of 2 January 2016. The perpetrators were from the Jaish-e-Mohammed founded by Maulana Masood Azhar, one of the terrorists India had released after the IC-814 hijack to Kandahar. A decade-and-a-half later, he continues to operate with impunity. The attack lasted 17 hours and casualties included seven security personnel. All six attackers were killed in the ensuing gun battle that lasted three days.

The Pathankot attack had once again laid bare the fact that the architecture of terror in J&K had symbiotic and deep roots in Pakistan. It was obvious that neither the deep state nor elements who operated from ungoverned spaces in Pakistan perceived the Modi-Sharif camaraderie as helpful to their agenda.

The attackers are believed to have crossed into Indian territory at Punjab's Bamiyal village that sits right on the international border at the tri-junction of J&K, Punjab and Pakistan. It is a well-known infiltration route.

The perpetrators of the Gurdaspur attack had also taken the same route. It is unfortunate that security forces were unprepared even after the Gurdaspur episode. Senior intelligence sources believe that there is a deeply entrenched politician-smuggler nexus at work that was responsible for keeping cross-border ingress channels in that area deliberately loose. Though intelligence advisory warnings about a possible attack and infiltration from Bamiyal had been issued in December, no appropriate action seemed to have been taken.

The Punjab police began to scan the area from midnight of 1 January, but were unable to locate the terrorists. The army personnel were unsuccessful in securing the perimeter of the airbase before the attack. The NSG, already on high alert around New Year's Eve, was deployed to protect installations in and around Delhi. Once information about infiltration in Pathankot became known, two NSG units were transferred there.

There has been a debate about the choice of deploying NSG units as their capability in interdicting terrorists is moot. These soldiers are trained in hostage rescue and interventions, and were not perhaps the best bet in securing an airbase.[10] Additional support for these NSG units was almost nil. Even though a large number of troops are stationed in that part of Punjab, none of them were called upon to assist in the interdiction process. As the attack ensued, there were reports of lack of coordination among various forces present at the site all of whom ostensibly answered to their own separate superiors. It only compounded the problem.[11]

The Pathankot attack could have been deadlier than it played out. Fortunately, the terrorists failed to reach and destroy tactical assets like MIG-21 fighter jets and MI-35 attack helicopters stationed there. Moreover, around 3,000 people including the families of armed forces who live there were unharmed. The entire attack was perhaps preventable if far more precise intelligence would have been available and proper procedures followed. It demonstrated once again India's unpreparedness for such an attack. A committee

---

[10]Asit Jolly and Sandeep Unnithan, 'The Blunders of Pathankot', *India Today*, 6 January 2016, https://www.indiatoday.in/magazine/cover-story/story/20160118-pathankot-attacks-pakistan-nawaz-sharif-narendra-modi-828272-2016-01-06. Accessed on 15 March 2021.
[11]Shashank Joshi, 'Pathankot Attack: India-Pakistan Peace Talks Derailed?' *BBC*, 7 January 2016, https://www.bbc.com/news/world-asia-india-35240272. Accessed on 15 March 2021.

under the chairpersonship of the former vice chief of the Indian Army, Lt Gen. Philip Campose, studied the security lapses and made recommendations to prevent a repeat occurrence.[12] The government subsequently did action the recommendations, especially as the Pathankot attack was unfortunately succeeded by the Uri attack in September 2016, Nagrota Airbase incident in November 2016 and the Sunjuwan army base attack in February 2018.[13]

What followed was even more bizarre. Perhaps embarrassed about the terror attack on the heels of the Prime Minister's 'out-of-the-box' visit to Lahore and Raiwind, the government allowed a Pakistani Joint Investigation Team (JIT) unprecedented access to the Pathankot airbase and the infiltration route to try and convince them that the terrorists who perpetrated the attack had indeed come from Pakistan. After visiting the above-mentioned areas on 29 March 2016, the team returned to Pakistan and promptly debunked the terror attack as a false flag operation, thereby maliciously implying that the Indian side had carried out the terror attack.

Strangely, the then NIA Chief, Sharad Kumar, was quoted by *Network 18* in an interview as having stated in response to the question, 'Have you found any evidence that government of Pakistan or any Pakistani government agency was aiding the terrorists to enter India and attack Pathankot?':

> No. So far no evidence to show that Pakistan government or Pakistani government agency was helping Jaish or Masood Azhar or his aides carry out Pathankot attack.[14]

---

[12]Sandeep Unninathan, 'New Inquiry Committee to Probe What Went Wrong in Pathankot', *India Today*, 14 February 2016, https://www.indiatoday.in/mail-today/story/new-inquiry-committee-to-probe-what-went-wrong-in-pathankot-308634-2016-02-14. Accessed on 15 March 2021.

[13]PNS, 'Ministry Okays ₹1,487 Crore to Boost Army Camps' Security', *The Pioneer*, 11 February 2018, https://www.dailypioneer.com/2018/page1/ministry-okays-rs-1487-crore-to-boost-army-camps-security.html. Accessed on 15 March 2021.

[14]Arunima, 'No Evidence of Pakistan Govt Hand in Pathankot Attack: DG NIA', *News 18*, 2 June 2016, https://www.news18.com/news/india/no-evidence-of-pakistan-govt-hand-in-pathankot-attack-dg-nia-1251256.html. Accessed on 15 March 2021.

It is inconceivable as to what the Government of India had hoped to achieve by giving access to a Pakistani JIT. This gesture was not even reciprocated by the Pakistanis by allowing access to the NIA of India. New Delhi was thrown off by the lack of reciprocation that exacerbated an already acerbic relationship.

Furthermore, the Pakistani media insinuated that Tanzil Ahmed, an officer of the NIA involved with the Pathankot investigation, had been 'murdered' because he ostensibly had reservations about the trajectory of the investigation.[15] A fact hotly disputed by the NIA. Undoubtedly, Tanzil Ahmed, a former BSF officer who had been with the NIA since its inception in 2009, was murdered. His wife Farzana Khatoon also succumbed to her injuries. Later, the alleged killers were also arrested by the police. The police were of the opinion that a domestic dispute was responsible for the murder.[16] [17]

On balance, the handling of the aftermath of the Pathankot attack did not cover the Indian state with any glory. Its handling once again demonstrated that as of January 2016, the approach of the government was still to give Pakistan a long rope. The policy of strategic restraint was still a present continuum.

MAYHEM IN URI

While the government was still grappling with the aftermath of the Pathankot attack, a much larger and graver terrorist incursion was in the making. Four heavily armed terrorists breached the robustly

[15]Ansar Abbasi, 'Muslim inspector probing Pathankot attack shot dead,' *The News,* 4 April 2016, https://www.thenews.com.pk/print/110192-Muslim-inspector-probing-Pathankot-attack-shot-dead. Accessed on 15 March 2021.

[16]Debobrat Ghosh, 'NIA Officer's Killing in UP: Terror, Drug Cartel Emerge as Possible Motives,' *Firstpost,* 4 April 2016, https://www.firstpost.com/india/nia-officer-mohammed-tanzils-killing-terror-drug-cartel-emerge-as-possible-motives-2710212.html. Accessed on 15 March 2021.

[17]PTI, 'Two Held in NIA Officer Tanzil Ahmed Murder Case, *Business Standard,* 12 April 2016, https://www.business-standard.com/article/pti-stories/two-held-in-nia-officer-murder-case-116041200423_1.html. Accessed on 15 March 2021.

guarded headquarters of the 12th Brigade in Uri town of J&K. They launched a massive grenade attack on 18 September 2016. Nineteen soldiers of the Indian Army were killed in the attack. Another 30-odd were injured. It was among the deadliest of attacks on the Indian Army in over two decades.

The attack came in the backdrop of considerable unrest in the Kashmir valley following the neutralization of a Hizbul Mujahideen terrorist Burhan Wani, who was masquerading as a self-styled commander of that outfit, in July of that year. Once again, SOPs were ignored, and the consequences were devastating.[18] The attack was cleverly orchestrated especially owing to its timing.

The chief minister of J&K, Mehbooba Mufti, said that the attack was targeted at creating a 'war-like situation' in the region. 'Unfortunately, people in Jammu and Kashmir, who are already mired in an agonizing situation, shall have to bear the maximum brunt of the fresh attempts being made to step up violence and trigger fresh bloodshed in the state.'[19]

It unfortunately had/has become increasingly difficult for an ordinary Kashmiri to remain neutral with each passing year in the past decades after a vicious cycle of violence commenced in 1989. Pakistan's promise to support their cause in the form of such attacks has acted as a catalyst for young Kashmiris to exacerbate their struggle in the Valley against the security forces. Whenever an encounter with terrorists would take place during those years in the Valley, civilians would come out in large numbers in support of the militants.

This self-reinforcing dynamic has been a no-win situation for

[18]Asit Jolly and Sandeep Unnithan, 'Designed to Provoke', *India Today*, 3 October 2016, https://www.indiatoday.in/magazine/cover-story/story/20161003-uri-attack-kashmir-jammu-loc-terrorism-india-pakistan-829604-2016-09-22. Accessed on 15 March 2021.

[19]PTI, 'Uri Attack Aimed at Creating "War-Like" Situation: Mehbooba Mufti', *Hindustan Times*, 18 September 2016, https://www.hindustantimes.com/india-news/uri-attack-aimed-at-creating-war-like-situation-mehbooba-mufti/story-kME6S0Hk3QLI5JQRNfqDkL.html. Accessed on 15 March 2021.

many years now. While on one hand, the militarization of Kashmir shot up monumentally, on the other, these frequent terrorist attacks emanating from Pakistan served to keep Kashmir in the international spotlight. Attacks on the scale of Uri, while pushing the Indian government to take kinetic action,[20] also further internationalized the Kashmir problem, thereby squarely playing into the Pakistani game plan.

Unfortunately, Pakistan has an ally in this action-reaction dynamic and that is India's rising young middle class that has not experienced the losses of war and is fed jingoistic notions by an increasingly acerbic television media. In times of grave national crisis, when sober reflection is the need of the hour to assess the pluses and minuses of any retaliatory measure, it mindlessly presses hard on the government to take military action against Pakistan.

Viewing a complex situation in black-and-white binaries, it has assiduously cultivated a narrative that India had been 'too soft' on Pakistan, and it was time to get tough.[21] Inflamed public passions are at a 180-degree juxtaposition from the calibrated responses that cold strategic and even tactical assessments would recommend under such circumstances.

Coupled with that, 'hard action', even if it is an optical illusion, is disproportionately glorified to substantiate the narrative cultivated and proliferated over the years. The balance that should be critical in such circumstances therefore becomes the primary, and not even a collateral casualty.

After the Uri attack—confronted with a ratcheting rhetoric of jingoism and prisoner to its 10-year campaign of accusing its predecessor UPA government of being 'weak on terror'—the NDA

---

[20]Ankit Panda, 'Gurdaspur, Pathankot, and Now Uri: What Are India's Options?' *The Diplomat*, 19 September 2016, https://thediplomat.com/2016/09/gurdaspur-pathankot-and-now-uri-what-are-indias-options/. Accessed on 15 March 2021.
[21]Prashant Jha, 'Uri Attack: Is India Getting Impatient with Delhi's Strategic Restraint?' *Hindustan Times*, 18 September 2016, https://www.hindustantimes.com/india-news/why-india-is-getting-impatient-with-delhi-s-strategic-restraint/story-MutvAqKiAXWWdP8GbEdf4K.html. Accessed on 15 March 2021.

government had to fashion a response that could not be too strong so as to inflict substantive damage on a nuclear-armed neighbour. Correspondingly, it had to be vivid enough to satiate both spiralling media passions and the genuine sense of outrage of an ordinary Indian citizen who had been at the receiving end of Pakistan-sponsored terrorism for over three-and-a-half decades now. The impact of such an action on the future of bilateral relations between India and Pakistan had also to be factored in while sending a clear message to the Pakistani deep state that India's strategic patience was at the end of its tether.

It was also evident that strategic restraint qua Pakistan practised over decades had not worked. However, since options under a nuclear overhang are both limited, if not risky, the cost of using conventional means to respond to the depredations of semi-state actors is always a tricky calibration that carries the intrinsic risk of uncontrollable escalation.

HOW INDIA AVENGED URI

The kernel of a surgical strike seems to have come from the Myanmar border operation of June 2015 where a National Socialist Council of Nagaland-Khaplang (NSCN-K) camp was hit and almost 60 insurgents were killed.[22] A similar strike was thus contemplated against Pakistan also. Even though the possibility of an air strike was floated, a shallow cross-border action was zeroed in as the best available option. The intelligence network cultivated by the Indian army in J&K, and that part of Kashmir illegally occupied by Pakistan, perhaps came in handy while carrying out the operation.

The strikes marked a major policy shift as the army crossed over to enemy territory and destroyed terror launch pads. Around 80 fatalities were inflicted in this operation executed by the Indian

---

[22]Nitin A. Gokhale, 'The Inside Story of India's 2016 "Surgical Strikes"', *The Diplomat*, 23 September 2017, https://thediplomat.com/2017/09/the-inside-story-of-indias-2016-surgical-strikes/. Accessed on 15 March 2021.

Special Forces. This information was gleaned ostensibly from the radio chatter picked up from across the LoC.[23] This operation was tactically distinctive, because even during the Kargil War, the army had been strictly instructed to remain on the Indian side of the LoC.

Even though the strikes jeopardized bilateral relations between India and Pakistan, although not to the point of a complete breakdown, there was limited or no gain in not taking any action or in other words 'exercising restraint'. Apart from mounting popular pressure, there were a number of other indicators that pointed to the need for a kinetic retaliation by the Indian state.

Sameer Lalwani and Hannah Haegeland in their comprehensive study 'Anatomy of a Crisis' ponder over the reasons why India operationalized this dynamic response.[24] Two major factors have been outlined in this study. One is the large number of casualties in a single incident of terror. The study suggests that certain circumstances increase the intensity of a crisis situation. Government responses to any terror outrage also have to factor in domestic political imperatives. This dynamic is further circumscribed by popular perceptions of a given situation.

Geography also plays a role in determining the magnitude of a crisis situation. A terror attack on a relatively safer place, say a hinterland city, dwelling habitats of civilians and armed forces personnel, establishments of strategic or tactical importance and economic or commercial nerve centres can be the prime drivers of a crisis situation meriting a strong riposte. Then comes the duration of the attack; the longer a property is in control of the adversary, the greater will be the push to take military action. An important consideration is the number of people killed in that one incident.

---

[23]Shaurya Karanbir Gurung, 'Surgical Strikes Took down 70–80 Pakistanis: Lt Gen. D.S. Hooda (retd)', *The Economic Times*, 29 June 2018, https://economictimes. indiatimes.com/news/defence/surgical-strikes-took-down-70-80-pakistanis-lt-gen-ds-hooda-retd/articleshow/64793589.cms. Accessed on 15 March 2021.

[24]Sameer Lalwani and Hannah Haegeland (eds.), *Investigating Crises: South Asia's Lessons, Evolving Dynamics, and Trajectories*, Washington, DC: Stimson Center, 2018, 23-55.

The Uri terrorist attack, therefore, had all the necessary ingredients that would impel a government into action. The location was an army base which is of tactical value to India's defence, and the number of Indian soldiers killed in a single incident was the maximum in over 20 years.

The second factor is the tendency of the adversary to practise salami slicing and attempt to launch smaller but humiliating attacks over time. The Mumbai attacks were in any case, literally or symbolically, massive in scale. While there hasn't been an attack of that proportion since then, there had been a number of smaller but very irksome attacks. The attacks on Gurdaspur, Pathankot and Uri all occurred within 15 months, and therefore definitely had a provocative trajectory to them.

The dilemma for India in the two attacks prior to Uri was that had it taken kinetic action it perhaps may have found it difficult to rationalize its reaction to international audiences. Not that Israel or other nations that are subjected to terror attacks, really care about such niceties as the situation in May 2021 in Gaza demonstrated. International public opinion is fickle and more often than not dictated by geography.

While an attack on the West can provoke two decades of 'virtual occupation' of Afghanistan, an attack such as the one in Mumbai in 2008 only attracts sanctimonious homilies from those whose positions are aggressively hawkish to begin with when it comes to attacks on their homeland.

A military response is always fraught with the risk of escalation. In the case of Uri, it could have also led to a general escalation along the LoC and even the International Border with Pakistan; therefore, the cost-benefit equation is something that had to be carefully weighed. Nevertheless, Uri was one such inflection point where the balance certainly seemed to weigh in favour of a kinetic cross-border response as should have been done in the case of 26/11.

A one-time response that sends a clear, calibrated message to the adversary was therefore an action worth initiating. While it cannot be ascertained with any degree of finality as to how much of a dent surgical strikes really make on the terrorist infrastructure along the LoC, the optics of the attacks, at least domestically, played out well for the NDA government. It also seemed to get the equilibrium right. Pakistan just dismissed the surgical strike out of hand and never responded.

It is another matter that former generals of the Army have told me, and also stated publicly, that shallow cross-border operations, including the nasty business of decapitating each other's soldiers, have been the norm rather than the exception going back to the Chattisinghpora massacre in 2000. Some other sources put the time stamp of such operations even further back to the year 1998.[25] [26]

On the diplomatic front, at the 71st Session of the United Nations General Assembly (UNGA) that opened in New York on 13 September 2016, India once again called out Pakistan for sponsoring terrorism from across the border. Concurrently, Pakistan tried to internationalize the Kashmir issue again. Given that the attack on the Brigade headquarters in Uri took place on the fifth day of the UNGA's annual assembly, i.e., 18 September, Indian diplomats were successful in rallying support from many key international players such as the UK, France and the US, all of whom condemned the Uri attack. Germany, Japan and South Korea issued official statements denouncing the attack and expressing support for India in its fight against terrorism. Similarly, many West Asian countries like Saudi Arabia, the UAE, Bahrain and Qatar showed support for India and censured the perpetrators of the attack in their official statements. These countries being important members of Organisation of Islamic Cooperation (OIC)

---

[25]Sobhana K. Nair, 'Surgical Strikes Held in Past Too, But Were Clandestine', *Mumbai Mirror*, 10 October 2016, https://mumbaimirror.indiatimes.com/news/india/surgical-strikes-held-in-past-too-but-were-clandestine/articleshow/54771709.cms. Accessed on 15 March 2021.

[26]'Operation Ginger: Tit-For-Tat across the Line of Control', *The Hindu*, 9 October 2016, https://www.thehindu.com/news/national/Operation-Ginger-Tit-for-tat-across-the-Line-of-Control/article15477494.ece. Accessed on 15 March 2021.

have been traditional backers of Pakistan.[27]

The international support in the aftermath of the attack was perhaps also important while taking the decision to launch these shallow cross-border incursions. It is hard to imagine that a big decision of entering enemy territory and taking out terrorist bases could have been made if international support had not been explicitly forthcoming or tilted towards the other side, i.e., Pakistan. This had been the case throughout the 1980s and '90s, going up to the 9/11 attacks in 2001. Those were the days when 'major powers' chose to be unsympathetic and even dismissive of India's lament that it was a victim of cross-border terror emanating from Pakistan.

After the 'surgical strikes', the US supported India for dealing decisively with terror. Russia also articulated that it stood for 'decisive struggle against terrorism in all its manifestations'. In South Asia, Bangladesh strongly supported the strikes, adding that any country has full right to respond to such a kind of terrorist attack. Afghanistan, the Maldives, Sri Lanka and Bhutan all pulled out of the SAARC summit due that year in Islamabad citing concerns over terrorism and lack of a 'conducive atmosphere'.

India had briefed top envoys from 25 countries on the context of the strikes after the operation had culminated successfully. The DGMO also got in touch with his Pakistani counterpart both post the Uri attack and after the surgical strikes to convey in unambiguous terms the reasons for the operation.[28]

The government in Islamabad conveniently denied that any strike had been conducted across the border and termed it as yet another incident of cross-border firing. It therefore absolved itself

---

[27]Vivek Chadha, Rumel Dahiya, Neha Kohli and Shruti Pandalai, 'Uri, Surgical Strikes and International Reactions', *Manohar Parrikar-Institute for Defence Studies and Analyses,* 4 October 2016, https://idsa.in/issuebrief/uri-surgical-strikes-and-international-reactions_041016. Accessed on 15 March 2021.

[28]'India's Surgical Strikes across LoC: Full Statement by DGMO Lt Gen. Ranbir Singh', *Hindustan Times,* 29 September 2016, https://www.hindustantimes.com/india-news/india-s-surgical-strikes-across-loc-full-statement-by-dgmo-lt-gen-ranbir-singh/story-Q5yrp0gjvxKPGazDzAnVsM.html. Accessed on 15 March 2021.

from taking immediate retaliatory measures against India. Even though Pakistan denied the strikes on terror camps located on its side of the LoC, the humiliation and embarrassment caused to the Pakistani deep state made a tit-for-tat response almost inevitable.[29]

OPERATIONS SHROUDED IN SECRECY

The Uri surgical strikes have certainly not been the only one. India has a history of dealing with problems on the border by launching such strikes into the enemy territory. The objective is to destroy terrorist infrastructure and all its related human and material elements, without causing any damage to civilian structures and people in whose villages and small towns these structures are set up for the purposes of active concealment in plain sight.

In the past, India's surgical strikes have been shrouded in secrecy. Some are even disputed as the government has refused to take ownership of them. The events leading up to the war of 1971 with Pakistan, including the Indian Army's training of and even joint operations with the Mukti Bahini deep inside Bangladesh, before the formal commencement of hostilities is well documented by historians. This could be termed as perhaps the earliest instance of a surgical strike by India. Similar strikes, although of differing scale and magnitude, had been carried out in 1971 in Pakistan and Pakistan Occupied Kashmir, in 2003 in Bhutan, 1995, 2006 and 2015 in Myanmar,[30] and sporadically along the LoC with Pakistan going back at least two decades as enunciated earlier.

The distinctive feature of the surgical strikes against Pakistan in 2016 is the way it was well advertised, with the government

---

[29]Sumita Kumar, 'Post-Uri Response by India', *Manohar Parrikar-Institute for Defence Studies and Analyses,* 30 September 2016, https://idsa.in/idsacomments/post-uri-response-by-india_skumar_300916. Accessed on 15 March 2021.

[30]Arshi Aggarwal, 'From 1971 to 2016: History of Surgical Strikes in India', *News Nation,* 29 September 2017, https://english.newsnationtv.com/india/news/from-1971-to-2016-history-of-surgical-strikes-in-india-anniversary-of-surgical-strike-on-pakistan-uri-attack-183212.html. Accessed on 15 March 2021.

taking complete ownership of the action, or series of actions, in an internationally televised presser anchored jointly by the DGMO and the official spokesperson of the MEA.

In the networked world that we live in, public ownership of the cross-border action slaked the public sentiment that wanted Pakistan to be punished. It also indicated a shift from the Government of India's erstwhile policy to keep such strikes under wraps. The NDA seems to have made the unfortunate assessment that these strikes pay political dividends. Accordingly, the marketing of such government action to domestic public opinion has regrettably attained paramount priority. While earlier the approach was to act with stealth and impose a cost that sends a clear message to the adversary, this model has been turned on its head with the post-Uri strikes.

Insofar as the Congress was concerned, it supported the action taken by the government against Pakistan. However, the chest thumping by the ministers of the NDA government and functionaries of the BJP was problematic. It was perhaps the most blatant use of national security responses for partisan political purposes. This in many senses would become the template for the future. This public gloating by important government and ruling party functionaries was rightly red-flagged and objected to by the spokespersons of the Congress even at the risk of being termed anti-national.[31] [32] [33]

A strange benchmark of nationalism had been unleashed on the nation since 2014—if you criticized the BJP, you were labelled

---

[31]"Surgical Strikes Politicised, Overhyped: Congress Thanks General Hooda for Exposing Modi', *India Today*, 8 December 2018, https://www.indiatoday.in/india/ story/surgical-strikes-ds-hooda-congress-modi-1405130-2018-12-08. Accessed on 15 March 2021.

[32]Siddharth Varadarajan, 'Chidambaram Interview Dropped as *NDTV* Censors News that "Compromises National Security"', *The Wire*, 8 October 2016, https://thewire. in/media/ndtv-censor-news-compromises-national-security. Accessed on 15 March 2021.

[33]M.K. Venu, 'Modi and BJP Are Openly Politicising National Security, After Saying They Will Not', *The Wire*, 13 October 2016, https://thewire.in/politics/modi-bjp-national-security. Accessed on 15 March 2021.

anti-national, if you critiqued the government, you were subversive and if you asked legitimate questions about the armed forces and the defence establishment, you were a downright traitor. One party seems to believe it has a monopoly on nationalism.

Nothing can be more unfortunate and discordant than to divide the nation on the lines of 'my nationalism is more than yours, my patriotism is better than yours'. The terms 'nationalism' and 'patriotism' have very distinct connotations and historical overtones if not experiences.

PULWAMA PAYBACK: RESETTING THE PAK PLAYBOOK

Once again, another lethal terror attack took place on 14 February 2019 in the Pulwama district of J&K. A JeM terrorist drove an SUV full of explosives into a convoy carrying paramilitary troops on the Srinagar-Jammu national highway. At least 44 CRPF personnel were killed and more than 20 injured in the suicide attack. India summoned the Pakistani High Commissioner and lodged a strong protest. PM Modi, in a statement, underscored that the security forces had been given freedom to operationalize a response.

The suicide bomber in this case was a 22-year-old named Adil Ahmed Dar, a member of the JeM, but resident of our legitimate part of Kashmir.[34] The part in illegal occupation of Pakistan including the Northern Areas constitutes illegitimate possession. His family said he began to harbour anti-India sentiments after he was injured in a protest following Burhan Wani's killing in 2016. It reflects how terrorist organizations have used the angst of the Kashmiri youth to achieve their malevolent objective of perpetrating terror.

The amount of warfare-grade explosives used in the attack could not have been purchased by legal means or obtained from the black market. The only possibility is that it came from across the border. Since the amount was large, it could have been done only over a

---

[34]"Kashmir Attack: Tracing the Path that Led to Pulwama', *BBC*, 1 May 2019, https://www.bbc.com/news/world-asia-india-47302467. Accessed on 15 March 2021.

period of time. This pointed towards serious intelligence lapses by the multifarious agencies that operate in J&K.[35]

In fact, a number of key questions still remain unanswered. For example, who allowed an unarmed, unescorted convoy to ply in a known area of terrorist activity? How was RDX and other explosives brought into J&K? Who assembled the car bomb? How many reconnaissance missions were carried out before the actual strike? How was Adil Ahmed Dar indoctrinated into becoming a suicide bomber? How many such human bombers are currently there in J&K waiting for the next set of instructions to blow themselves up?

The NIA had filed a charge sheet in the above incident in August 2020. Whether it satisfactorily answers all the above and more questions, only the outcome of the trial and the consequential judgement[36] would judicially determine.

As expected by now, India retaliated with an air strike on Balakot on 26 February 2019 at a large JeM camp where many key personnel of the group, senior commanders and trainers were reportedly located. Balakot falls in Pakistan's Khyber Pakhtunkhwa province and naturally the air strike was seen by Pakistan as violation of its sovereignty. The Pakistani air force also attempted to strike Indian military installations in J&K, but failed either by default or design maybe not wanting to escalate an already inflamed and deteriorating situation. Wing Commander Abhinandan Varthaman piloting a MiG-21 Bison aircraft was hit while in hot pursuit of a Pakistani aircraft. Upon ejecting, he landed in POK. He was captured by the Pakistani Army but released two days later due to both Indian resolve and ostensibly some international pressure operating behind the

---

[35]Prabhash K. Dutta, 'What We Don't Know about Pulwama Attack that Almost Brought India-Pak to War', *India Today*, 14 February 2020, https://www.indiatoday.in/news-analysis/story/what-we-don-t-about-pulwama-attack-that-almost-brought-india-pak-to-war-1646413-2020-02-14. Accessed on 15 March 2021.

[36]Ananya Bharadwaj, 'NIA Files 5,000-Page Chargesheet in Pulwama Terror Attack, Names Jem Chief Masood Azhar', *The Print*, 25 August 2020, https://theprint.in/india/nia-files-5000-page-chargesheet-in-pulwama-terror-attack-names-jem-chief-masood-azhar/488798/. Accessed on 15 March 2021.

scenes to calm an impending escalation.[37]

The extent of damage done by the Balakot air strike is not in the public realm and has been the subject of an animated debate. A report published by the Australian Strategic Policy Institute (ASPI) concluded based on satellite imagery that these strikes 'missed', failing to hit the actual targets.[38] Fortunately, the site chosen for the strike was on a hilltop and not in the densely populated areas of POK where most Jaish camps are located. Missing the target in a densely populated area would have resulted in mass civilian casualties and severe loss of face for India.

Another report by the Digital Forensics Lab (DFRL) of the Washington-based think tank, Atlantic Council, also independently reached a similar conclusion that the strike had perhaps more optical than substantive value in denuding the infrastructure of terror.[39] In fact, the DFRL Report was headlined 'Surgical Strike in Pakistan a Botched Operation?'

In October 2020, a member of National Assembly of Pakistan and leader of the Pakistan Muslim League (N) Party, Ayaz Sadiq, revealed in his assembly speech that the Pakistani government had released IAF Wing Commander Abhinandan fearing another attack by India.[40] To that, Foreign Office spokesman of Pakistan, Zahid

---

[37]ET Online, 'Pulwama terror attack: What happened on Feb 14 and how India responded', *The Economic Times*, 14 February 2020, https://economictimes.indiatimes.com/news/defence/pulwama-terror-attack-what-happened-on-feb-14-and-how-india-responded/articleshow/74128489.cms. Accessed on 15 March 2021.

[38]Marcus Hellyer, Nathan Ruser and Aakriti Bachhawat, 'India's strike on Balakot: a very precise miss?' *The Strategist*, 27 March 2019, https://www.aspistrategist.org.au/indias-strike-on-balakot-a-very-precise-miss/. Accessed on 15 March 2021.

[39]Michael Sheldon@DFRLab, 'Surgical Strike in Pakistan a Botched Operation?' *Medium*, 1 March 2019, https://medium.com/dfrlab/surgical-strike-in-pakistan-a-botched-operation-7f6cda834b24. Accessed on 15 March 2021.

[40]Nilavro Ghosh, 'Pakistani Lawmaker Ayaz Sadiq Stands by Indian Wing Commander Abhinandan Varthaman's Release Statement', *Hindustan Times*, 31 October 2020, https://www.hindustantimes.com/world-news/pakistani-lawmaker-ayaz-sadiq-stands-by-indian-wing-commander-abhinandan-varthaman-s-release-statement/story-NbZVF2aVYoZNjl2erh6p8H.html. Accessed on 15 March 2021.

Hafeez Chaudhri, said that there was no pressure on Pakistan to release Abhinandan and it was a gesture of peace.[41]

Given the charged nature of the situation at that time, it is plausible that India would have attacked Pakistan across a border front. Whether that would have been a wise choice, considering the possibility of quick escalation between two nuclear-armed states is moot.

What Pulwama-Balakot demonstrated was that there were no institutional off-ramps that could have been accessed to deescalate the situation. Had Wing Commander Abhinandan not been released under Indian pressure or otherwise, or if the Balakot strike would have had unintended collateral consequences, an escalation would have been inevitable.

ENTERING A NEW REALM

The continued use of terror by Pakistan and the conventional responses now institutionalized by India in the absence of any sustained, structured and substantive conversation is very tricky. India and Pakistan have entered a new realm in their seven-decade old adversarial existence.

The Pulwama attack highlighted once again Pakistan's continued use of terror tactics and jihad as a military strategy to inflict damage on India. The four wars fought between the two sides have underscored that India could not be defeated in conventional warfare, and hence the semi-state actor strategy has been employed since the 1980s.[42] Punjab was the first frontier in 1980, followed by J&K in the 1990s and then the paradigm was upscaled to the rest

---

[41]PTI, 'Abhinandan Released for Peace, says Pakistan', *The Hindu*, 29 October 2020, https://www.thehindu.com/news/international/wing-commander-abhinandan-varthaman-iaf-pilot-was-released-as-a-gesture-of-peace-says-pakistan/article32976316.ece. Accessed on 15 March 2021.

[42]Yudhijit Bhattacharjee, 'The Terrorist Who Got Away', *The New York Times Magazine*, 19 March 2020, https://www.nytimes.com/2020/03/19/magazine/masood-azhar-jaish.html. Accessed on 15 March 2021.

of the country, as evidenced by the attack on the Indian Parliament in December 2001.

The ISI was instrumental in training these non-/semi-state actors in Afghanistan to fight the Soviet Union. When the Soviet Union left Afghanistan in 1989, this strategy seemed successful in achieving geopolitical objectives. It is, therefore, unsurprising that Pakistan decided to take full advantage of the unrest and turmoil that took an ugly turn in Kashmir from the late 1980s. At the heart of the Pakistani strategy to bleed India with a thousand cuts is the unquenched desire for revenge over the creation of Bangladesh in 1971. That is a humiliation that the Pakistani Army has not been able to live down. It is a collective scar on the institutional psyche of the Pakistani military establishment.

The Pakistani deep state and the ISI are also responsible for upscaling the model of suicide bombers in South, West and Central Asia. A phenomenon that was unique to the Liberation Tigers of Tamil Eelam (LTTE) in Sri Lanka has been fine-tuned by the Pakistani deep state into a strategy where it becomes difficult for those at the receiving end of terror attacks to find an effective antidote against religiously motivated young men for whom their life is an immaterial commodity in the quest of achieving some notion of Jannat (heaven). Lest it be forgotten that as late as 1987, the CIA-Pakistan deep state mujahedeen could not find a single human bomber to blow up Salang Pass that would have cut off the most vital Soviet supply route to Afghanistan.

However, there is one basic flaw in Pakistan's assumption that the terror strategy will work in the case of its relations with India. The Soviet Union was a foreign power ruling over Afghanistan from far-off Moscow, unfamiliar with the terrain, culture and people of Afghanistan. J&K, on the other hand, has been an integral part of India since time immemorial and has been administered by democratically elected governments for substantive periods since 1947. Politicians in J&K and the bureaucrats working there are familiar with the culture, ethos, terrain and people of Kashmir.

HOW THE MILITARY HIJACKED PAKISTAN

The dysfunction in Pakistan is a result of the disproportionately large military resource being allocated to the state in 1947. This skew right from the inception has allowed the military to strong-arm the civilian government ever since. To maintain an undisputable position, it has vilified India and painted it as the demon which wants to destroy Pakistan. Nothing could be further from the truth. The narrative of an evil India coupled with the 'Masla-e Kashmir' issue has provided much required legitimacy to the Pakistani military for grabbing power in the country and a disproportionate stake over its national resources.

The coups post 1947 have meant that Pakistan in its entire post-independence history of 72 years was ruled by the military for a good 33 years. That is enough time for any institution as powerful as the military to develop deep roots in the governance mechanism. The Pakistani deep state is therefore an offspring of the ghastly and completely ill-conceived partition of India.

The Pakistani military constantly seeks to avenge the humiliation of the 1971 war where more than 90,000 Pakistani soldiers were taken prisoners of war after a crushing defeat by the Indian military. It constantly seeks to undo that ignominy by attempting to operationalize and deploy sub-nationalistic and now religion-based violence in J&K to sever it from India. The hauntingly beautiful vale of Kashmir is a Muslim-majority region that in the Pakistani estimation should have been a part of Pakistan after the partition of the Indian subcontinent.[43] The Pakistani deep state has therefore trained, armed and financed militants to wage a war against India to take Kashmir back. It created the Taliban in Afghanistan that has now survived for two decades sheltered by Pakistan and kept operating successfully in the Afghan countryside. It defied all American, NATO and International Security

---

[43]Shivam Vij, 'Why the Pakistani Deep State Sponsors Terrorism in India', *The Print*, 18 February 2019, https://theprint.in/opinion/why-the-pakistani-deep-state-sponsors-terrorism-in-india/194395/. Accessed on 15 March 2021.

Assistance Force (ISAF) efforts to neutralize it and with stunning speed has seized almost the entire Afghanistan.

What is however moot is whether it is the Taliban or regular/ irregular Pakistan army personnel who are/were in the vanguard of the blitzkrieg in Afghanistan. The meltdown of the Afghan National Defense and Security Forces (ANDSF) would keep strategic scholars in business for at least the next decade. However, the regional and even international implications especially for Pax Americana of the Taliban takeover would be gargantuan to say the least.

TOWARDS PERMANENCE IN CONFLICT

The Indian response after the Uri attack had changed the very nature of the bilateral relationship, at least temporarily. This action-reaction dynamic will lead to more frequent collisions between the two states not limited to the border alone. The new paradigm of launching terror attacks and strikes against each other, however, does not address the problems between the two countries in any way.

An article by V. Sudarshan in *The Hindu* calls out the normalizing of strikes and attacks in the bilateral relationship between India and Pakistan.[44] It also brings into question whether at all such a strike has an impact on the terror structures which have waged a continuous war against India. The support they have received has been consistent and strikes haven't created the desired impact. It has pushed the government into advancing the level of such punitive action to even launching airstrikes. This is a dangerous trend as it tries to resolve an ethnic, geopolitical and historical problem compounded by the use of terror by Pakistan through coercive means.

It will surely escalate tensions in the neighbourhood and focus unwanted attention from outside. As a result, the region will become

---

[44]V. Sudarshan, 'The Magical Effects of a Good Surgical Strike', *The Hindu*, 27 February 2019, https://www.thehindu.com/thread/politics-and-policy/the-magical-effects-of-a-good-surgical-strike/article26385830.ece. Accessed on 15 March 2021.

more volatile and given that it is densely populated, humanitarian crisis of gargantuan proportions could unfold.

India can launch determinative action against its adversaries but it is highly doubtful whether with its current economic situation it can sustain a prolonged conflict especially where even China would inevitably be involved. Even though India's efforts in the betterment of its defence on the northern borders will irk both Pakistan and China and invite reactions as has happened since April 2020, it is indispensable for protecting its sovereignty in the region. India's spending on defence will have to continuously increase given the vast borders in conflict and superior technology and manpower needed to be deployed there. However, it is essential to point out that India's defence expenditure as a percentage of GDP has been constantly declining since 2014. Various reports of the Parliamentary Standing Committee on Defence and even the Estimates Committee have flagged this very disturbing trend.[45]

In a rather unusual development, the DGsMO of India and Pakistan declared a ceasefire on 25 February 2021 at noon. The terse joint statement reads as follows and deserves to be quoted in full.

> The Director Generals of Military Operations of India and Pakistan held discussions over the established mechanism of hotline contact. The two sides reviewed the situation along the Line of Control and all other sectors in a free, frank and cordial atmosphere.
>
> In the interest of achieving mutually beneficial and sustainable peace along the borders, the two DGsMO agreed to address each other's core issues and concerns which have propensity to disturb peace and lead to violence. Both sides agreed for strict observance of all agreements, understandings

---

[45]PTI, 'Parliamentary Panel Slams Centre for Inadequate Funds in Defence Budget', *NDTV*, 25 July 2018, https://www.ndtv.com/india-news/parliamentary-panel-slams-centre-for-inadequate-funds-in-defence-budget-1889736. Accessed on 15 March 2021.

and cease firing along the Line of Control and all other sectors with effect from midnight 24/25 Feb 2021.

Both sides reiterated that existing mechanisms of hotline contact and border flag meetings will be utilized to resolve any unforeseen situation or misunderstanding.[46]

It is believed that this ceasefire was a result of sustained back-channel diplomacy, and the chronically corrosive environment in the region perhaps may have compelled the governments to look beyond the theatre of perennial conflict. One formulation in the joint statement lends itself to multiple interpretations. It reads as follows: 'In the interest of achieving mutually beneficial and sustainable peace along the borders, the two DGsMO agreed to address each other's core issues and concerns which have propensity to disturb peace and lead to violence'. The reference to core issues and concerns obviously means terrorism in the case of India and J&K for Pakistan.

The question of whether this opens the door for a revival of the composite/resumed dialogue (or whatever other nomenclature it may be draped in), remains open ended. However, were that to happen, both countries would have to guard against hard-line elements within the Pakistani establishment who would work overtime to scuttle this overture. History bears testimony to the fact that over the past two decades whenever India and Pakistan have moved to normalize their relationship, a terror attack has halted the process dead in its tracks.

We will have to see if this process that has commenced on 25 February will be more than just a ceasefire, given the fact that from 2004 to 2014, there have been 550 ceasefire violations. The last ceasefire in 2003 that effectively held the field till 2008 had brought down ceasefire violations.[47] Subsequently this number went up to

---

[46]'Joint Statement', *Ministry of Defence*, 25 February 2021, https://pib.gov.in/PressReleasePage.aspx?PRID=1700682. Accessed on 15 March 2021.

[47]Christophe Jaffrelot, 'Ceasefire Violations in Kashmir: A War by Other

2,936 in 2018, 3,299 in 2019 and 5,133 in 2020 respectively. Given the enormity of the increase, even a stand-alone ceasefire that mitigates or totally eliminates the mutual exchange of fire on the border is more than a step forward.

This is a street that both India and Pakistan have walked down before. They have declared multiple ceasefires in the past, and every one of them has failed. These ceasefires have come after a period of intense crises, so the recent one is no surprise. For it to stick and allow any productive engagement between the two countries, it would need the backing of formalized mechanisms that prevent repeated violations of this ceasefire agreement.[48] It remains to be seen whether the ceasefire will be followed up and an institutional mechanism put in place by both the nations to bring about some degree of depth to the process. A disinterest or apprehension to pursue would put the ceasefire in constant risk of collapse, returning the situation to the earlier precarious state of play in the bilateral relationship.

India's Pakistan policy for a few decades before 2016 had been one of strategic restraint. The objective behind that was to not disrupt the rather intricate balance in the region and escalate tensions between the two nuclear-armed nations. The Pakistani deep state, that has tried to destabilize India even more aggressively after 1971, unfortunately perceived it as a license to operationalize its 'bleed India with a thousand cuts policy'. The policy shift in 2016 meant that India was moving away from its earlier 'reserve' and was willing to use conventional means overtly to impose a cost on Pakistan for its shenanigans.

However, kinetic action to engage with neighbours cannot be a permanent state of play. Sustained dialogue over issues such

---

Means?' *Carnegie Endowment,* 24 October 2019, https://carnegieendowment.org/2018/10/24/ceasefire-violations-in-kashmir-war-by-other-means-pub-77573. Accessed on 15 March 2021.
[48]Happymon Jacob, 'The Anatomy of a Spring Ceasefire', *The Hindu,* 3 March 2021, https://www.thehindu.com/opinion/lead/the-anatomy-of-a-spring-ceasefire/article33974369.ece. Accessed on 15 March 2021.

as Kashmir, border resources, terrorism and other outstanding obstacles is the only way forward to create a shared future.

The Indian establishment therefore must re-examine the very nature of the relationship it seeks with Pakistan and try and locate it in the context of wider approach to the neighbourhood. It also must factor in that South Asia is the least integrated region in the neighbourhood with one of the worst human development parameters in the world. Is this a sustainable solution for over 2 billion people who call South Asia home?

TEN

KASHMIR: THE DORMANT VOLCANO

It was 5 August 2019. As the proceedings in Parliament commenced on that Monday morning, there was widespread apprehension of a major move by the NDA government as several political leaders in the erstwhile state of J&K, including two former chief ministers, had been detained the night before. There was a complete communication blackout in the state (internet, mobile phones and other modes). Thousands of security personnel had been deployed in J&K. There were restrictions on civilian movement, and even the ongoing Amaranth Yatra had been called off citing security concerns. However, the speculation was that the government, at best, would repeal Article 35A. Nobody in their wildest dreams imagined that the government would go any further than that.

A few days prior to that, I ran into Home Minister Amit Shah in a corridor of the Parliament. He was headed to his chamber and I was going to meet another minister for constituency work.

I casually asked him, 'Are you bringing a bill to repeal Article 35A of the Constitution?'

'You do not need Parliamentary approval for that,' he replied.

It was a chance conversation and I did not make much of it. Finally, however he did introduce a Constitutional Order in the House to supersede the Constitution (Application to Jammu and Kashmir) Order, 1954 that had originally inserted Article 35A into the Constitution of India.

By way of context, it would perhaps be instructive to point out that Article 35A was inserted into the Constitution of India through the Constitution (Application to Jammu and Kashmir) order, 1954 Constitution Order Number-48. It was promulgated by the then President Rajendra Prasad under Article 370, on the advice of the Nehru-led Union Government, without being actually introduced as a bill in Parliament to amend the Constitution as laid down in Article 368 of the Constitution. The Supreme Court, at that point in time, was seized of a bunch of petitions challenging the Constitutionality of Article 35A. In its defence, it was argued that the provision was validly inserted and that the Supreme Court had, in 1961 and 1969, upheld the powers of the President under Article 370(1)(d) of the Constitution to enact such constitutional orders.

In the Lok Sabha chamber, news soon started filtering in that Amit Shah had introduced two resolutions and two bills in the Rajya Sabha. Someone rushed to the Rajya Sabha to get a copy of the bill and soon it became evident that the government had gone far beyond repealing Article 35A.

There was stunned disbelief at least in the Opposition benches and almost equal surprise in the Treasury benches in the Lok Sabha as members pored over the only copy of the bill available in the House and consulted with each other trying to make sense of what the government was doing. Soon, the bulk of the Opposition was in the well, protesting and strongly deprecating the move. The bedlam continued well into the afternoon and the evening.

In the Rajya Sabha, the Home Minister had introduced the Constitution (Application to Jammu & Kashmir) Order, 2019 {Ref. Article 370(1) of Constitution of India—issued by the President of India to supersede the 1954 order related to Article 370, Resolution for Repeal of Article 370 of the Constitution of India {Ref. Article 370 (3)}, Jammu & Kashmir (Reorganisation) Bill, 2019 {Ref. Article 3 of Constitution of India} and Jammu & Kashmir Reservation (2nd Amendment) Bill, 2019.[1]

---

[1]'Government Brings Resolution to Repeal Article 370 of the Constitution', *Press Information Bureau*, 5 August 2019, https://pib.gov.in/PressReleasePage.

The Constitution (Application to Jammu and Kashmir) Order 2019 – CO 272 stated that all the provisions of the Indian Constitution would now apply to the state of J&K, thereby effectively terminating the special status of the state.

The Jammu and Kashmir Reorganisation Bill bifurcated the state and created two separate Union territories—Jammu & Kashmir with a legislature, and Ladakh without a legislature. This meant that the Constitution of India would now apply in full measure across J&K and Ladakh. The J&K legislature would henceforth have no discretionary powers notwithstanding the fact that J&K has or had a Constitution of its own. The resolution, Constitutional order and the bill were passed in the Rajya Sabha on that very day despite vociferous resistance from the Opposition.

The next day, they were introduced in the Lok Sabha. As the lead speaker from the Opposition benches, I opened the debate recounting the entire history of the state before dealing with the unconstitutionality of the government's actions. In a 27-minute speech, I laid out the opposition of the Congress to the proposed resolutions and the J&K Reorganisation Bill.[2] Since the government had the numbers in the Lok Sabha, the bills and the resolutions were passed but not before the Opposition called for a division to register its dissent by voting against the government's machinations.

Following the resolutions passed by both Houses of Parliament, the government issued a further Constitutional order 273 on 6 August, declaring all the clauses of Article 370 to be inoperative. The amended Article 370 would now read as follows:

> 370. All provisions of this Constitution, as amended from time to time, without any modifications or exceptions, shall apply to the State of Jammu and Kashmir notwithstanding anything contrary contained in article 152 or article 308 or any

aspx?PRID=1581308. Accessed on 15 March 2021.
[2] The same can be accessed at http://loksabhaph.nic.in/Debates/Result17.aspx?db sl=776&ser=&smode=t#4430*2. Accessed on 15 March 2021.

other article of this Constitution or any other provision of the Constitution of Jammu and Kashmir or any law, document, judgment, ordinance, order, by-law, rule, regulation, notification, custom or usage having the force of law in the territory of India, or any other instrument, treaty or agreement as envisaged under article 363 or otherwise.

There was a moment of levity during the debate. After I finished my speech, Amit Shah stood up and asked whether I supported or opposed the abrogation of Article 370. To which I replied: '*Ek angrezi ki kitaab hai, har cheez kali aur safed nahi hoti* (There is an English novel, everything is not in black and white'), there are 50 shades of grey in between.'

From that moment onwards, that was the only thing about my speech that social media trolls picked on and had a party at my expense. *Fifty Shades of Grey* is an erotic trilogy. However, more than just the erotica, it is about complexity, subtlety and nuance also. However, all that was lost on the 'intelligent' users of social media. The *Business Standard* reported, 'Manish Tewari seems to have read #fiftyshadesofgrey last night, and climaxed vigorously in Lok Sabha'. Another wrote, 'Congress's Manish Tewari suggests not everything is black or white, there are 50 shades of grey in between. And the best part is HM Amit Shah's laughter during the statement. Best debate ever.'[3]

As an aside, I do doubt that despite his laughter being noticed by the social media trolls and which, frankly, I did not see as we stood on opposite sides of the aisle with eyes locked onto each other, Amit Shah would have read the contentious book. He perhaps was laughing at my avoiding a cryptic yes or no answer, and instead answering through a metaphor.

---

[3]ANI, 'Congress' Manish Tiwari trolled for mentioning "Fifty Shades of Grey" in LS', *Business Standard*, 6 August 2019, https://www.business-standard.com/article/news-ani/congress-manish-tiwari-trolled-for-mentioning-fifty-shades-of-grey-in-ls-119080600621_1.html. Accessed on 15 March 2021.

What I had in mind when I used that analogy was that if the government thinks that the 'Masla-e-Kashmir' can be resolved by merely abrogating Article 370 or 35A, and stripping J&K of its statehood, then they do not understand both the layered and tenacious nature of the problem. Later, I wrote a piece explaining the context of that remark, not for the benefit of bhakts, trolls and perverts, but for those who were genuinely perplexed by my use of a metaphor that seems to be synonymous with sexual violence in the public mind.[4]

MOVING THROUGH CONTROVERSIAL WATERS

The state of J&K, as we knew it till 5 August 2019, came into existence when first Jammu, then Kashmir and subsequently Ladakh were taken by the armies of Maharaja Ranjit Singh, the Sikh ruler of what is colloquially known as the Lahore Durbar. In 1808, Ranjit Singh attacked Jammu and expelled Raja Jit Dev, the ruler of Jammu state who first found sanctuary in British India and later received in appanage the estate of Akhrota, modern-day Pathankot, for the upkeep of his dependents and himself.

Till around 1816, Maharaja Ranjit Singh kept Jammu as a tributary of the Lahore Durbar. However, Ranjit Singh's rule was successfully challenged by Mian Dido, a popular leader of Jammu. He then decided to utilize the services of Gulab Singh, a Dogra chieftain in his service from that region, to preserve his rule in Jammu. Gulab Singh acquitted himself honourably and consolidated the hold of the Lahore Durbar in the Jammu hills. It brought rich bonuses for both Gulab Singh and his family. Quickly, almost every part of the Jammu region was assigned to Gulab Singh and his kinfolk as jagirs. Kashmir was taken by the Lahore Durbar in 1819.

The region came under non-Islamic rule for the first time in

4Manish Tewari, 'The 50 Shades of Grey in J&K', *The Tribune*, 20 August 2019, https://www.tribuneindia.com/news/archive/comment/the-50-shades-of-grey-in-j-k-819908. Accessed on 15 March 2021.

close to 500 years. At the time, not only was Kashmir vital to Sikh control of its territory, but it also appeared as strategically important in the three-way struggle between the British, Russian and Chinese for control of Central Asia.

On 17 June 1822, Gulab Singh was personally coronated by Ranjit Singh as the Raja of Jammu at Akhnoor on the western (right) bank of the Chenab River.[5] Gulab Singh was granted complete autonomy. He maintained his own army which was headed by an able warrior, Zorawar Singh Kahluria.

In 1834, Zorawar Singh captured Ladakh. Gulab Singh kept expanding the Sikh empire further north to Baltistan, Gilgit and Gartok near the source of the River Indus right up to Lake Mansarovar. By 1841, Gulab Singh controlled all the lands south and east of the Kashmir Valley and as a consequence, the lucrative shawl-wool trade as well. One year later, both the Emperor of China and the then Dalai Lama signed the Treaty of Chushul with Gulab Singh to maintain status–quo. This resulted in the loose delineation of the borders between Ladakh and Tibet, then under Chinese suzerainty.

The death of Maharaja Ranjit Singh on 27 June 1839 shook the foundations of the expansive Sikh Empire. Gulab Singh, with considerable astuteness carefully planned to consolidate his position within this declining Sikh Empire, and began to harbour designs on the Kashmir Valley. From a position of strength, he inserted himself in the politics of Punjab by offering his military services first to the British against the Sikhs in the Anglo-Sikh wars, and then his negotiating services to both once the British had secured a victory in the wars of 1846. These negotiations only served to further consolidate Gulab Singh's authority over the territory he now controlled. For the Sikh Empire that he had served earlier, it only added insult to injury.

---

[5]'Nation Remembers Gulab Singh—the Founder of Jammu and Kashmir on His Coronation Day', *Newsroom*, 17 June 2020, https://newsroom24x7.wordpress.com/2020/06/17/nation-remembers-gulab-singh-the-founder-of-jammu-and-kashmir-on-his-coronation-day/. Accessed on 15 March 2021.

As a consequence of the Treaty of Lahore between the Sikhs and the British signed on 9 March 1846, and the Treaty of Amritsar signed between the British and Gulab Singh on 16 March 1846, the independent possession of Kashmir was handed over to Gulab Singh in return for a total sum of ₹75 lakh—₹50 lakh to be paid by 1 October 1846 and the rest subsequently.[6]

Fast forward to a century later, the maharaja of J&K at the time of Independence and partition of India was Hari Singh, a descendent of Gulab Singh. He had ascended the throne in September 1925. While the rest of India was fuelled with ideas of nationalism against British rule, in Kashmir it was directed against the Maharaja under the aegis of a popular movement for socio-political reforms. In 1939, Sheikh Abdullah formed the All Jammu and Kashmir National Conference that included both Hindus and Muslims, asking for a representative government based on universal suffrage. As the movement gathered momentum, the Sheikh grew popular across the state, especially in Kashmir. In 1946, he was incarcerated,[7] the Maharaja declared martial law and had the Sheikh sent to prison for sedition.

While all of this was going on, it was also becoming evident that the British would soon be departing the subcontinent. The dream of an independent state started taking a firm grip of the Maharaja's mind. He loathed the Congress, so he was reluctant to consider joining India. But the fate of his Hindu dynasty would have anyway been sealed if he would have joined Pakistan. Sheikh Abdullah, who was released from prison on 29 September 1947, called for a full transition of power to the people of Kashmir. For him, a popular government in Kashmir was not going to be the government of any single group. It would be a joint government of Muslims, Hindus and Sikhs.

Pakistan, with its Muslim majority, naturally wanted Kashmir

---

[6]Chitralekha Zutshi, *Oxford Short Introduction Series: Kashmir*, Oxford University Press, 2019.
[7]Ramachandra Guha, *India After Gandhi: The History of the World's Largest Democracy*, Picador India, 2017.

to accede to it. India estimated that because the leading political party, the National Conference (NC), was considered to be non-sectarian, the religious aspect was inconsequential. As for Maharaja Hari Singh, the hope of freedom always clung to him. 'The only thing that will change our minds is if one side or the other decides to use force against us,'[8] his deputy prime minister said in Delhi. His words proved prophetic. Two weeks later, a force of several thousand-armed men invaded the state from the north.

On 22 October, armed tribesmen actively aided and abetted by the nascent Pakistani state, crossed the border between NWFP and Kashmir, and made their way towards the capital, to wrest the princely state by force. Once in Kashmir, the tribesmen moved quickly down the Jhelum valley, stopping only to steal, rape and loot. The Maharaja realized that he would need India's help to foil Pakistan's attack. He urged India to immediately send troops to push back the invaders. India secured Hari Singh's accession to the new dominion before committing troops to repulse the tribal invasion. Subsequently, the Maharaja formally signed the Instrument of Accession to India on 26 October 1947 at Jammu, thereby acceding the state of J&K to India. It was lawfully accepted by then Governor General of India Lord Louis Mountbatten on 27 October 1947, thereby paving the way for the integration of the princely state of Jammu and Kashmir into the dominion of India.

The war between India and Pakistan raged on the frontlines in J&K all through the remainder of 1947 and well into 1948. As Srinath Raghavan explains,

> The truce of January 1949 came into effect only because each side was exhausted and convinced that it could no longer make significant territorial gains against the other. The Indian side was able to preserve and protect the Kashmir Valley and the areas of Jammu and Ladakh. The Pakistanis illegally grabbed a long strip running from north to south in the western part of the

---

[8]Ibid.

state comprising Azad Jammu and Kashmir, Gilgit Baltistan and Skardu (in Ladakh). This came to be known as Pakistan Occupied Kashmir or (POK). The Kashmir dispute was thus born.'[9]

The Kashmir dispute reached the international arena in January 1948. This resulted in a series of UNSC resolutions calling on both Pakistan and India to demilitarize and then hold a plebiscite to decide the future of the state of J&K (which has yet to take place because the essential precondition for its operationalization was the withdrawal of all Pakistani troops and other elements from areas they continue to illegally occupy since 1947). India was also asked to maintain law and order and to install an interim government with all genuine stakeholders. The interim government was set up and led by Sheikh Abdullah as the prime minister. But the status of the territory was still under dispute.

FORMATION AND EROSION OF ARTICLE 370

The Constitution that came into effect on 26 January 1950 incorporated J&K into the Indian Union. However, it guaranteed the state a certain autonomy; thus, giving birth to Article 370. Article 370 gave special rights to the state of J&K. It stated that the president would have to consult the state to take any decision on matters other than defence, foreign affairs and communication. It also allowed the state to form a constituent assembly which would decide both the constitution of the state and its relation with the Constitution of India.

The special autonomy given to the state was derived from Clause Seven of the Instrument of Accession, which stated clearly that the state of J&K does not need to accept any future constitution of India. It was a temporary provision, and was to last till the state gave itself a new constitution; however, 'because the State's constituent assembly dissolved itself in 1957 without recommending anything on the

---

[9]Ibid.

future of Article 370, it became a permanent feature of the Indian Constitution—an iron clad guarantee.'[10]

By the summer of 1952, however, Sheikh Abdullah started drifting away from the 'powers that be' in Delhi. Serious differences had cropped up between his government and the Praja Parishad party.[11] This party formed in 1947, aimed to represent the interests of the Jammu Hindus, was now starting to vociferously raise its voice for the Jammu region, where majority of the Hindu population resided. By 1950–2, there was a growing conflict between the Muslim-majority Kashmir Valley and the Hindu-dominated districts in the Jammu region.

It would be instructive to note that the 1961 Census revealed that Muslims comprised 68.31 per cent of the state's population, while Hindus made up 28.45 per cent. Nearly 50 years later, these percentages have not changed much as the 2011 Census logged Muslims again at 68.3 per cent and Hindus at 28.3 per cent.[12]

The spike in sectarian tensions, spurred in part by the Praja Parishad agitation in the winter of 1952–3, created reservations in Sheikh Abdullah's mind and he perhaps started having qualms about his decision to support the accession of J&K to India.[13] [14] [15] The NC

---

[10]Srinath Raghvan, 'Kashmir—The State and The Status', *YouTube*, 7 October 2019, https://youtu.be/OgXVMO5rdHg. Accessed on 15 March 2021.
[11]Ibid.
[12]Zeeshan Shaikh, 'Share of Muslims and Hindus in J&K Population Same in 1961, 2011 Censuses', *The Indian Express*, 30 December 2016, https://indianexpress.com/article/explained/share-of-muslims-and-hindus-in-jk-population-same-in-1961-2011-censuses/. Accessed on 15 March 2021.
[13]Zahir ud-Din, 'August 9, 1953: When Sheikh's Arrest Changed Kashmir for Ever', *Greater Kashmir*, 10 August 2016, https://www.greaterkashmir.com/kashmir/august-9-1953-when-sheikhs-arrest-changed-kashmir-for-ever. Accessed on 15 March 2021.
[14]Arun Sharma, 'BJP Proved Sheikh Abdullah Right: He Apprehended India Would Go Back on Article 370', *National Herald*, 4 August 2020, https://www.nationalheraldindia.com/opinion/bjp-proved-sheikh-abdullah-right-he-apprehended-india-would-go-back-on-article-370. Accessed on 15 March 2021.
[15]M.J. Aslam, 'August 9 1953: Why Sheikh Abdullah Was Removed', *Kashmir Life*, 17 August 2018, https://kashmirlife.net/august-9-1953-why-sheikh-abdullah-was-removed-183655/. Accessed on 15 March 2021.

in October 1948 had incidentally passed a resolution supporting the accession of J&K to India.

The Sheikh was sceptical about right-wing elements in Nehru's government. He worried about what would happen to the commitments that had been made to J&K by the Union Government post Nehru's departure from the scene. He was of the view that Nehru's secular convictions were really the only bulwark preventing India's slide towards majoritarianism.[16] His fears came true, for post Nehru, India skid down the slippery slope of trying to formally accommodate religious impulses in the public space rather than treating it as a pure pursuit in the private domain.

Nehru's intellectual commitment and firm conviction was that secularism meant the clinical separation of the church and the state.[17] It is not a zeal either shared with that degree of cerebral rigour nor understanding by his ideological inheritors who reinterpreted secularism to mean *Sarva Dharma Samabhava* (equal respect for all religions)—the implicit patronage of religion by the state that ultimately has paved the way for the spectre of undeclared majoritarianism that characterizes the Indian milieu today.[18] [19]

In Delhi, the Sheikh met Nehru and also had a round of meetings with other ministers. In exchange for sovereignty far greater than that enjoyed by other states of the Union, they worked out a deal known as the Delhi Agreement of 1952 whereby, not only would

---

[16]Ibid.

[17]Vivek Kumar Srivastava, 'Nehru and His Views on Secularism', *Mainstream Weekly*, 15 November 2014, http://www.mainstreamweekly.net/article5316.html. Accessed on 15 March 2021.

[18]Harinder Baweja and Aurangzeb Naqshbandi, '"Congress Has to Confront the Question of Secularism", Says Manish Tewari', *Hindustan Times*, 6 September 2020, https://www.hindustantimes.com/india-news/congress-has-to-confront-the-question-of-secularism-says-manish-tewari/story-Y8VDBuhjBmiErsgldwFvQN.html. Accessed on 15 March 2021.

[19]Rafiq Zakaria, 'Secularism as Practised by The Indian Political Class Has Been of No Use to Indians', *India Today*, 8 April 2002, https://www.indiatoday.in/magazine/cover-story/story/20020408-secularism-as-practised-by-the-indian-political-class-has-been-of-no-use-to-indians-796637-2002-04-08. Accessed on 15 March 2021.

state subjects become full citizens of India, but the new flag of the state would be hoisted alongside the national flag. Without the approval of Srinagar, Delhi would not send in forces to quell internal disturbances. If residual powers rested with the Centre with respect to other states, they would remain with the state in the case of J&K. The Delhi Agreement, in many senses, institutionalized the relationship between the state and the central government.[20]

However, Machiavellian politics coupled with unbridled ambitions of some and a complete misread of the mind of a complex personality that the Sheikh was, led to a series of missteps that would cast a long shadow on the relationship of J&K with the Indian Union for decades to come. Rumours were deliberately spread that Sheikh Abdullah would declare independence on Friday, 21 August 1953, on the occasion of Eid al-Adha.[21]

On 8 August 1953, the then Sadr-e-Riyasat, Yuvraj Karan Singh, dismissed the Abdullah government and arrested him. Simultaneously, the faction of the NC labelled pro-India by agent provocateurs, for reasons of both convenience if not mischief and then led by Bakshi Ghulam Mohammed, was sworn into power. However, P.N. Haksar would write to Indira Gandhi much later on 2 June 1972, in the context of the Sheikh's release from yet another spell of incarceration. He correctly described the arrest of Sheikh Abdullah and his dismissal as prime minister in 1953 as the 'original sin.'

The J&K Constituent assembly reaffirmed the state's accession to India. However, on 14 May 1954, while the Constituent Assembly was still in session, several articles of the Indian Constitution were extended to the state of Jammu & Kashmir by a Presidential Order. Ostensibly, this was done to give effect to the Delhi Agreement of 1952. This Presidential Order is considered the basic order that commenced the process of the hollowing out of Article 370.

[20]Ramachandra Guha, *India After Gandhi: The History of the World's Largest Democracy*, Picador India, 2017.
[21]'Securing Kashmir', *ERE Now*, https://erenow.net/exams/indiaaftergandhi ramachandraguha/13.php. Accessed on 15 March 2021.

Interestingly, as A.G. Noorani mentions in his book *Article 370: A Constitutional History of Jammu and Kashmir*, 'The Constituent Assembly had given its concurrence three months earlier in a quaint manner on 15 February 1954 while adopting the report of the drafting Committee.'[22]

The events that followed strongly suggested a contractual relationship between Bakshi Ghulam Mohammed and the Indian state. While New Delhi could get Kashmir integrated with the Union of India under its own terms, Bakshi Ghulam Mohammed got unfettered powers to run the state. The result was threefold: it undermined the faith of the ordinary Kashmiri in the sanctity of New Delhi's word, crippled democratic institutions and eroded J&K's autonomy.

Subsequently, 13 steps were taken to extend various provisions of the Indian Constitution to the J&K State. This began in 1954 with the Constitution (Application to Jammu and Kashmir) Order, 1954, also called the Basic Order.

By this legislative fiat, the central government could now legislate on a majority of subjects in the Union List qua J&K also. In J&K, the Supreme Court of India now had absolute jurisdiction. The constitutional rights of people protected by the Indian Constitution would now be upheld in the territory, but with a central caveat: these civil liberties could be suspended at any time in the interests of 'protection' at the discretion of the authorities in Srinagar, and no judicial examination of the suspensions would be permitted.[23]

Article 370 had effectively been dead in letter and in spirit ever since the Presidential Order of 1954. Even after the constituent assembly had convened, adopted a separate constitution for J&K on 17 November 1956 (which came into effect on 26 January 1957) and then dissolved itself, provisions of the Indian constitution continued to get extended to the state. They were done in a manner

---

[22]A.G. Noorani, *Article 370: A Constitutional History of Jammu and Kashmir,* Oxford, 2011.

[23]Ramachandra Guha, *India After Gandhi: The History of the World's Largest Democracy*, Picador India, 2017.

that, for the purposes of academic argument, could be termed as antithetical to the spirit of both Article 370 and the fact that the state had a legally adopted Constitution of its own by January 1957, which needed to be respected. J&K was the only state that was given the liberty to convene its own constituent assembly, draft, pass, adopt and promulgate its own Constitution. If that Constitution was not to be respected, it was not worth the paper it was written on.

In November 1964, Article 356 was extended to the state of Jammu and Kashmir. In March 1965, the constitution of the state was changed to make the elected Sadr-e-Riyasat, a Centre-appointed governor. In 1975, a Presidential Order was issued during the Emergency, which said that the state legislature and its power over defining the role of the governor would be absolutely curbed, making the governor even more of a central government appointee than he ever was.[24] As a point of view holds:

> The second half of 1953 signalled a decisive turning point in the basis and nature of the relationship between Kashmir and India. The old NC [National Conference] conception had viewed that relationship as an honourable partnership of equals. After 1953 this conception became history. From August 1953 onward, any defiance of New Delhi's absolute supremacy in the relationship guaranteed not only a swift passage to political oblivion but criminalization as an enemy of the state. The fate suffered by a leader of Sheikh Abdullah's stature sent out a very powerful—and unambiguous—message. Only those who unequivocally agreed to follow the Indian state's agenda in Kashmir could aspire to office, or indeed, could play any sort of role in institutionally sanctioned politics.[25]

---

[24]Express News Service, 'Explained: When Jammu & Kashmir Had Its Own Prime Minister and Sadr-e-Riyasat', *The Indian Express*, 15 April 2019, https://indianexpress.com/article/explained/when-jammu-kashmir-had-its-own-prime-minister-and-sadr-e-riyasat-5675554/. Accessed on 15 March 2021.
[25]Sumantra Bose, *Kashmir Roots of Conflict, Paths to Peace*, Harvard University Press, 2005.

While the erosion of Article 370 continued from the 1950s all the way into the 1990s and beyond, the fact that it continued to exist as a Constitutional guarantee, providing a special status to J&K, at least gave the Indian state a leg to stand on. India could at least say, both domestically and internationally, that it had not reneged on the commitments it had made to the people and the political elites of J&K on 26 October 1947. Moreover, going all the way up to 1952, the relationship between J&K and the Indian Union could always legitimately be termed as a 'special relationship' considering the peculiar circumstances of its merger with India. Even this minimum modicum of Constitutional 'nicety' was buried on 5 August 2019.

Article 370 gave a sense of both autonomy and uniqueness to the people of J&K with regard to their place in the Indian Union. In this regard, they were not alone. The Union of India, over time, had engrafted into the Constitution of India special provisions in the form of Articles 371 (A) to 371 (J) to give special rights to the people of Nagaland, Assam, Manipur, Andhra Pradesh and Telangana, Sikkim, Mizoram, Arunachal Pradesh, Goa and even Maharashtra, Gujarat and Karnataka. The rights may not have been that exacting as the ones delineated in Article 370, but nonetheless, they were rights that set these states on a separate, if not exclusive, pedestal in contradistinction to other states in the Union of India.

A TRAVESTY OF THE CONSTITUTION

The legal issues surrounding Kashmir's accession to India are extremely intricate. While the manner in which the Jammu and Kashmir Reorganisation Bill was passed, and what transpired in the Parliament on 5 August 2019, is unprecedented, with all 103 clauses and all the five schedules being put to vote together, with no member submitting any amendments and voting on a bill that they could not even read, analyse or discuss,[26] puts the constitutionality

---

[26]Maansi Verma, 'Diminishing the Role of Parliament: The Case of the Jammu and Kashmir Reorganisation Bill', *Economic and Political Weekly*, 16 November 2019,

of the abrogation under question.

Article 370 can be abrogated by the president, but only by following the recommendation of J&K's constituent assembly. Now this assembly was dissolved in 1957. This meant that there was an iron clad guarantee given to Article 370. However, the Presidential Order passed on 5 August ascribed fanciful interpretations: 'State government was now to include 'Governor' under Article 367 and by clever sophistry the 'Constituent Assembly of the State' mentioned in clause 3 of Article 370 which had dissolved itself in 1957, was now to be read as the 'Legislative Assembly of the State.'

However, the government, in haste perhaps, overlooked the obvious. Even going by its own constitutional order of 2019, it was precluded from doing what it ultimately did and that was nothing short of a constitutional coup. Section 2 of the said order states:

2. All the provisions of the Constitution, as amended from time to time, shall apply in relation to the State of Jammu and Kashmir and the exceptions and modifications subject to which they shall so apply shall be as follows:

To article 367, there shall be added the following clause, namely:

(4) For the purposes of this Constitution as it applies in relation to the State of Jammu and Kashmir—
  (a) references to this Constitution or to the provisions thereof shall be construed as references to the Constitution or the provisions thereof as applied in relation to the said State;
  (b) references to the person for the time being recognized by the President on the recommendation of the Legislative Assembly of the State as the Sadar-i-Riyasat of Jammu and Kashmir, acting on the advice of the Council of Ministers of the State for the time being in office, shall be construed

https://www.epw.in/engage/article/diminishing-role-parliament-case-jammu-and-kashmir. Accessed on 15 March 2021.

as references to the Governor of Jammu and Kashmir;

(c) references to the Government of the said State shall be construed as including references to the Governor of Jammu and Kashmir acting on the advice of his Council of Ministers; and

(d) in proviso to clause (3) of article 370 of this Constitution, the expression 'Constituent Assembly of the State referred to in clause (2)' shall read 'Legislative Assembly of the State.'[27]

It is thus fairly evident the governor could not have made any recommendation to extend the Articles of the Indian Constitution to Jammu & Kashmir because if the provisos to Article 370 (1) (d) are read in conjunction with the newly introduced Article 367(4)(c), it is clear that the governor must act only on the advice of his council of ministers. This ipso facto implies the existence of a popular government that was not there as the state was under president's rule when this constitutional jiggery-pokery was done.

Moreover, by no stretch of imagination could the word 'Constituent Assembly' be stretched to mean Legislative Assembly. For the sake of argument, if it is accepted that Constituent Assembly could mean Legislative Assembly, it certainly could not mean the Parliament of India in whom the legislative functions of the state stood vested as the state was under President's rule.

Effectively, what Parliament did, because the incumbent government had a brute majority, was to get the Union Legislature to step into the shoes of the state legislature under the amended Article 367 (4) (d), and recommend to itself the repeal of Article 370. It then sanctified it itself by approving through a division C.O. 273—Declaration under Article 370 (3).

This was an insidious if not vile way to fulfil a long-standing political commitment of the BJP and its political predecessor, the Bharatiya Jana Sangh, that proclaimed that once it got an

---

[27]Co 272, The Constitution (Application to Jammu & Kashmir) Order—2019.

opportunity, it would abrogate Article 370.

What makes this opportunism all the more despicable is that when the BJP and People's Democratic Party (PDP) got together to form a government on 1 March 2015, they formulated an Agenda of Alliance to provide a subterfuge to the chicanery manifest in that arrangement. It stated, 'While recognizing the different positions and appreciating the perceptions, BJP and PDP have on the constitutional status of J&K considering the political and legislative realities, the present position will be maintained on all the constitutional provisions pertaining to J&K including the special status in the Constitution of India.'[28] This was committed by the BJP four years, five months and five days before the constitutional coup of 5 August 2019. As the adage goes, even a week is a long time in politics.

What was done on that day of August in 2019 was nothing short of a deliberate death blow to the intrinsic flexibility in the Indian model of federalism. The Supreme Court should have stayed this Constitutional coup right away but in its wisdom chose not to do so. The matter hangs fire in the Supreme Court, with no date fixed as yet for the next set of hearings even two years later at the time of writing.

The government's narrative had always been that Article 370 was the root cause of corruption and militancy in the state of J&K. These reasons were based on hollow fables. It was undoubtedly because of the existence of Article 370 that the state had done much better compared to others when it came to the implementation and execution of land reforms.[29]

Certainly, the education and health system in J&K should be

---

[28]PTI, 'Mehbooba claims PM's support on status quo for Article 370', *Outlook India*, 11 August 2017, https://www.outlookindia.com/newsscroll/mehbooba-claims-pms-support-on-status-quo-for-article-370/1121722. Accessed on 15 March 2021.
[29]Happymon Jacob, 'A Year on, Article 370 and Kashmir Mythmaking', *The Hindu*, 4 August 2020, https://www.thehindu.com/opinion/lead/a-year-on-article-370-and-kashmir-mythmaking/article32262654.ece. Accessed on 15 March 2021.

further strengthened, but Article 370 is not the justification for underperformance in the education and health sector in Kashmir. It is not the case that private investors cannot set up shop in the state because of Article 370; they can always lease land, as they have done over the years. The real reason that stops them is the rising militancy in the state.[30] If anything, Article 370 played a role in suppressing this militancy and its abrogation might progressively worsen the state's development agenda.

While revoking Article 370 was a long-standing political commitment of the BJP, the current situation of the state is a consequence of the continuous effort of myth-making regarding Kashmir that has been peddled and encouraged by the ruling party.

TWO YEARS ON

Domestic Implications

The abrogation of statehood and the bifurcation of J&K into two Union Territories, an unprecedented first in the constitutional development of India was premised on an illusion that it would transform the Valley into a vale of prosperity. More than two years have elapsed since the abrogation of Article 370, and things look much the same, not just for Kashmir but also for Jammu and Ladakh. Operations against militants continue, internet and communication shutdowns continue, the targeting of civilians and political workers by extremists has not ceased, border areas have not become any more tranquil, infiltration and ceasefire violations have not stopped and there is no flood of fresh investments. The NDA government's action has instead disrupted the cultural fabric of the state.

Since August 2019, the Valley faced the longest internet shutdown perhaps in any democracy, with 55 territory-wide internet shutdowns, and the destruction of 48 properties on the pretext that militants might be hiding inside. Restoration of the internet has

---

[30]Ibid.

not offered any relief, since internet speeds were stuck at 2G. 4G services were finally restored on 6 February 2021, 17 months after they were suspended. However, the long hiatus caused by curfews and restriction on the movement of people to and from the state has wreaked havoc on the bread and butter of Kashmir's economy.

'Less than 50,000 tourists visited the U.T. between August and December 2019 with the Kashmir Chamber of Commerce and Industry projecting losses of around $6 billion.'[31][32]

On the LoC, cross-border firing had seen a tremendous increase with 2,300 ceasefire violations within the first six months of 2020—a 75 per cent rise in such incidents.[33] In fact, Pakistan has gone back to its old methods of propping up new insurgent groups with a new 'non-sectarian' outfit surfacing in the Valley, called The Resistance Front (TRF).

Has the situation changed on the border? The answer is an unequivocal no. There is a flawed reasoning at play here. Article 370 is not the cause for terrorism, and its abrogation does not have a consequential relationship to the reduction of the turmoil in the state, which by all means has not taken place even after two years. However, it must be logged that the ceasefire agreement of 25 February 2021 between India and Pakistan has provided some limited relief from the continuous cross-border shelling that had made the lives of villagers in the habitats close to the border a living hell.

Even those who had initially celebrated the move in J&K to abrogate Article 370 and decapitate the statehood initially, have now developed second thoughts about the wisdom of such a gambit. This

---

[31]Khalid Shah, 'J&K One Year Later: Not Quite a Success (Part I)', *ORF*, 5 August 2020, https://www.orfonline.org/expert-speak/jk-one-year-later-not-quite-a-success-part-i/. Accessed on 15 March 2021.

[32]Anees Zargar, 'J&K Lost ₹40,000 crore', *Newsclick*, 23 July 2020, https://www.newsclick.in/Jammu-Kashmir-Lost-40 per cent2C000-Crore-Govt-Imposed-Lockdowns-Post-Article-370-Abrogation. Accessed on 15 March 2021.

[33]Khalid Shah, 'J&K One Year Later: Not Quite a Success (Part I)', *ORF*, 5 August 2020, https://www.orfonline.org/expert-speak/jk-one-year-later-not-quite-a-success-part-i/. Accessed on 15 March 2021.

is courtesy the legal amendments brought in by the Centre to alter the definition of who is enumerated as a 'domicile'. This had the effect of authorizing non-residents to purchase land in the territory of the erstwhile state of J&K. These modifications stipulate that a person who might have dwelled in the erstwhile state of J&K for a period of 15 years, or whose children may have gone to school, college or university in the erstwhile province for a period of seven years or more and had appeared either for the grade 10 or 12 exam, would be eligible to the status of a 'domicile'. This would qualify them for both employment and the right to even acquire property in that erstwhile domain.

Many see this as a window for the integration of security forces, bureaucrats and scholars into state services, public-sector corporations, state-run educational establishments, etc., dramatically decreasing the prospects for local citizens who had historically been eligible for these jobs before the abrogation of Article 370, Article 35A and the statehood of J&K.

Even the Jammu unit of the BJP underscored their antipathy to these new rules.[34] It was almost reminiscent of the decade of the 1920s, when Kashmiri Pandits were at the forefront of preserving the unique ethos of the state. They rallied to the mantra 'Kashmir for Kashmiris'.[35]

For the Naya Kashmir project, the only good news is the faith reposed in the democratic system of the state. The District Development Council (DDC) elections of 2020 won by the People's Alliance for Gupkar Declaration (PAGD) (an alliance of the major and minor political parties including the PDP and NC)

[34]Nistula Hebbar, 'Jammu BJP Raises Concerns over New J&K Domicile Rule with National Leadership, Amit Shah', *The Hindu*, 3 April 2020, https://www.thehindu.com/news/national/other-states/jammu-bjp-raises-concerns-over-new-jk-domicile-rule-with-national-leadership-amit-shah/article31245991.ece. Accessed on 15 March 2021.
[35]Badri Raina, 'It's Been 9 Months. What Did the Revocation of J&K's Special Status Achieve?' *The Wire*, 27 April 2020, https://thewire.in/rights/jammu-kashmir-article-370. Accessed on 15 March 2021.

has clearly demonstrated through a people's mandate that any misconceptions that the BJP had in mind in terms of its position in the state politics, especially in the Kashmir valley, were purely illusionary. In the DDC elections, the BJP ran full-blown campaigns attempting to discredit the NC, PDP, Peoples' Conference and other smaller regional parties who make up the alliance. This election and its result are defiantly and definitely a dampener on such disinformation.

The abrogation was projected as a remedy that would magically solve all the ailments of the state. The Kashmir dispute is a result of complex historical grievances; it can only be termed as obtuse to even imagine that it could be settled by Constitutional chicanery.

International Challenges

The Modi government's decision has set in motion a diplomatic challenge the likes of which can be compared to what India faced after the Pokhran-II nuclear tests (1998). The abrogation of Article 370 has yet again internationalized the Kashmir issue after nearly half a century.

This is, indeed, the maximum global attention that Kashmir has received since the 1990s. India had persuaded much of the world before August 2019 that the main problem in J&K was cross-border terrorism perpetrated by Pakistan. However, the current narrative presents other concerns for both domestic and foreign viewers. In the months after the repeal, the UNSC, a first in several decades, convened not once, but twice, for consultations on the abrogation of Article 370 and the situation in Kashmir. The consultations fortuitously took place behind closed doors.

The US Congress, in a scathing indictment, passed two house resolutions on the issue of Kashmir, condemning New Delhi's move and the subsequent internet and communications shut down. The House Resolution 745 was successful in gaining 36 co-sponsors.[36]

---

[36]Khalid Shah and Kriti M. Shah, 'Kashmir After Article 370: India's Diplomatic Challenge', *ORF Occasional Paper* 259, 2020 .

The UK too, in September 2019, passed a resolution calling for 'international intervention' and a 'UN-led referendum.'[37]

This increased focus on the situation in Kashmir forced New Delhi to embark on a massive diplomatic outreach. The government mobilized its foreign missions to counter the Kashmir narrative set by Islamabad and Beijing. A MEA team met members of the UNHRC to put forward India's position. The External Affairs Minister travelled through Europe and Southeast Asia; NSA Doval handled West Asia; Modi personally spoke to US President Trump and other world leaders in what can be jocularly termed as acrobatic diplomacy to try and set the Indian narrative on Kashmir.[38]

New Delhi also invited foreign diplomats to Kashmir on 'fact-finding' trips. European Union (EU) lawmakers were invited to the Valley in October 2019; those who came represented some of the EU's extreme far-right political parties. This made the EU legislators the first group to enter the Valley after the abrogation of Article 370, well before even Indian lawmakers and legislators were allowed to enter the state.[39]

The events that have unfolded post August 2019 in J&K substantially dented the image of 'Brand India' globally, notwithstanding the NDA's protestations to the contrary. With Kashmir attracting negative international attention, two nations stood to gain the most—China and Pakistan.

Statements by the Chinese Foreign Ministry did not bode well for New Delhi. China's Foreign Ministry spokesperson, Hua Chunying, stated that, 'The parties concerned should exercise restraint and act with caution, especially to avoid actions that unilaterally change the status quo and exacerbate the tension. We call on the two sides to peacefully resolve relevant disputes through dialogue and consultation and safeguard regional peace

---

[37]Ibid.
[38]Ibid.
[39]Ibid.

and stability.'[40] Chinese President Xi Jinping even suggested an India-China-Pakistan trilateral 'free from the influence of third parties'[41] to PM Modi during the Mamallapuram informal summit.

Being a permanent member of the UNSC and an ally of Pakistan, the Chinese government went to the extent of requesting a closed consultation of the UNSC on Kashmir. For both the nations, the fact that Kashmir was taken up by the UNSC and internationalized, after five decades, was an achievement in itself. But China's attempts at shepherding a unanimous statement through the Security Council on the transformed reality in J&K and against the actions of the Indian government were foiled by Indian diplomats based at India's Permanent Mission to the UN in New York.[42]

China had stated clearly that any move to unilaterally change the status of the former state was 'illegal and invalid.' These responses stemmed not just out of solidarity with its closest ally, Islamabad, but also from its concern over Ladakh becoming a Union Territory. China believes that it would directly impede its sovereignty. Its strategic interests in terms of the CPEC corridor running through POK would also be affected by the abrogation of Article 370, especially as they think the balance of power has shifted towards India with the united state of J&K now becoming a figment of history. However, these concerns are totality misplaced notwithstanding the other constitutional questions with regard to the abrogation of statehood and Article 370.

China Institutes of Contemporary International Relations (CICIR), a Chinese think tank affiliated to the Ministry of State Security, was more direct in its imputation. It went to the extent of linking the current Ladakh stand-off as a direct consequence

[40]Ghazala Wahab, 'What Kashmir Has to do with the India-China Stand-off in Ladakh', *The Wire*, 10 July 2020, https://thewire.in/security/india-china-kashmir-ladakh. Accessed on 15 March 2021.

[41]Ibid.

[42]'UNSC Discusses Kashmir', *UN News*, 16 August 2019, https://news.un.org/en/story/2019/08/1044401. Accessed on 15 March 2021.

of the move to abrogate Article 370. The think tank had described the move as a joint challenge to China and Pakistan, attacking the sovereignty of both the states.[43]

Islamabad reacted sharply by outrightly rejecting India's move to abrogate Article 370. It suspended all bilateral trade with India and expelled the Indian High Commissioner to Pakistan. Prime Minister Imran Khan—speaking a day after the announcement of the decision—called the move 'unconstitutional', and even went to the extent of threatening India with another Pulwama. Islamabad did not stop here and went all out, when its ambassador to the US stated that any such action might force Pakistan to redirect Afghan troops to the Kashmiri frontier.

However, Pakistan's hypocritical outrage over Kashmir is astoundingly ridiculous. Over the last seventy years, they have repeatedly demolished, dismantled and resurrected Constitutional and administrative arrangements in POK. Gilgit-Baltistan under Pakistani tutelage has virtually suffered political abandonment. The region does not find any mention in Pakistani constitution and its domiciles are not even awarded citizenship. All of them are quasi-citizens of the Gilgit-Baltistan province and not Pakistan. In fact, over the years, the cultural identity of the people has been systematically undermined by the Talibani colonization, and it was all encouraged by the State. It therefore becomes pertinent for Islamabad to first look within before shedding crocodile tears over the abrogation of Article 370.[44]

For India, both its credentials as the largest democracy in the world and its global stature as a beacon of liberalism, unfortunately, stand undermined. The foreign press across the world vociferously critiqued the abrogation of Article 370 and the division of J&K.

[43]Ghazala Wahab, 'What Kashmir Has to do with the India-China Stand-off in Ladakh', *The Wire*, 10 July 2020, https://thewire.in/security/india-china-kashmir-ladakh. Accessed on 15 March 2021.

[44]Kriti M. Shah, 'Article 370 and Pakistan's false outrage', *ORF*, 12 August 2019, https://www.orfonline.org/expert-speak/article-370-pakistan-false-outrage-54344/. Accessed on 15 March 2021.

India has had to walk the extra mile to rally international opinion in its support. This is notwithstanding the fact that most countries have been rather measured in their public response regarding the developments in that troubled paradise.

New Delhi's chronicle about the need to carry out these constitutional and legal changes has been adversely influenced.

India had control over the portrayal of the Kashmir crisis for the better part of three decades before 5 August 2019. It had successfully and not incorrectly focused the problems plaguing the state to unremitting cross-border terrorism sponsored by Pakistan. Even internationally, Pakistan was recognized as the primary aggressor destabilizing not only J&K, but also being at the root of most of the region's problems. However, the way in which the constitutional amendments were carried out has opened a Pandora's box. The implications are grave and the fallout will occupy the collective energies of Indian policymakers, security officials and strategic experts for decades to come.

POSTSCRIPT AFGHANISTAN

The takeover of Afghanistan by the Taliban in August 2021 represents a victory for the Pakistani deep state, namely the ISI-Military combine. The Taliban was conceived, created, nurtured, armed, resourced, protected and patronized by the above-mentioned clique. Even while it played footsie with the US during the War on Terror in Afghanistan for two long decades, Pakistan assiduously safeguarded its assets in Afghanistan. They are not limited to the Taliban alone and include the Haqqani network and other such semi-state actors. While the US can be faulted for abandoning Afghanistan, the fact remains that it would have been naïve to expect the US to perennially remain in Afghanistan. However, the manner in which the Doha process led by Ambassador Zalmay Khalilzad systematically undermined the government in Kabul, squandering the gains of 20 years of US effort and investment defies imagination.

In a rather startling claim that has portentous implications for the region, US Republican Congressman Jim Banks, stated that 'due to the negligence of this [Joe Biden's] administration,' the Taliban possess more than $85 billion worth of US military equipment including 75,000 vehicles, more than 200 airplanes and helicopters, and more than 600,000 small arms and light weapons. 'The Taliban now has more Black Hawk helicopters than 85 per cent of the countries in the world,' Banks added.[45]

In addition to weaponry and other heavy machinery, Banks opined that the Taliban also have access to tools such as night-vision goggles, body armour, medical supplies and biometric devices containing fingerprints, scans and other biographical information of the US's Afghan allies.

'We don't have a complete picture, obviously, of where every article of defence materials has gone, but certainly, a fair amount of it has fallen into the hands of the Taliban,' NSA said shortly after the collapse.[46]

If even a fraction of what Banks claims is true, it is obvious where those weapons are headed—into the hands of semi-state actors. Given the chaotic situation in Afghanistan, they obviously may have fallen into the hands of myriad bad actors operating in that country. Why would the US by default or design leave their state-of-the-art military hardware in a war-torn country where no one is in charge and a civil war seems to be the obvious state of play? Unless, of course, the Sunni Taliban is the latest US ally in South Asia as a counterweight to the Shia Crescent that has grown in strength as a consequence of earlier US follies in Iraq, Libya and Syria which

[45]Jordan Davidson, 'The Taliban Now Has $85 Billion Worth Of Taxpayer-Funded US Military Equipment', *The Federalist*, https://thefederalist.com/2021/08/27/the-taliban-now-has-85-billion-worth-of-taxpayer-funded-us-military-equipment/. Accessed on 15 March 2021.

[46]Ibid.; Idrees Ali, Patricia Zengerle and Jonathan Landay, 'Planes, Guns, Night-Vision Goggles: The Taliban's New U.S.-Made War Chest', *Reuters*, 19 August 2021, https://www.reuters.com/business/aerospace-defense/planes-guns-night-vision-goggles-talibans-new-us-made-war-chest-2021-08-19/. Accessed on 15 September 2021.

made unintended victors out of the US-created quagmire in the region. The US finds it difficult to now maintain even a semblance of diplomatic presence in some of the nations it has destabilized from the turn of the millennium onwards. The new actors in the wider West Asia are Russia and China.

It would perhaps take a generation of scholars to make sense of it precisely as the aftermath of the US involvement in Vietnam did from the mid-1970s onwards.

Be that as it may, a triumphant Taliban that can claim that just as the fighting and fiercely independent people of Afghanistan had vanquished the Soviet Union, a superpower in the penultimate decade of the twentieth century, thereby paving the way for its subsequent collapse, they had similarly defeated the only remaining hyper-power, the US, in the second decade of the twenty-first century through guile, cunning and military tactics. It would have profound consequences on Pax Americana and the US's reliability qua its allies around the world.

The implication of such an assertion and the unfolding situation in Afghanistan is that it would give a huge fillip to all kinds of militant and terrorist organizations in West and South Asia from the Islamic State—Daesh and al-Qaeda to the LeT and JeM respectively. Both radicalism and extremism would be exacerbated. This will have implications on the security situation in J&K and the other north-western border states also.

INDIA'S STRATEGIC INTERESTS IN AFGHANISTAN

Consider the following vignettes. A child born in the December of 1979 in Afghanistan would be 42 years old today. Across four decades, that middle-aged person now has known strife, violence and bloodshed as the only normal. A new phase in that tragedy has been inaugurated on 15 August 2021. India's Independence Day for an overwhelming number of Afghans would now become the moment that marked their return to medieval and reactionary occupation, subjugation, oppression and virtual enslavement.

It all began on 24 December 1979. Soviet Tanks had rolled across the Amu Darya to commence a brutal nine-year occupation of that antediluvian acreage situated at the crossroads of time.

It was the year 2016. For 15 long years now Afghanistan had been free of the malevolent influence of the Taliban. At a Track-2 event, I ran into a former chief of the Afghan National Army early one morning. I asked him how the situation in Afghanistan was like then. He said that they had a democratic government, a free and vibrant press—print, TV, radio and digital—encompassing over 1,800 media outlets, and girls and women in schools and colleges. It was a learning to see that a former military man was calculating the achievements of the past decade-and-a-half in intangibles rather than gain or loss of territory qua the Taliban. Sadly, all that is history. The Afghan Generals must atone for creating a phantom defense force that just collapsed like a house of cards and melted away in the face of the Pakistan-Taliban onslaught.

In a letter to the now fled president of Afghanistan Ashraf Ghani, the US Secretary of State Antony Blinken had virtually read out the riot act to fall in line with the latest US approach to the Afghan quagmire. The letter had been made public by the Afghan news outlet Tolo News. It had neither been denied by the US nor the Afghan government, respectively.[47]

The missive sketched out the following modes for an across-the-board settlement to the Afghan imbroglio pegged on the desirability of an enduring ceasefire by the Taliban. It, therefore, envisaged ministerial-level parleys under the auspices of the UN between Russia, China, Pakistan, Iran and India and the US to deliberate upon a unified approach to supporting peace in Afghanistan, and a senior-level meeting between the Taliban and the Afghan government hosted by Turkey to take place shortly to finalize a peace agreement between the two.

---

[47]Letter to Ashraf Ghani from the US Secretary of State Antony Blinken. Available at https://tolonews.com/pdf/02.pdf. Accessed on 15 March 2021.

It mentioned a revised plan to operationalize a 90-day reduction in violence programme predicated upon thwarting a spring offensive by the Taliban. The dispatch further called upon President Ghani to consider US proposals for a road map targeted at a new and inclusive Afghan government.

The letter closed with a rather portentous caveat stating: 'We are considering the full withdrawal of our forces by May 1st, as we consider other options. Even with the continuation of financial assistance from the United States to your forces after an American military withdrawal, I am concerned the security situation will worsen and that the Taliban could make rapid territorial gains.'

Only the last part of Blinken's prophecy ultimately came true. It demonstrates how US intelligence and operational assessments were disconnected from reality. Either they did not have a measure of the ground situation or they had decided to deliberately suspend realism.

Since India will have to deal with the Taliban now, it must seriously consider what 'real' strategic interests it has in Afghanistan.

Writing a decade earlier on the same question, veteran journalist Shekhar Gupta opined,

It will still be a country of great strategic importance. But for whom, is the question. It will be of no strategic importance to us. None of our supplies or trade comes to Afghanistan. None of our bad guys hide there. No Afghan has ever been involved in a terror attack on India. In fact, almost never has a terror attack on us been even planned in the more precise Af-Pak region. They have all been planned and executed between Muzaffarabad, Muridke, Karachi and Multan. Almost never has an Afghan, Pakhtun, Baluch, Tajik, any ethnicity, been involved in a terror attack in India.

It's always been the Punjabis. Ask anybody in the Indian army who has served in Kashmir and he will tell you that the intruders he fought were exactly of the same ethnic stock as the bulk of the Pakistani army he may have to fight in a real war: the Punjabi Muslims. Leave Afghanistan to the

Pakistanis. If the Pakistani army thinks it can fix, subdue and control Afghanistan, after the British, Soviets and Americans have failed to do precisely this at the peak of each one's superpowerdom, why not let the Pakistanis try their hand at it? If they pour another ten divisions and half of the ISI into that hapless country now, isn't it that much of a relief for us on our western borders?[48]

The assessment above is perhaps as relevant even today as it was a decade ago. However, the Pakistan-backed Taliban may not really be the masters of their destiny. What was therefore true a decade ago may not really be the beacon of illumination for the decades ahead in their entirety. Notwithstanding that, hard questions with regard to our 'real interests' in Afghanistan were never asked then and are not being asked even now. Would a foothold in Afghanistan have helped us in the event of a two-front war with China and Pakistan? Highly unlikely till the time we were not willing to put boots on the ground in Afghanistan. An impossibility given the current situation. Would it be desirable to put boots on the ground even if the new players in the region or the UN were to request us to do so in the foreseeable future?

The last time India had seriously considered such a request was in early 2003 to deploy Indian forces in Iraq. Prime Minister Vajpayee had rightly refused to do so. Would a relationship with the new dispensation in Kabul open up new vistas for India in Central Asia? Not really, especially after Iran dropped India from the Chabahar-Zahedan Railway Link project just before it (Iran) inked a $400 billion 25-year strategic partnership with China.[49] There is no free lunch in

[48]Shekhar Gupta, 'Why India Should Get out and Leave Af to Pak', *The Print*, 10 November 2018, https://theprint.in/opinion/why-india-should-get-out-and-leave-af-to-pak/147786/. Accessed on 15 March 2021.
[49]Suhasini Haider, 'Why Is India out of the Chabahar Rail Project?' *The Hindu*, 19 July 2020, https://www.thehindu.com/news/international/the-hindu-explains-why-is-india-out-of-the-chabahar-rail-project/article32126361.ece. Accessed on 15 March 2021.

life. There will be costs and implications to doing business with the Taliban. India needs to be careful therefore. The level of engagement needs to be calibrated after a hard-headed assessment about our real stakes and interests in Afghanistan.[50]

Given the chaos and turmoil in Afghanistan that may continue interminably, the NDA government would therefore be well advised to resolve the situation in J&K to the satisfaction of the people and the mainstream political forces who have stood by India since 1947. It would require surmounting ideological dogmas in the broader security interest. Would the NDA have the conviction to prioritize national interest in J&K above everything else? Only time would tell...

---

[50]Manish Tewari, 'Does India Have Strategic Interests in Afghanistan?' *Deccan Chronicle*, 14 March 2021, https://www.deccanchronicle.com/opinion/columnists/ 130321/manish-tewari-does-india-have-strategic-interests-in-afghanistan.html. Accessed on 15 March 2021.

EPILOGUE

The book began with a central question: have India's responses to the myriad security challenges it faced over the past two decades made the nation any safer today than it was when those situations manifested themselves?

The preceding chapters make it abundantly clear that the answer is unfortunately in the negative. Our institutional learnings are at best tenuous and at worst, non-existent. But even though this book may have reached a pessimistic conclusion, this laborious stocktaking was essential, for the sake of our sovereign and our nation.

A classic example of that is the shocking manner in which the Chinese intrusions in the summer of 2020 caught the BJP-led government napping. What makes it worse is that this is a repetition of what happened exactly 20 years ago when India had faced a similar situation in the form of the Kargil intrusions in the high Himalayas about 500 kilometres from where the present stand-off with China is playing itself out. When Kargil intrusions took place, it was another NDA government that was caught napping! Eternal vigilance is the price of national security.

It is therefore obvious that no real lessons with regard to border management in terms of preserving and protecting its inviolability were internalized by the national security establishment post the Kargil war. How else could one explain the occurrence of the same sequence of events in eastern Ladakh 21 years later?

Similarities don't stop there. Consider this: Pakistan made an attempt to change the territorial status quo in 1999 by occupying the heights that could interdict the traffic on old National Highway 1-A. Similarly, the Chinese occupied heights that overlook the DSDBO road, thus giving them the latitude to target critical Indian troop movement and logistics vital for resourcing both Sub-Sector North (SSN) and the DBO Brigade.

Similarly, statements emanating from China after the decision to abrogate Article 370 and transform the state of J&K into two Union Territories post August 2019 was in many ways similar to the rhetoric that was cacophonous from the Chinese against the Forward Policy adopted by India close to the end of September 1961. Obviously, there seems to be no institutional memory in the MEA that could have juxtaposed both the situations and deduced how the Chinese might react in the physical space post such utterances. Or, perhaps, politicians in charge today don't bother with institutional inputs.

Another example is the uncanny parallel between the Parliament terror attack in December 2001 and the Mumbai terror attack seven years later in November 2008. Though both the attacks may have been normatively different in terms of targets and execution, their similarity lay in the fact that both were fedayeen attacks predicated only on one objective—creating a spectre of unrestricted terror through high-visibility outrages.

Given that the security establishment had lessons from both the terror attack on the J&K Assembly in October 2001 and the Parliament attack in December 2001, how could something as audacious as the 26/11 attack have escaped the radar of our intelligence structures? After all, months, if not years of planning, would have preceded the execution of such a complex operation. How had no electronic chatter or human intelligence manifested itself? Does it not tantamount to taking your eye off the proverbial ball?

Another striking parallel that was ignored is that whenever there is an outreach to Pakistan by India, it is inevitably followed by a terror attack to derail any such initiative. After Prime Minister Modi flew to Raiwind in December 2015 to greet Prime Minister Sharif's family on his granddaughter's wedding, the security establishment should have been cognizant that a terror attack would already be in the works and therefore vigil needed to be enhanced. Despite that, the Pathankot Air Force base was attacked exactly a week later.

A fortnight after the meeting between the Indian and the Pakistani prime ministers in Ufa in July 2015, the Gurdaspur terror attack had unfolded. In the past too, there were many such unfortunate precedents. It is therefore self-evident that India's national security responses are episodical, reactive and, at best, tactical. It is also evident that we are not in a habit of learning from history.

Another issue that was flagged in the Prologue was about how prepared India is to deal with the technological and digital revolution that has transformed the canvas of battle in the past two decades, and will continue to do so in the future. Unfortunately, the situations that India dealt with in the past 20 years provide no clear road map or markers. It is still virgin territory. Except for the October 2020 attack on Maharashtra's power grid, nothing in the past two decades really provides a clear template of how to react to a major attack on India's critical infrastructure.

The doctrinal question of when a cyber-attack qualifies as an act of war meriting a response by conventional means is still evolving theology, not only in India but in many other geographies as well. It would however need to be addressed sooner than later.

Saudi Arabia chose not to respond, at least overtly, to the drone attacks on their oil facilities in March and May 2021. This drone situation is worrying because over the past two years, drones have become the preferred vehicle for Pakistan to drop arms and ammunition into India. The drones and arms seized in Punjab testify to this threat. The drone attack on Jammu airport in June 2021 once again underscored that weapons of terror are also becoming increasingly autonomous. How to contend with semi-state actors who have access to new technologies will be a challenge for all those nation states who have to deal with terror being used as an instrument of state policy.

Most importantly, the overarching rubric for India underscored by the COVID-19 pandemic is that it must craft a national security doctrine for the coming decades which ensures that it has peace on its periphery to cater to its human and developmental imperatives.

The COVID-19 pandemic has exposed rather brutally India's internal vulnerabilities. Great power aspirations need to be backed by a robust economy populated by healthy and happy people.

The twin challenge, therefore, is to craft its own template of Jacksonian exceptionalism in external engagement that gives both space for consolidation, strategic autonomy and yet is not an act of Jeffersonian isolationism. This is a high-wire trapeze act that would test the skills of our best minds in the years ahead.

The contours of that exceptionalism would be determined by the calibration of India's external economic dependence, especially its maintenance imports such as crude oil, fertilizer, etc., that are crucial for keeping the economy ticking.

Would India be able to become Atmanirbhar (self-reliant)—the latest catchphrase of PM Modi? For Atmanirbhar is just a rehash of the self-reliance mantra that India pursued during 1947–91. Would it walk down that street again or would it stay on the path of economic liberalization and globalization adopted in 1991 while augmenting its internal capacities? This would be the practical test of our creed of exceptionalism.

India must develop a national security doctrine keeping in mind that the world today sits on the intersection of a physical civilization that evolved over the millennia and a virtual civilization that is still taking shape. The future of humankind lies on this crossroads. The question is whether we are ready to face this challenge.

ACKNOWLEDGEMENTS

First and foremost, my profound gratitude to Professor Happymon Jacob, who inspired me to write this book and provided feedback on the various drafts.

My sincere thanks to my two very enterprising and diligent collaborators Harshit Kacholiya, who served as my Legislative Assistant to Members of Parliament (LAMP) and Akash Sahu, who was my research associate. Both of them researched and referenced this book based upon the inputs that I provided while running and walking at unearthly hours of the mornings either in Delhi, Ropar or Chandigarh.

I owe a debt of gratitude to Nicholas Rixon who, during the second wave of COVID-19 while his mother was in hospital in Kolkata and sister was also unwell, still found time to do the first edits of the book before it went to the publishers.

I would also like to thank Gaurav Saini and the entire team at Council for Strategic and Defense Research (CSDR), who provided valuable support during the conceptualization and writing of this book. My thanks to my old classmate and senior journalist Dinesh Kumar, who was kind enough to read some of the initial chapters of this book.

My heartfelt gratefulness to Kapish Mehra, managing director of Rupa Publications India, for being extremely patient with me. I would be failing in my duty if I do not thank Yamini Chowdhury, senior commissioning editor at Rupa and a fellow competitive swimmer, whose valuable suggestions and editing tightened and focused the book. I would be remiss if I do not thank N.N. Anjasi, assistant copy editor at Rupa Publications, who did the final copy edit on this manuscript.

My sincere thanks to *The Asian Age, Deccan Chronicle, The Indian Express, The Hindu, The Tribune, Hindustan Times, Outlook*, Observer Research Foundation (ORF) and every other publication that has generously allowed me to write in their columns. The present book draws from some of my columns on these media platforms. I hereby acknowledge that wherever I have quoted from these writings, they first appeared in the respective publications where they were published.

Penultimate, my eternal gratefulness to my colleagues Pawan Dewan, Arvind Chowdhary, Praveen Wadhwa, N.S. Krishna Mani, Jaspal Singh, Manoj Kumar and Ganesh Kumar, who have always been eternal pillars of support.

Finally, I would be way out of line if I do not express my full-throated appreciation and gratefulness to my wife Naaznin Shafa and daughter Ineka Tewari, my fiercest critics and dearest friends. They stoically took it in their stride that I would come back from my parliamentary commitments and professional obligations as a lawyer and start pecking away at my laptop rather than spending time with them. They must have often wondered why this lawyer-politician is trying to write a book on national security. I hope the book does justice to the time not spent with them.

INDEX